FAITHFUL FOR LIFE

God bless you!

Rev Paul Marx OSB

25 aug '97

FATHER PAUL MARX, OSB

Published by
Human Life International

Cover design by Christy Sharafinski
© 1997 Human Life International
4 Family Life
Front Royal, VA 22630
USA

1-800-549-LIFE • Fax: 540-636-7363
E-mail: publications@hli.org • Internet: http://www.hli.org

Contents

$\mathcal{D}$edication

his book is dedicated to Mrs. Harold (Virginia) Gager. For years Virginia edited my newsletter, *Love, Life and Death Issues*, for the Human Life Center at Minnesota's St. John's University. There she also edited the *International Review of Natural Family Planning*. She similarly edited my bestsellers *The Death Peddlers: War on the Unborn, The Mercy Killers* and many other publications, including this volume.

Virginia Gager

Her wisdom, diligence, and common sense have been so helpful to me for so many years, that I wish to recognize this publicly and thank her for her many hours of unpaid work in fostering the pro-life/pro-family movement across the world.

> Rev. Paul Marx, OSB
> January 2, 1997

(I wish also to recognize the skilled typing of my faithful assistant, Miss Brenda Bonk, who for more than a decade has patiently put up with impatient me. Also, I would like to acknowledge the care shown to me by Mrs. Bernice Kowalik, whose healthy cooking has certainly added years to my life! Finally, I would like to thank HLI's first employee, Bernadette Ethen, for her tireless efforts on many lifesaving projects throughout the years. —Rev. Paul Marx, OSB)

Preface

"*V*eni Sancte Spiritus*," the monks intoned. Or so I imagine. "Come, Holy Spirit, fill the hearts of thy faithful and enkindle in them the fire of thy love." On 15 June 1947, Father Paul Marx was ordained a priest of the order of Saint Benedict.

A few months ago, friends asked Father Paul to mark the fiftieth anniversary of this solemn occasion by writing the story of his life. (Friends have a way of doing that sort of thing, not fully comprehending the toil and tribulations they are setting in motion.) At first reluctant to commit himself to the venture, Father Paul Marx, OSB, finally turned on his tape recorder. The rest, as they say, is autobiography.

His story is hardly a saga of rags to riches. Riches? I doubt that Father Paul has ever lived in more than one or two rooms at a time since he left his seven-bedroom farm home in Minnesota for the no-frills dormitories or monastic cells of St. John's College Preparatory High School, University, Seminary, and Abbey. He once ran his vast international pro-life organization from a single room in a Washington, D.C. priory; later he moved to spartan headquarters in a converted warehouse. Only recently (in August 1996) did he advance to a room with a view, that of the Blue Ridge Mountains of Virginia from the perspective of the beautiful Shenandoah Valley.

No rags, either. Father grew up in a family that was large—fourteen children lived past infancy—but well-enough off, at least by Great Depression standards. Probably the closest he came to true, worrisome poverty was when he left St. John's University sixteen years ago at the wheel of a little car, bound for our nation's capital with only $7,000 to his name.

Still, Father's life story does inspire one Horatio Alger spin-off that is realistic: From NFP to HLI, that is, from teaching Natural Family Planning to students and married couples to serving as chairman of

"You are doing the most important work on earth." — Pope John Paul II to Fr. Marx, 17 November 1979.

Human Life International, the world's largest and most effective pro-life, pro-family ministry.

The progression from NFP to HLI was natural for Father Paul, because it is only a short step from respecting the holiness and integrity of the marital embrace to defending human life itself from fertilization to natural death. (From here to eternity, one could say.) It was Father's genius to recognize, very early in the monumental struggle against the forces of evil, that it is an equally short step from abusing the sexual faculty to attacking unborn babies and, down the line a bit, declaring that some other lives are simply not worth living any more.

Therefore, to be authentically pro-life and pro-family means opposing not merely abortion and euthanasia but contraception and sterilization as well. That, as the Bible notes in another context, is indeed a "hard saying." The "benevolence" of birth control in its various guises is a concept firmly ingrained in the American—not to mention the global—psyche. Contraception is a subject diligently avoided by almost every right-to-life group, because attacking it is considered either politically dangerous or just plain irrelevant. It is a moral offense hardly ever addressed even from the Catholic pulpit, although it does seem that the topic of Pills and IUDs as abortifacients could well be injected into the obligatory annual homily on abortion.

In the early 1980s the late Cardinal Joseph Bernardin of Chicago articulated a "consistent ethic of life" that indiscriminately wove together such "pro-life" issues as hunger, poverty, capital punishment, and the nuclear-arms race with abortion and euthanasia, appearing to give all of them equal status as moral aberrations. Popularly known as the "seamless garment" theory, Cardinal Bernardin's proposal turned out to be especially mischievous with regard to politics. If hugging trees was as meritorious as opposing abortion, it seemed to the rank-and-file Catholic that he could with clear conscience vote for a candidate who opposed capital punishment for convicted murderers even as he supported funding of the execution of innocent preborn babies.

It now appears that the consistent ethic of life is really a consistent culture of death, marked by contraception, sterilization, infanticide, child and spousal abuse, broken or never-formed marriages, euthanasia, and so on—not equals in iniquity, of course, but all of them elements in a slow-developing chain reaction set off by the initial disrespect for God's gift of life. The seamless garment is in fact a shroud.

As you might expect, Father Paul has attracted many enemies from a rich variety of sources, notably (from one side) Planned Parenthood and radical-feminist types and (from another) faithless theologians and over-cautious or ignorant men of the cloth. Interestingly, perhaps prophetically, his first significant opponent was the Minnesota bishop who, many years ago, tried to snuff out Father's NFP programs. Father has been accused of being a bishop-basher, a racist, an anti-Semite, an anti-Muslim, and a woman-hater. (That is only a partial list!) His decision not to address the last charge gives me the chance to do so myself.

Father Paul a woman-hater? That is an insult that could have been hurled at him only by unlicensed practitioners of the "celibate male" mythology that has served the anti-life cause so well. As you will read in his autobiography, among Father's earliest memories are those of his mother as a "wise and holy" woman and of his parochial-school teachers as devoted, unselfish nuns whose supervisors (male! maybe celibate!) often failed to appreciate them.

I suspect that his early impressions were solidified as he labored to write his doctoral treatise on Father Virgil Michel, a pioneer in the liturgical movement of the 1920s and 1930s. Referring to Father

Virgil, Father Paul says: "The proponents of the feminist movement, he insisted, were not the first champions of women's rights, freedom, and higher status. Only ignorance of Christian tradition could allow so false and facile an assumption. It was precisely Christianity that had rescued woman from the more or less qualified slavery and subjugation to men in pagan Greece and Rome. The fact of Christ's coming through the instrumentality of a woman and Mary's role in the work of redemption already indicate women's true position and dignity in Christian society."

Father Paul's writings are full of adjectives like "incomparable," "magnificent," and "splendid" applied to women of his acquaintance. Most important, Father has always paid women the ultimate compliment of asking, even urging, them to do something, big or small, to advance the pro-life movement.

He has plucked some of these "volunteers" from the kitchen and recruited others in the halls of commerce, science, and academia. To Bonnie Manion he might have said something like this: "Why don't you start an NFP center? I'll help you." To Magaly Llaguno: "You should head our HLI branch in Miami." To countless other women: "Why don't you write to your bishop? Call on your congressman? Organize a Birthright chapter?

I had known Father for about a year when I received my own summons to serve. A few months later he phoned to say that he had just mailed me proofs of *The Death Peddlers*.

"Have you ever seen galley proofs?" he asked.

"No. Can I make any major changes at this stage?"

"Yes, if necessary. It's easy. Just cut and paste."

Cut and paste! I wonder if that isn't a metaphor for some of the difficult parts of Father's life as a priest. When circumstance hands you a flawed script, as it has to Fr. Marx—he lost his staff and some friends, his tenure, his health insurance, his newsletters and other publications, his library, his mailing list, even his Human Life Center at St. John's University; he was vilified from right and left—just discard what is no longer useful, salvage what is good, and rearrange what is left by pasting it in a better location. Father Paul Marx, OSB: ground breaker, prodigious worker, determined warrior, deadpan humorist, inveterate night owl, and, above all, God's good and faithful servant.

Veni Sancte Spiritus. "Come, Holy Spirit. . . . Send forth thy spirit and they shall be created, and thou shalt renew the face of the earth." Let the altar bells peal, the candles burn, the banners sway, the censers swing, the odor of incense rise to Heaven. Let the angels chant in jubilation as Father Paul Marx completes his fiftieth year as a priest of the Order of Saint Benedict.

Virginia Gager

Introduction

Many friends and acquaintances have asked me to record highlights of my apostolic travels and experiences over some thirty-five years of pro-life/pro-family work in ninety-one countries. Some people join the Navy to see the world; I joined a Benedictine Abbey instead and have seen more than most sailors have—much of it for an unwelcome reason: the worldwide anti-life, anti-family, anti-God movement.

I have met very many significant persons in the various countries. While I cannot always remember names and dates without prompting, the personalities and events I discuss or describe here are accurately portrayed. I tried to keep a diary of all my foreign excursions. At this writing I am still quite a bit ahead of Pope John Paul II in travels. By the way, he was born ten days after I was, on 18 May 1920.

CHAPTER 1

Starting Out. . .

*I*t all began about nine months before my birth, on 8 May 1920, to George and Elizabeth Marx in a seven-bedroom house on a 200-acre dairy farm three miles from the village of St. Michael, Minnesota, which is now almost a suburb of Minneapolis. I was baptized with the name Benno, the German for Benedict, and given the name Paul when I later entered St. John's Abbey.

My mother once told me that she had prayed to have a large family; she was indeed a very good pray-er, for I was the fifteenth in seventeen pregnancies! Three babies died shortly after birth, including the last one. At the age of four, then, I watched my mother weeping over that small white coffin bearing her seventeenth child. I shall never forget it. What a contrast this experience is to the hedonistic, pagan climate of today, where the attitude of even Catholic parents so often is, "A girl for you and a boy for me, and heaven help us not to have three."

Our large family was not unusual in this small, German Catholic community. We were all safely delivered at home by a Masonic bachelor, Dr. Alfred Ludemann, who hopped around on one crutch, having lost a leg while riding a horse too close to a tree. Once Dad and Ludemann met in the local bank. Said Ludemann: "George, you should not have so many children. Stop it." Retorted my father, "Don't worry, Dr. Ludemann, you're getting paid for each one."

Of the fourteen surviving children, eleven were girls and three were boys. We could never take a vote in our family: it would always have been eleven to three. My father had eight daughters before Joseph came along to help him on the farm—but not for long, because Joseph left at fifteen for boarding school in preparation for becoming a Benedictine priest of St. John's Abbey, fifty miles away.

In 1941 I joined the Abbey too. I have been joking ever since that my brother and I became priests to get away from the eleven girls! But

My paternal grandparents: John Baptist and Barbara Marx.

two of the sisters outwitted us by becoming nuns, members of St. Benedict's Convent only four miles away from St. John's Abbey. By that time, St. John's and St. Benedict's had become the two largest Benedictine institutions in the world. Most unfortunately, both seem to be dying out now, wilted by a deadly modernism, a questionable theology and a radical, secular feminism that has devastated so many religious institutions today.

Of my two sisters who joined St. Benedict's Convent in St. Joseph, Rosina (now Sister Dorothy Ann) became a missionary among the Indians in northern Minnesota, and Cecilia (now Sister Virgene) became a nurse and anesthetist, ending up as a pastoral counselor at St. Benedict's Hospital (now Ogden Regional Medical Center) in Ogden, Utah, where she is a member of Mount Benedict Priory.

My grandparents on my father's side emigrated with six children from Zweibrücken, Bavaria, in 1851. Why they emigrated is not clear. My great-grandfather, who accompanied them, became ill, died, and was buried at sea. With their six children my grandparents settled in McHenry, Illinois. In 1856 they boated up the Mississippi to St. Anthony Falls (located today within Minneapolis). From there they traveled by barge and boat until they arrived near their claim along the Crow River, three miles south of the present village of St. Michael.

Here the early immigrants built a log church and raised their large families. My first cousin, Leander Goeb, compiled a remarkable anthology (1851-1981) of the *Descendants of John Baptist Marx and Barbara Huder*, my grandparents, from whom came many religious and priestly vocations, as we shall see. In 1857 Uncle Andreas Marx was shot over a land dispute.

My maternal grandparents were Hubert and Theresa Rauw; they left Europe from German-speaking Malmedy in Belgium. My mother was one year old when her parents emigrated to Minnesota. Looking for greener pastures some years later, they again emigrated, this time to cold, snowy, underdeveloped Saskatchewan, Canada. My mother, who had married by that time, stayed behind. As homesteaders in Saskatchewan, her parents lacked the usual institutions and conveniences. With the severe Canadian winters, much snow, and virtually no roads, life must have been very hard indeed, and they suffered a great deal. In the Humboldt area of Saskatchewan they helped to found the Benedictine Territorial Abbey of St. Peter.

Minnesota became a state only in 1858. The pioneer monks of St. John's Abbey had arrived in 1856 from St. Vincent's Archabbey in Latrobe, Pennsylvania, and founded St. Michael's parish in 1857 to care for German Catholic immigrants. Their existence was primitive and severe, and these transplanted Benedictines died rather young. My paternal grandfather fought in the American Civil War, even though he had three children. Grandmother saw him off at the train station in Minneapolis. She walked forty miles with him and then back home with a baby in her arms and two toddlers straggling through the bush (there were no roads).

My mother was an excellent amateur nurse, gardener, canner of fruits and vegetables, cook, and bread maker. Rarely were any of us ill. If we were indisposed, Mother would give us a spoonful of castor oil sweetened with a little sugar—a terrible-tasting concoction, but Mother claimed it "tasted good." She spoke a very broken English. My father raised mainly milk cattle, hogs, chickens, and potatoes. Strangely, I never acquired a backache from picking up all the potatoes that we duly marketed for much-needed income. With an abundance of fresh meat, vegetables from my mother's large garden, poultry, and fruit, we ate well, even through the Great Depression that began in 1929.

I vividly remember the presidential campaign waged in 1928 by New York's Governor Alfred E. Smith, who may have lost because he was a Catholic. So, too, I remember the notorious kidnapping and murder of the Charles Lindbergh baby in March 1932. In fact, blessed

My maternal grandparents, Hubert and Theresa Rauw with their many children. My mother, Elizabeth, is in the center at the back.

with a good memory all my life, I recall my oldest sister Anna's wedding that took place when I was only two years old.

I distinctly remember also the anxieties of my parents, particularly of my father, who though gentle, calm, and "gemütlich" (jovial), was also a worrier. He was afflicted with frequent migraine headaches, a malady he kindly did not pass on to any of his children. My mother was somewhat high-strung; she rarely complained but did her own share of worrying without inflicting it on her children. But who wouldn't worry, with fourteen children to raise in the economically depressed pre-World War II years? I clearly recall my father's grief at losing $6,000 (in those days a lot of money) because of a local bank closure, of which there were many during the Great Depression. I also recall how during the dust storms of the 1930's he agonized about the difficulty of paying his $176 tax bill.

Although a somewhat inept farmer, my father was in many ways a modern man: Early on he bought electric milking machines that reduced milking by hand; we were one of the first families in the community to have a modern (then!) refrigerator, indoor toilet facilities and a fashionable car (an Oakland). My dad used only the first and second gears for a long time before he discovered the third (high) gear—poor car!

Family vacations? There were none. On a dairy farm there is no escaping the daily care of the animals. While Minnesota has 10,000 lakes and a number of rivers, including the mighty Mississippi starting in northern Minnesota and running south through the state, I went fishing only once. I never had the patience to wait for a fish to bite my line. I could have used a baseball glove (one of my brothers had one) and a bicycle, but my parents could not afford many luxuries. On the Fourth of July they bought us tiny firecrackers that we lit from a little

bucket of coals and then threw into the air to explode. My mother churned her own butter (cheaper) and in the winter concocted home-made ice cream, which we avidly ate with saltines. Cookies, I suppose, were too expensive to buy or to bake in huge quantities in those Depression days. Later, at home from boarding school, I read books after daily farm work and chores.

Although there were two public grade schools, each about three miles away, for one of which my father had to pay heavy taxes, my parents would

My parents, Elizabeth Rauw and George Marx were married 11 November 1901.

not think of sending any of their children into public education, and so we walked to and from school every day—three miles each way in snow, rain, or shine—to attend the Catholic parochial school at St. Michael. I arrived a little late now and then but did not miss a single day of school between grades two and eight. How well I remember seeing mother, up early in the morning, making breakfast and a boxed lunch for each of us! At 7:00 a:m. we left for the long walk. She always insisted that we go to daily Mass at 8:00 a.m. The last thing she told me and my sister Cecilia when we embarked for school was, "Be sure you're on time for Mass." One of the first questions at the end of the day after I returned home was, "Were you on time for

The Marx family farm near St. Michael, Minnesota.

Mass?" Later, when my parents had retired to St. Michael, they attended daily Mass as long as they could walk.

Minnesota undergoes thunderous rainstorms, nearly always preceded by lightning. A keen memory: When these storms came, my mother would light a blessed candle, put it on the dining table, and serenely go back to work. My little sister and I would crawl under the table for protection; we did not have Mother's confidence in her burning candle.

The Catholic school in St. Michael was taught by the School Sisters of Notre Dame of Mankota, Minnesota; their dedication was abundantly repaid through the years with the many vocations issuing from that school. Eventually, too, this large community was to be decimated by a radical feminism.

I still remember Sister Mary Corolla, the erstwhile second-grade teacher who broke a few rulers over fingers in keeping an iron-clad discipline. At times she convincingly boxed an ear or two. She must have set a record in getting her pupils to contribute pennies, nickels, and dimes to save the black babies in Africa. For this cause, dutifully charting every cent for us to see, she cleverly had the boys compete against the girls to see who could contribute most. Of course, we boys won most of the time—sometimes by stealing the girls' money!

The nuns were amply rewarded by the parents, who were most grateful for their humble, devoted, unselfish services. How well I remember all the eggs and fresh produce I carried to those seven or eight nuns in the school and to the pastor, as did others! How well I remember the nuns saying their prayers, walking outside in their black habits in hot weather! How well I remember the sisters' chapel lit up early in the morning as they said their prayers and attended Mass before teaching a full day's school!

Shown here in 1923 are the fourteen
children of the Marx family (I'm the
second child from the left).

Our seven-bedroom Marx family
farmhouse near St. Michael,
Minnesota.

My parents were hard-working, faith-
filled, simple folks. They are shown
here during their later years.

Twenty-eight years later, all fourteen Marx children were still alive, shown here at my parents'
Golden Wedding Anniversary in 1951 (I'm the fifth from the left in the back row).

Here I am outside St. Michael's parish—the "priest factory"!

Incidentally, I learned my first catechism in German and heard many a German sermon as I grew up. And how handy that German came in later on, after I had forgotten most of it (except my authentic German accent), when I had to lecture in German against abortion. (German is by far the most commonly spoken language in Europe.) In 1972, when I began these lectures, I did not even know the German word for abortion. It is very descriptive: *Die Abtreibung*—meaning "the chasing of the child away."

The Catholic church of St. Michael was known as a "priest factory" because of all its vocations. I was the twenty-fourth priest to have come from this parish of 230 families in 1947, when I was ordained on the fifteenth of June. By that time over 100 local nuns had taken their vows! The saintly Archbishop John Gregory Murray of St. Paul once said that no other American parish could outdo St. Michael's in producing vocations. It was actually a German Catholic enclave. There was not a single Protestant student in the eight grades of my schooling!

As I have noted, the Catholic church of St. Michael was founded in 1857 by pioneering Benedictines, but it was in the hands of a diocesan priest of the Archdiocese of St. Paul as I grew up. This unusual man, a Slovakian immigrant by the name of Anthony Miks, pastored the parish more than thirty years, and died there. In his last sickly years he had a well-liked young assistant, Alphonse Schladweiler, who later became the first bishop of New Ulm. Father Schladweiler impressed me enormously.

Father Miks was a thoroughly good priest who ruled the parish almost like an autocrat. He certainly had his virtues. I still see him kneeling in thanksgiving every morning after Mass. Never late for

Mass, always totally dedicated, ever concerned about the spiritual welfare of his people, he had a unique way of teaching religion. Every
week he taught every grade-school class in church for at least one
hour. He would sit on a pew facing his anxious little flock, would pop
a question, would look searchingly at each cringing pupil; after asking,
for example, how many commandments there were and eyeing each
child, he would point to (for example) "Marx." Since you never knew
when you would be pounced upon, you could not afford to fall asleep
or lose attention. Needless to say, he attracted total attention at all
times. But overall he was kind, never cruel, and I do not recall his ever
hitting anyone.

Father Miks perhaps had a unique way of preparing people for
marriage. My sister explained how he patiently ran them through the
ceremony the night before. Then he invited the couple to be married
to the parish-house for "instruction." Not even inviting them to sit
down, he instructed them: "Tomorrow after Mass everything that
was wrong before marriage will be right." He then invited them to the
door, bidding them "good night."

I have often been asked what Father Miks said or did to have generated so many vocations. In fact, for my master's degree in sociology
at the Catholic University of America, I was expected to analyze the
socio-economic base of this small, vocation-producing parish. When I
learned that I was to interview every family, I said, "No go."
Incidentally, the parish produced two abbots and an impressive array
of monsignors.

I cannot recall that Father Miks ever explicitly urged anybody into
the priesthood or religious life. Perhaps it would be accurate to say
that he inspired others by his marvelous example, because he was a
priest from head to toe. Nor were there ever any priestly or religious
scandals in the parish. (Enough of those came later.) We servers rever-
entially feared the pastor; he was not above embarrassing you at the
altar if you made a mistake in serving. If he came down our way on a
sidewalk (in those days a dirt path), we would take another route.

Every other year Father Miks would drive his servers in his large
old car to St. John's Abbey/University fifty miles away, to attend a
graduation or a baseball game. In alternate years he would take us to
walk the grounds of St. Thomas College or Seminary in St. Paul. I

guess this visit was intended to remind us to become priests or religious. I can still see him juggling the big wheel of his ancient rattletrap, hardly ever saying anything, buying us an ice-cream cone on the way to our destination and a candy bar on the way back. At Easter and Christmas our gift from him as his servers was an apple and ten cents, duly extracted from the Sunday collection. He was a bee-keeper, and once a year he treated his grade-school children to honey on dry bread in appreciation for our honoring his name-day.

When the parish grew to 400 families, it built a Catholic high school; that was the end of vocations, except for a straggling few. I think one explanation for all the vocations before the Catholic high school was built was that the young often went away to minor seminaries or Catholic boarding schools. Incidentally, there were fifty-five religious/priestly vocations in three generations of the Marx and related clans.

In both school and home, religion was paramount. We dutifully went to Confession every month, received Communion every day during Lent, and attended the Stations of the Cross after school every Friday. The pastor again conducted Stations in the evening for those who could not get there in the afternoon, with Confession before and after, along with the inevitable Benediction.

There was hardly a week during the school year when there wasn't some religious, nun, priest, monk, or missionary at home visiting his (or her) family. Talk about reminders of the priesthood and religious life! We who were growing up in a vocations parish surely had them. On the other hand, my parents never explicitly promoted religious or priestly vocations. Their religious example was quite sufficient.

Criticism of religious or priests was strictly *verboten* in our family. Dad explained that anyone who spoke unkindly about a priest or hindered his work in any way would die without one in attendance. He offered a few luscious—invented or real—examples to illustrate his warning. He himself died with all fourteen children around his bed, my priest-brother leading the prayers for the dying, my nurse-nun-sister attending him, and I absolving him periodically. On the other hand, Mother died suddenly, before any of us could reach her bedside at the St. Cloud hospital. Both of my parents lived to be seventy-five. Weeks before my dad died, I gave him the last rites. When I had fin-

Two priests (myself and my brother, Fr. Michael) and two nuns (Sr. Virgene and Sr. Dorothy Ann) in one family! We had all gathered to celebrate my parents' 50th wedding anniversary in 1951.

ished, he turned to me and said touchingly, "I'll never forget this." Because I had been a very mischievous lad (nothing serious!), he never quite believed I would make it to the altar. Most likely he did not believe it until I was actually ordained.

In so many ways my father was an admirable man. He greatly loved the missions and was generous in his financial support of missionaries. How well I remember the many thank-you and begging-for-more letters I carried home from the mailbox a half-mile away! Dad was a supersecret giver. About once a year some missionary from a far-off country would come to visit and thank him. We all knew why. But my dad was always embarrassed. Late in life my mother inherited $10,000. There was no doubt as to how my father secretly spent it— on the missions. When my brother Reinhart bought the farm in 1939, my father gave him only this piece of advice: "Because I always tried to be good to the missions, God has been good to me. You do that too." And he did.

Just as we never began any class in schools I attended without a prayer or ended without one, so at home we religiously prayed before and after meals. We always ate together, and no one left the table until all were finished and had prayed or had been properly excused. Finishing all the food you put on your plate was sometimes a stern duty. I recall how my brother Joe once threw a piece of bread across the table to my brother Reine. Mother admonished her wayward son that "bread and all food is a gift of the Lord and thus is sacred—and wouldn't the poor in China be glad to have it?" "Give it to them," chanted Joe, precipitating another sermonette.

Attached to our usual prayers after breakfast were special prayers for the day. During Lent we said the rosary on our knees together with the Litany of the Saints in the evening. Again the rosary in October and May, but not at other times. Every night before we went to bed, we recited night prayers together, unless my parents were entertaining visitors, in which case my older sisters conducted prayers upstairs. I shall never forget how my father's eyes were fixed on the crucifix during those prayers. On my ordination day I told my parents I would remember them in every Mass I would ever be privileged to offer. Tears came to my father's eyes. I have never forgotten that promise, nor have I ever forgotten at Mass the good, unknown woman who paid my tuition, room, and board ($400 per year) through high school and college.

Nor shall I ever forget the old-time Lent as it was strictly observed in our home and family. Adults fasted and abstained. The very young were urged to practice self-denial in their own way. From my older brothers and sisters I learned to deny myself candy during Advent and Lent (saving it up to gorge myself on Christmas Day and Easter Sunday).

My father and mother had what must have been the equivalent of a grade-school education. Dad read German and English publications two or three hours every night. At meals and other times he would relay to us what he had read. I think from that practice grew my lifelong interest, almost a kind of fanaticism, in knowing what's going on in Church and world. On occasion he would sit me down to read an article with the admonition, "Dass ist schön zu lesen" ("that is good to read").

My mother did not do much reading, because she had no time. But she was an excellent housekeeper, endowed with all those talents and virtues that mothers attain when they love their children and revel in their own vocation. She was really a wise and holy woman. I'll never forget the afternoon before I received my First Holy Communion at age ten. She kindly suggested that I go upstairs and think about what I was going to do the next day! And I did. The Catholic upbringing of all her children was always her first concern; she was totally unselfish. All too late I was to realize that my parents were (and are) really saints; I pray every day for their intercession on behalf of my welfare and my work.

It is an old idea that every Catholic home should indeed be a little church (*ecclesiola*), characterized by common prayer, good reading, healthy and joyous interaction, and the domestic education and formation for which there is no substitute. Our home was like that. A truly Christian home, like ours, should follow Christian customs and be decked out with Christian symbols and pictures. A holy-water font was strategically placed at the head of our stairs. On Ash Wednesday and Good Friday we received for breakfast dry toast without butter or jelly, and oatmeal without milk or sugar. (To this day I cannot abide oatmeal, a standard Depression food!) But on Easter there were hot cross buns and other special things to eat. And for Christmas breakfast we usually had chipped beef.

My mother needed no wise theologian or scholarly liturgist to tell her that feast days should be celebrated in *Missa* (Mass) *et mensa* (dinner table). To this day I still try to observe this Ash Wednesday/Good Friday tradition I learned in my early years. When I do not succeed, I feel that something is missing. And I still miss having chipped beef on Christmas morning, too. Good habits start early and perdure.

Being assisted at my first Mass by classmate Fr. Raymond Schulzetenberge. I have never forgotten my parents at any of the thousands of Masses I have since said.

In many ways life on the farm was hard, and a certain built-in asceticism prevailed. Imagine my father, getting up at 3:00 a.m. to feed the horses that would draw the sleigh through the snow for an hour

It's hard to keep up with the Marx clan—there's so many of them! I have 92 nieces and nephews. Here I am with one of my grand-nieces resting comfortably in my arms.

on unreliable roads to Midnight Mass ("Midnight Mass" actually began at 5:00 a.m.). Home for breakfast; and after caring for the cows and other animals, my father would again hitch up the horses for the 10:00 a.m. High Mass, three miles away! I have a clear memory of my father and mother going to Confession every month. When that car rolled out of the yard on a Saturday night, there was only one place they could be going: to Confession, and to the rosary and Benediction that, in those days, preceded Confession. Although we had Methodist and Lutheran neighbors with whom we collaborated in grain threshing and the like, none of my sisters married outside their religion. My parents made it very clear that mixed marriages are hazardous. "Do not start what you should not do in the first place" was their repeated, gentle admonition. And when boyfriends sat with my sisters in the car too long after bringing them home, my dad would turn on the yard light to curb any excessive romantic enthusiasm. At times he had occasion to warn my sisters of "too short" skirts. He was a wise man. What would he say of mini-skirts today?

To this day the Marx clan is a big one: one of my sisters has eighteen living children. I have over ninety nieces and nephews, among whom are one priest and two nuns. So far as I know, all attend Mass regularly; there has been one civil divorce with a subsequent annulment; one devout sister joined a fundamentalist group. Of the original fourteen children who lived past infancy, six have died at the time of this writing.

Through the years I have often asked priests and religious what the chief source of their vocation was. Virtually always the answer was "parents" or "home." That was surely true in my case.

CHAPTER 2

Schooling

n the fall of 1935, at fifteen years of age, having been educated in an excellent primary school and raised in a solidly Catholic home, I entered St. John's College Preparatory High School in Collegeville, Minnesota, to study for the priesthood. I recall having one date in high school, and one in college. I also recall a Franciscan retreat master's telling us pre-divinity students that among God's most beautiful creatures were young girls and women. But then he thundered, "But they are not for you!" I have always found the fair sex attractive, especially those who are "easy on the eyes." But I was fixed on becoming a priest.

My teachers were mostly monks of St. John's Abbey; they conducted St. John's University, a major seminary, a college preparatory high school, and the Liturgical Press on the same campus. All these activities generated a rich spiritual, intellectual, and cultural environment. Students and many visitors came from all parts of the world; each year we heard lectures by men of renown. I was active in school plays, track, and football, and was elected co-captain of the football team in my senior year, when I was also president of my class and of the student council. I held the school record for the 100- and 220-yard dashes. My writing career began with a column ("Did You Know?") in the weekly school paper, *The Prep World*. In my junior year I won the coveted medal in the annual elocution contest, and in two of the four years I received the gold medal for highest scholastic achievement. In 1939 I graduated second in my class as salutatorian.

In about my sophomore year, I developed a strong case of scrupulosity that persisted through the seminary. Of all the pains and sufferings of my seventy-seven years, none was more excruciating. I know the stark reality of mental agony. But in the Providence of God, it brought its benefits. Later, as confessor, I sensed and understood the scrupulous penitent's painful turmoil as soon as he had uttered his first sentence.

I attended the St. John's Preparatory High School in Collegeville, Minnesota. Shown here is my high school's student council, of which I was the president. I am pictured second from the right in the front row.

During my senior year I also served as president of the Johnny Prep players, the school's theatre group. Our first play was "The Flight of the Gull," a comedy in three acts. I had the lead role as an old German sea captain, Captain Brandt. (I'm the first one seated on the left.)

All of my extra-curricular activities kept me busy. I worked as the associate editor of The Prep World. Eldred Cleare and I took our work very seriously. I am grateful for all the experience I received in working with publishing. It has sure come in handy during later years!

I was co-captain of the high school track and field team. At this time (1938-39), I was the 100- and 220- yard dash record holder. (I'm in the front row, third from the left.)

During my senior year I was co-captain of my high school's football team with Robert Johnson. (I'm number 40 — small, but fast.)

My football career continued in college; here I'm pictured as guard for St. John's University. And as one monk said, "Marx spends his Saturday afternoons in the enemy backfield."

I hope I've been helpful to many victims. My advice to the scrupulous? Find a wise, sympathetic, experienced confessor and obey him.

AT ST. JOHN'S UNIVERSITY

*T*he next step in my educational journey was to enter St. John's University on the same campus, in the fall of 1939. Given the machinations of the sports-inclined monks, I had taken enough college courses in my senior year of high school to meet the requirements for playing quarterback on the university football team in my freshman year, and guard in my sophomore year. I was elected captain of the team for the next year but declined. I had other plans.

After two years of college, the custom for divinity students interested in joining the Abbey was to enter the novitiate; this I did in July of 1941 with ten others. Guiding us in our secluded lives was the ascetic, saintly Benedictine theologian and scholar, Father Basil Stegmann, OSB. He had been rector of the Catholic Fujen University in Peking, China, which the American Benedictines founded in 1924 at the request of the Holy See and later turned over to the Society of the Divine Word. Of the eleven novices in my class, nine survived—that is, took temporary vows for three years!

MY NOVITIATE AND ORDINATION

I do not think anyone ever forgets his novitiate year. Surely I will not. Our novice master, Father Basil, was a demanding, though very human, spiritual guide who drummed into us the spirit of St. Benedict's ancient Rule. He was anxious for us to learn the 1500-year history of the Benedictine Order and cultivated a Benedictine spirituality in a wise program of lectures, reading, meditating, working outside one hour a day, and praying. We wrote short articles on spiritual/religious topics. From day one, we recited the Divine Office with the larger monastic community.

The novitiate was no lark! Cooped up and isolated, not permitted to talk to other monks, and allowed only one shower per week, we prepared ourselves for a lifetime of *ora et labora* (pray and work), the Benedictine motto. I remember losing seven pounds during the Lenten fast. We intensively studied the Rule of St. Benedict with its common-sense directives, and the twelve steps of humility featured in many a lecture. Through the years I have always found praying harder than working.

In the novitiate and the seminary, and for years thereafter, we arose at 4:10 in the morning, recited Lauds and the small Hours, and then attended conventual Mass; next we attended the abbot's Mass; meanwhile, the priest-monks offered their own private Mass. Breakfast was most welcome at 7:00. The monks on the faculties of the three schools then taught their classes. In those days of numerous confessions to be heard, many faculty members would help out in neighboring parishes on weekends, only to come back Sunday night to get ready for Monday's classes—and another day beginning at 4:10 a.m.! That was my life for years.

Father Basil was a realist. Speaking of a healthy religious life, he urged us continually to face facts fearlessly all our lives. To this day, when we meet a fellow novice (five of us are still living), we ask each other, "Are you still facing facts fearlessly?" Later, monitoring courses in psychiatry at then-famed St. Elizabeth's Hospital in Washington, D.C., I heard a renowned Jewish psychiatrist emphasize that, while no one ever fully faces reality—that would be too uncomfortable—we are psychologically healthy to the extent that we confront the realities of our lives. As T. S. Eliot observed, "Mankind cannot tolerate much reality." So in both the natural and supernatural dimensions of human life, it is ever the facing of truth that makes us free and brings us peace of mind.

Father Basil held very distinctive ideas about Benedictinism and what Benedictine monks should be doing and how they should be living. In Father's view, to live the monastic, Benedictine life was to do the work that the Church most needed to be done, consonant with pursuing the common life and reciting the Office together. He often emphasized that, if the Benedictines had always been what they should have been according to the Rule of St. Benedict, there would have been no need for Jesuits, who came along ten centuries later, after the Reformation. (He carried no grudge against Jesuits, though; he valued all religious orders in their variety of apostolates.)

The only luxury our novice master allowed himself was smoking an occasional cigar or, now and then, an ancient pipe that had seen many better days. But he almost always insisted that every Sunday his novices smoke a cigar; he had the odd notion that cigarettes were far too worldly and out of place in the mouth of monks. He wisely emphasized spiritual reading of all kinds, study of the Bible, and pursuit of Benedictine spirituality. He had a great respect for the intellectual life and later, as our prefect guiding us through the seminary, allowed us to use gift-money to buy books we thought important. Secular newspapers and magazines were taboo in both the novitiate and the seminary. And so, every day except Sunday, Father Basil carried on classes with us, preaching and lecturing.

In 1964, St. John's Abbey had a total of 404 monks, including almost 300 priests (today's total membership is 221). Father Basil thought the community far too large for the Benedictine ideal. He preferred monasteries with small schools and/or various apostolates consistent with the common life. He prayed that he would die in a poor abbey, but he did not.

He and I clashed fiercely for months in private evaluations: I for one could not see how obedience could be human and reasonable and even religious unless one fully understood and thus truly accepted a command or assignment. St. Benedict had allowed a skeptical monk to discuss with his abbot a given command or position three times; after a third such discussion, if the abbot did not give in, the monk was to accept the task cheerfully as a genuine religious act of obedience. Father Basil insisted that I was a proud rationalist, having to certify a reason for every position, procedure, or command, whereas humility and confidence in God should characterize a Benedictine's life. He emphasized, "A superior can give a bad command and make a mistake, but *you* cannot go wrong in obeying, after mildly explaining your point of view that the assignment or command seemed unsuitable, for whatever reason." My best friend in the monastery once told me, "If you make up your mind about something, you will go through the wall to defend and foster it." I guess he was trying to tell me I was a stubborn German.

Father Basil stressed again and again the importance of faith, observing that true faith locks one into God's knowledge and wisdom;

An aerial view of the St. John's Abbey campus (Collegeville, Minnesota) with four separate facilities: a high school, the university, the seminary and the Liturgical Press. This picture is from 1994. The campus has grown significantly since my undergraduate days in the 1940s.

he explained that Divine Wisdom far exceeds the best of human reasoning, insights, and machination. History is full of mere reason's shipwrecks, he added. In religious life, he pointed out, one must often bend one's reason and must sacrifice one's will to God, working through superiors. Trust in God and in His Divine Providence, and cultivate a healthy skepticism about your own abilities, he advised.

Eventually I saw the light; at least, I survived the novitiate and resumed my college education, majoring in philosophy, at that time my favorite subject. Despite all difficulties, I had enjoyed the novitiate experience so much that I was not anxious to resume formal studies.

I clearly recall 7 December 1941 and our entry into World War II, a horrible war in which fifty-seven students of St. John's University died, some of them my cherished, talented classmates. During the war three hundred pre-flight Air Force cadets lived on campus. As novices we were allowed to see films of the war in progress, and I remember well the Battle of Britain, when Britain's Royal Air Force bravely staved off defeat against the gigantic German onslaught. About the brave British pilots, the great Winston Churchill rightly observed, "Never have so many owed so much to so few."

Because we were exempt from the military, we had to go to school

*First Vows,
1942, with my
parents.*

eleven months of the year; therefore, I went through a truncated major-seminary period of five rather than the normal six years. During those years I did not read a single newspaper. It was forbidden. But at least the Air Force films gave us an understanding of the broader aspects of the war.

After three months of piano lessons, my teacher, Father Innocent Gertken, OSB, gave up on me, saying, "You played too much football; your fingers are too stiff." Apparently my fingers were not too stiff to push the keys of the tuba I played in the college band, even if the "um pah pah" that came out of that huge animal might indicate otherwise.

In 1944 I graduated from college *cum laude* with a bachelor's degree in philosophy. Three years after completing the novitiate training, we took solemn vows binding us to the Abbey forever. Then we were off to a ten-day vacation at home, the first in four years of monastic life.

During my seminary days and for five years thereafter I helped coach football in the college-preparatory high school. During that time

I also prefected, that is, monitored the boys in a study hall and dormitory. Life was very, very busy but engrossing, and theology became a whole, new, exciting world. Summers were filled with reading, learning a foreign language, and doing some outside manual work. On weekends we filled the needs of retreatants, mostly married couples.

On 15 June 1947, I was ordained, and life became even more interesting and fascinating. Never had I wavered about my priesthood, although in my youth I'd toyed with the idea of becoming a medical doctor.

My early years in the priesthood increased the great respect I always had for girls and women and, for whatever reason, have always admired the enormous potential for good that truly Christian women possess. Perhaps that is why I shudder with revulsion over the modern secular feminism that has weakened or destroyed so many fine institutions, including many women's religious orders, our Catholic school system, and now our Catholic hospitals, while making so many women, by and large, dissatisfied or unhappy.

I am convinced that one reason for the feminist rebellion and anger is the shoddy treatment given them all too often by thoughtless men. Even many priests took for granted the great work of devout and devoted nuns; that has always troubled me. Now and then I

Newly ordained as Father Paul Marx, OSB on 15 June 1947.

served as chaplain to a group of nuns; for two summers I taught them a basic course in liturgy. For years I was a confessor at the neighboring St. Benedict's Convent. I always kept up a healthy correspondence with many sisters. Both in those years and later I came to understand the pain many sisters experience from ungrateful, at worst rude and at best casual, treatment of their often heroic, and too often unsung efforts.

The next five years were very challenging, rewarding, and busy: teaching in Prep School (at different times) ancient and modern history, English, and religion to sophomores, and sociology to seniors.

Ordination Day, pictured here with my brother, Fr. Michael.

I recall how, teaching a sophomore religion class, I had given what I considered a super-explanation of the virtue of chastity. I thought I had answered all questions, when a brave lad put up his hand at the back of the room to ask, "Well, how far can we go?" My response: "Not very far; in fact, you can't even start!"

My first assignment as a newly ordained priest was to replace a pastor in northern North Dakota for one month. The pastor seemingly had become involved with a seventeen-year-old girl and had abandoned the parish. This delicate assignment was for me a rather sudden immersion into priestly, parochial work; I enjoyed the challenge. My intensive two years of French came in very handy in this partly French-speaking parish. At the same time, I was also chaplain to a small group of nuns who ran a small high school for girls in the parish. These young ladies really must have learned their faith, because they converted many of the Lutherans whom they later married.

After sixteen years of Catholic schools I experienced my first secular education in the summer of 1948, when I took various courses at the University of Minnesota. At that time the university's excellent Newman Center was headed by Father Leonard Cowley, who was later to become auxiliary bishop of St. Paul. Conversations with him were most enlightening. On campus during the regular school year were 7,000 Catholics, not a few of them nuns, whom the secular students called "the DARs," that is, "the damn average raisers." Today many Newman Centers, unfortunately, seem to have gone sour theologically.

A non-Catholic professor of psychology, whose course I was taking, loved to chat with a priest about serious things in life; we often had meals together. Because he counseled many Catholic students, I once

Processing in to say my first Mass at my home parish.

My first Mass at St. Michael's.

asked him what his overall impression of Catholics was. He gave me an answer I shall never forget: "When it comes to achieving peace of mind, Catholics seem to have a monopoly." "Explain that," I said. Said he, "How wise you Catholics are in preparing people for marriage! My wife and I had no preparation; we have divorced; we have both remarried other partners; we are both unhappy; we still love each other. Had we received some kind of preparation and warning about possible pitfalls, we would still be together today." Catholic marriage preparation at that time was not all that great, but it is far worse today.

He then spoke about the wisdom of confession: "I can think of nothing more helpful for a healthy psychological life than periodically to unload one's sins and infractions, and then to start all over." Unfortunately, as a fledgling priest I was too green to stay in touch with him. I have often regretted it. Perhaps I could have "fished" him into the Church.

In the summers of '49, '50 and '51, I took courses in the social sciences at the Catholic University of America in Washington, D.C. Here I first met ugly racism. One Saturday I came to help in a parish in Hyattsville, Maryland. The pastor was terribly upset. He told me that an awful thing had happened to his brother that week in Baltimore: a black family had moved into the block where the brother lived. "What's so bad about that?" this innocent Minnesota farm boy asked. Then came his shouted blast: "Would you want to live with niggers? I'll hear their confession and give them Communion, but there I draw the line!" I was all the more incredulous because I had gone through the novitiate with a Bahamian black who became Father Prosper Meyer, OSB, a great missionary in the Bahama Islands. St. John's University always accepted black students; and St. John's Abbey pioneered the Church in the Bahama Islands, where 98 percent are black.

While teaching in Prep School I also helped coach football with Chub Ebnet, a college classmate; we won one state Catholic championship, beating, with our 240 students, huge Twin Cities Catholic high schools taught by the Christian Brothers. I likewise coached the track and field team, which won five consecutive state crowns.

Very close to students in this college preparatory boarding school from athletic coaching, prefecting and teaching, I learned something that may surprise the reader. From all indications, certain fairly bright students, very much interested in becoming priests, had great difficulty learning the mandatory Latin; they dropped their vocational plans. Americans, generally, have a notorious difficulty with foreign languages, especially Latin and Greek.

Of all my teaching years, I have the conviction that I did the most good in Prep School. Eighty 14-year-old freshmen came in every fall from good Catholic homes, often headed by professional parents. It was great to teach, prefect, counsel, and coach them as immature freshmen and then watch them stumble through their awkward sophomore year and on to their more stable junior and senior years. By graduation they had grown into young, thinking, Christian men, spiritually and intellectually ready to go to college, which almost one hundred percent did. Among them today are prominent doctors, lawyers, and priests. I left that work in 1952 with heavy heart, although I must admit that loud, immature freshmen had started to get on my nerves!

In 1952 my superior, Abbot Alcuin Deutsch, informed me that he was going to send me to the Catholic University of America to get a Ph.D. in sociology. Here is how he dispatched me: "Father Paul, you have a very bad name—Marx; we're sending you to study sociology so you can undo some of the evil your namesake Karl Marx perpetrated in the world." Actually, Karl Marx was not so much a sociologist as an economist/social philosopher. In any case, now I knew my academic mission!

Although I missed teaching in Prep School, I was thoroughly fascinated with graduate school. I breezed through classes, auditing courses in anthropology, psychology, and psychiatry that were not required. I knew these subjects would be helpful in teaching family sociology and counseling married couples. Having monitored married retreatants earlier, I vowed to equip myself in every possible way to teach marriage preparation and parenting, and to help married couples in retreats, especially in the matter of the birth-control problem, about which I had heard and read so much.

A wonderful remembrance is the many retreats I conducted for married couples in the summers of the late 1940s, 1950s and 1960s. Many of the husbands had served in the armed forces. Then, and throughout my life, I learned from the married couples I counseled, as they from me—it has always been a two-way street.

MY DOCTORAL DISSERTATION

I chose for my doctoral dissertation the life and work of Father Virgil Michel, OSB, a monk of St. John's Abbey. Father Virgil had received his Ph.D. in English from the Catholic University of America with a dissertation on the writings of the convert Brownson, who became a great apologist for the Catholic Church; he once wrote that

Fr. Virgil Michel was the pioneer of the liturgical movement, as well as founder of Liturgical Press. Were he living, he would be a voice of sanity in the "reform of the reform" of the liturgy that is going on today.

"Catholicism is as logical as hell." Perhaps Brownson's yen for apologetics rubbed off on Father Virgil, who had a lifelong interest in that subject, as have I. Father Virgil took education courses in several summer sessions at Columbia University. Later Abbot Alcuin sent him to Europe to study philosophy in Rome and Louvain. In Europe he discovered the budding liturgical movement, and while Thomistic philosophy—particularly social ethics—was by far his first love, he foresaw the need of establishing a liturgical movement in the English-speaking world. With the collaboration of Abbot Alcuin, he founded on his return the Liturgical Press and *Orate Fratres* (now *Worship*). During the Depression years of the 1930s, he initiated a pioneering School for Catholic Social Thought at St. John's University.

He undoubtedly was the leading exponent of that subject when he prematurely died (at the age of forty-eight) on his patron saint's feast day, 16 November 1938, of a neglected streptococcus infection. He was the personal friend of then-young Mortimer J. Adler, with whom he discussed philosophy late into the night whenever they met.[1] Michel toyed with the Great Books Movement but died before he could implement it in Catholic university education.

A prolific though poor writer interested in everything, in his short life he wrote enough books, pamphlets, articles, and reviews on a great variety of subjects to make up a title-list of fourteen pages. All of these works I read, along with twenty-two years of preserved correspondence. This project took me all over the world. One of his collaborators, Father Walter Reger, OSB, observed, "When Virgil Michel

---

[1]   See Adler's glowing tribute to Father Virgil Michel in *Orate Fratres*, vol. 13 (22 January 1939), 123-129.

died, the monastery was tired for months. In his quiet way, he inspired many, who then could not escape writing or working." As a senior in high school I had often heard him lecture. Although he was a dull, emotionless speaker, thought poured out of him, and he was one of the best discussion leaders I have ever witnessed.

Driven by ideas and seemingly interested in everything, Father Virgil anticipated the feminist movement. He frequently wrote on the role of the Christian woman and the family in modern times.

In 1929 Michel stated:

> The Christian woman is as it were a natural sacrament in the world, an external sign of inner grace radiating good-ness everywhere. She is a power for good in the world to which only the most debased men will fail to respond, and whose active influence the world never needed more sorely than today. [2]

Actually, according to Father Virgil there are two possibilities for woman in regard to man: either she plunges him deeper into hell than man would descend by himself, or else leads him farther up into heaven than man would ascend by himself. If man's weapon of domi-nation in a pagan civilization was brute force, woman's in a Christian culture is the strong one of spiritual influence. By temperament, incli-nation, and ability, she is in many ways better fitted for God's battles and the cause of the Church, Father Virgil explained, and that is why wherever the Church has triumphed, woman has played a major role. And that is also precisely why, as he told the Minnesota Council of Catholic Women in 1936, "The worst that can happen to a civilization is that its women descend to the moral depths of the unchristian men of the age. We are at that stage today."[3]

The great Jesuit Father John LaFarge, then editor of *America*, warned Father Virgil about the pitfalls of journalism: "Write about the weather, and surely someone will write to object." Later, Father

---

[2]   "Liturgy and Catholic Woman," *Orate Fratres*, vol. 3 (1929), 274.

[3]   Synopsis of Address of Virgil Michel to the Minnesota Council of Catholic Women (in Michel papers), p.2.

Teaching at St. John's University.

Virgil was to tell his many collaborators "never to exaggerate. All exaggeration is a kind of lie." This policy may explain why he escaped acrimonious controversy even while lecturing and writing on highly sensitive subjects.

This pioneer of the liturgical apostolate would be appalled by all the craziness in liturgical practice going on today. Although a thorough intellectual, he also had a practical sense. Were he living, he would be a voice of sanity in the "reform of the reform" of the liturgy that is going on. As early as 1920 he spoke and wrote about the vernacular in the liturgy; he didn't push it, because he perceived the times were not ready for it. He used to say that "he is no leader who is too far ahead." So too his correspondence shows that he held advanced ideas about a truly Christian ecumenism, which he quietly promoted. (Perhaps some of this rubbed off on me. As a deacon in the seminary I organized weekend theological conferences with my fellow seminarians and those of Luther Theological Seminary in St. Paul, Minnesota.) Among Father Virgil's many collaborators at the time were Monsignor Martin Hellriegel of St. Louis and Monsignor William Busch of St. Paul.

Advancing the idea in modern times of the Church as the Mystical Body of Christ, he hoped to interest a contemporary, Monsignor Fulton J. Sheen, in the liturgy. In 1936, Sheen feebly attempted to comply, writing *The Mystical Body of Christ*, which was put together with the careless research of students. Father Virgil found the book so inadequate that, starting with "Sheen's grammar and ending with his theology," as one commentator wrote, Father Virgil tore it to shreds so thoroughly in a review[4] that Sheed and Ward, the publishers, immediately withdrew it.

AT HARVARD

*I*n the summer of 1954 I took courses in cultural anthropology, economics, and finance at Harvard, the best school I ever attended. I could not believe the demands made by the professors. My Roman collar seemed to draw a number of students on campus, especially one bright agnostic who delighted in ridiculing Catholic teaching in lengthy, sometimes heated discussions. I enjoyed those encounters, as did the inevitable little audience around us. Eventually my antagonist and I became great friends. At the end of the summer, he touchingly poured himself out to me as to a long-lost friend because he had just flunked two vital courses. I could be thoroughly sympathetic because I too almost flunked a course in anthropology. Unfortunately, preoccupied with my doctoral dissertation, I failed to remain in touch with him, just as I had failed a few years earlier with the psychology professor at the University of Minnesota.

I lived in a Boston parish where the Irish priests shocked me by making narrow-minded, intolerant comments about Protestants. I guess I was not ready for that, having grown up with good Protestants in Minnesota, which is thirty percent Lutheran, thirty percent other Protestant, twenty-seven percent Catholic, and two percent Jewish. In this state Lutherans and other Protestants operate excellent seminaries, colleges, and other institutions. The Billy Graham Evangelistic Association, with its 30-million dollar annual budget, has its headquarters in Minneapolis. This city is also home to the huge Lutheran Social Services headquarters. As the saying goes, if Lutheranism died, the funeral would be in Minneapolis. I never wanted it to die. In Minnesota, Catholics and Protestants get along famously, with great

---

[4] *Orate Fratres*, vol. 10 (18 April 1936), 281-285.

respect for each other. Anyway, I think that is why I was shocked by the uncalled-for comments of Bostonian Irish priests.

Instead of taking a vacation after that intensive summer at Harvard, I immediately went back to Washington, D.C. to write my doctoral dissertation, which I vowed to finish as soon as possible. In my fool-ishness I excluded *all* other activities, even reading the daily newspa-pers. Resting/vacationing has never been my cup of tea. (Abbot Alcuin Deutsch always said that vacations are not the lot of monks.) I even made the enormous mistake of giving up the chaplaincy of my "Cana Club," a group of wonderful married couples who met weekly in their homes to discuss the vocation and spirituality of marriage. Before long I almost suffered a psychological breakdown.

In this predicament, I recall that once I did not sleep for an entire week. In a situation like this, you do not know what is happening to your inner self; you have to be rescued. Some kind soul reported my condition to my superior, Abbot Baldwin Dworschak, who wrote me the kindest and most understanding letter in withdrawing me tem-porarily for rest, assuring me he would send me back—which he did. Let me say here that I owe very much to Abbot Baldwin for his wise discerning of my situation, his fatherly handling of a monk who was quite ill without knowing it and, in any case, would have been too stubborn to admit it. Well, after months of recharging at the abbey I went back to Washington to complete my thesis and gain my doctorate in family sociology, with minors in Catholic social thought and cultural anthropology, the architectonic science, a supremely fascinating subject.

UNIVERSITY TEACHING

*H*aving completed my doctorate, I began teaching at St. John's University in the fall of 1956. Here I organized the department of sociology. At various times I taught introductory and industrial sociology, and I taught family sociology each semester until 1974. The latter subject amounted to mostly a comprehensive, semester-long course in marriage preparation and parenting. After taking my first family-sociology course at St. John's, three students entered the seminary. I guess the Benedictine nuns at the neighboring College of

St. Benedict for women wanted religious vocations too, and so they invited me to teach that course to their students—whereupon one of my female students entered the convent!

I always began these family courses by voicing a lifelong conviction: marriage is the only vocation and profession in which amateurs are allowed to ply their trade with little or no preparation and with the sad results that we know. Long before Pope John Paul II examined this principle in his *Letter to Families* (1995), I knew that most social problems have their roots in a dysfunctional family life.

The remaining 1950s, 1960s, and beginning 1970s were wonderful years of making student contact, teaching, and lecturing on various topics throughout the country, especially on liturgical and social subjects, a reflection of my work on Virgil Michel.

An aside: One of my favorite lectures in the family-sociology course and in retreats for the married was on the subject of the differential psychology of men and women. I clearly recall one time I told my college girls that men tend to be more cold, materialistic, and indifferent to suffering, while women are more inclined to be empathetic, sympathetic, and sensitive to pain and tragedy. Thus, when a husband and wife witness a car accident, he is likely to say, "I wonder whether they have insurance?" The wife, on the other hand, may well say, "I wonder if anyone is hurt?" Well, I do not think the girls were over-impressed by what I said.

The day after that class I was a passenger on a six-seater, two-engine airplane when it crashed into a frozen, plowed meadow in eight-below-zero weather near Rolla, North Dakota. The engines had suddenly stopped because the gas line froze; as we fell some 1,500 feet out of the sky, I was in total despair, for we were surely heading for death. "O Lord, only eleven years of priesthood," I thought in my anguish. Selfishly, I forgot to absolve anyone in the perhaps twenty-five seconds of our drop.

We missed by inches several telephone wires and bounced at least twenty feet after hitting the icy ground. The experienced World War II pilot kept the front wheel off the ground for as long as he could as we lost momentum. The plane finally made a complete about-face and came to a stop. We hurriedly and thankfully scrambled to safety fifty yards away before we looked back, afraid of an explosion. A bundled-up farmer who had witnessed the whole episode came to meet us as we stood on the frozen field, luggage in hand, cold and uncomfortable, but glad to be alive. His first question: "Is the plane badly damaged?" When we entered the farmhouse, the wife's first query was, "Is anybody hurt?" She had coffee and cookies waiting on the table for us.

Two days later in class I told my girl-students what had happened, emphasizing that I never again wanted to go this far to prove my point. Years later, in 1988, because I had missed an earlier connecting flight in India, I failed to catch the Pan Am Flight 103 that went on to explode over Lockerbie, Scotland, killing all aboard. Five times I escaped the jaws of death: twice I almost drowned, twice I could have died in plane crashes, and once I almost died of altitude sickness in La Paz, Bolivia—to be described in the next chapter.

Except for the near-disaster in North Dakota, my millions of miles of flying in ninety-one countries were uneventful. For these flights I always tried to be on time. On one occasion, however, I was late, the plane was waiting, and I was the last one to board. As I confronted the hostile faces turned toward this dumb and tardy priest, I quipped, "The last shall be first and the first shall be last," and tension disappeared. On another occasion, an old woman told me that she felt safer because a priest was on the plane. When I got off later and she stayed behind, I told her, "Now you are on your own."

To continue: Upon my return from graduate school in 1956, John Gagliardi (now the second-most-winning college football coach in the country) asked me to be his line coach. I was flattered but had to tell John that I quit high-school coaching when I found myself working out plays during Mass and I couldn't go back to that. He understood, and we have been great friends ever since. I continue to admire his genius; John is truly a great coach and a gentleman. Coaching football is a terribly nerve-wrenching profession, ever-filled with painful anxiety and constant tension. But believe me, as coach you learn all about human nature.

In the 1960s I was awarded a summer-long grant to study the concepts of liberalism and conservatism at the University of California at Berkeley, an institution with many on-campus libraries. In my report I maintained that conservatism was not a doctrine, and surely not an ideology. Later someone summarized my own findings:

> Far from being an ideology, conservatism is more a disposi-
> tion, a general preference for traditional and tested ways,
> an affection for what human beings have created so far and
> a mistrust of efforts to tear those things down in the name
> of untested and potentially dangerous futures.[5]

In short, a vast group of problems can be solved by past human experience. I concluded that I was an extreme centrist: maintaining respect for the best of the tried and tested (the best of the past) and still open to all the possible things of the future. Of course, this disposition requires a mature discernment, a knowledge of history, and a broad intellectual background.

Another grant brought me one summer to American University in Washington, D.C. Here I heard fascinating lectures and discussions on the relation between science and religion. Very interesting were the collaborators of Albert Einstein, who told us how that great mind functioned: "He was always thinking." I recall stopping one aimless discussion by suggesting that perhaps the order in the universe implied an intelligent creator. Had not the historian of science, Alfred North Whitehead, asserted that every scientist assumes order in the universe? The point seemed well taken.

Two memories of university teaching I am especially proud of: I secured the largest number of graduate scholarships for my students; also the Jewish provost Dr. O. William Pearlmutter several times told me that, upon asking alumni who, of all their teachers, had influenced them the most, he found that I constantly ranked in the top three. But, then, I had a great advantage: my course in family sociology, because it amounted mostly to marriage-preparation and parenting, dealt with a highly personal subject that easily invited student confidences.

TOURING EUROPE

*T*he summer of 1959 was interesting and unique. I was chaplain, general tour guide, and guardian of the virtue of thirty-four women Catholic-college graduates and nurses in a 64-day tour of ten

---

[5] E. J. Dionne, Jr., *Washington Post*, 12 March 1996.

countries in Europe. One lucky lad did manage to join this bevy of females, and I remember that Bishop Leonard Cowley expressed the hope that this young man was "a good and nice guy." He was. We went over by ship and back by ship. It was a truly magnificent experience. When Abbot Baldwin read the list of girls, he said that he would never have allowed me to accompany them had he known my charges were virtually all women. "Have you ever heard of any complaints about me in that regard?" I asked him. "No," he assured me, and then requested that I write him a card every day. I did.

The tour was exceedingly well organized. A shy, trustworthy Austrian graduate-school student took charge of all the tickets and hotel arrangements. In every city a special tour guide showed us around; we saw and experienced a lot! For instance, the girls were to have no dates except by my permission, and no girl could leave the group by herself. There were several rules. I went on many "dates" accompanying the girls to various places that summer, since I was their overall chaperone.

One night in a beerkeller in Innsbruck, after a night of convivial beer-drinking, three young Austrian men entered the scene; they bought several bottles of champagne, with which the girls duly topped off the beer. I had earlier left the party, believing that the group was in the good hands of the three other men of our party. But several girls got drunk and had to be helped back to the hotel.

The next morning I sensed that something had gone wrong and that sooner or later I would find out. Indeed, at our next stop, Venice, I did find out. We four men—the Dutch bus driver Hennie (carefully chosen for his trustworthiness, I learned later), the "nice guy" Bob of New Jersey, the Austrian treasurer Franz, and I—were sitting at table when Hennie in his broken English told me what had happened the night before. Although the girls had, as it turned out, suffered only intoxication, Hennie warned me about what could have happened. He concluded: "Now, Fodder, girl go home; modder find girl p-r-e-gnant; modder no blame Franz; modder no blame Bub; modder no blame me; modder blame you!"

At that point I fully realized my totally delicate responsibilities. I can claim that one of my notable priestly achievements was to bring thirty-four red-blooded girls through ten countries of Europe over sixty-four days, having a great *and* chaste time. Alas, I learned very much that summer! I confirmed what I had always known and taught: that there is a vast, inherent, God-planned, emotional and psychological difference between male and female. This truth, of course, is sadly and vehemently resented and denied by die-hard feminists, who hate Freud's dictum "Anatomy is destiny." How right was the marriage counselor Professor Al Clemens in graduate school: "Seventy-five percent of marriage counseling consists of explaining him to her and her to him"!

THE AMERICAN LAW INSTITUTE PROPOSAL

*M*y life changed enormously in 1959, when the American Law Institute drafted a proposal to the state legislatures permitting abortion for rape, incest, fetal defects, mental or physical health, and the mother's life. When the proposal came to my attention I recognized it immediately as abortion-on-demand.

But no one foresaw the future tragedies of legal abortion earlier or more clearly than Professor Eugene Quay of Georgetown University's Law School. Though very ill, he wrote two long, magnificent, and insightful articles predicting and describing the dangers of what was to come. The articles were published in *The Georgetown Law Review*.[6] In the middle 1960s I began my own writing and lecturing against baby-killing while continuing to teach a full load of classes.

In 1972, seeing the ominous clouds foreshadowing the massive war on the unborn, I founded the Human Life Center at St. John's University with a $50,000 grant from the De Rance Corporation in Milwaukee. The idea had come to me as early as 1970, but I faced much local opposition stemming from ignorance of what was happening in society and of what abortionists were poised to do. This developing culture of death would preoccupy me for the rest of my life and would take me to many countries of the world.

But I am getting a little ahead of myself. First comes the story of my fascinating infiltration of the fantastic world of an abortion symposium.

---

[6] "Justifiable Abortion," *Georgetown Law Review*, vol. 49, no. 2 (Winter 1960), 173-256; vol. 49, no. 3 (Spring 1961), 395-538.

CHAPTER 3

That Meeting

For almost ten years I had been following the abortion movement when across my desk came a flyer announcing an incredible full-three-day symposium at the International Hotel (now
Wyndham) near the Los Angeles Airport; this meeting was to
be an assemblage of eminent doctors, heads of hospitals, Planned
Parenthood officials, lawyers and judges, health-insurance executives,
Protestant ministers, Senator Robert Packwood, and many other significant persons in the legal and medical fields. The program was entitled
"Therapeutic Abortion—A Symposium on Implementation." It was to
run Friday, Saturday, and Sunday, 22-24 January 1971. (It is important
for the reader to remember this date: a full two years before *Roe v.
Wade.*)

The central point of the meeting was the question of how to implement abortion-on-request in the United States, how to change society
to accept it, how to change state laws, how to oppose religious and
other opposing forces, and how to influence the United States Supreme
Court! This announcement, listing its case of prominent professors,
lawyers, doctors, and notable opinion-molders, was mind-boggling in
its nefarious aims.

I was determined to take part. First I had to secure written permission just to attend and special written permission to record any part of
the meeting. For the first time ever I called myself "Dr. Marx" in my
machinations to get in; nor was I lying, since I had obtained my doctorate in family sociology. A careless secretary wrote me permission to
attend, and another, still more careless, secretary granted me the special written permission to tape. With recorder on shoulder I was
checked carefully at the door each time for the three days, the first

time by two huge men who must have been football players. A notorious doctor-abortionist about whom I had just been reading felt sorry for me on that first entrance, telling the two checkers, "For all you know he could be the editor of the proceedings." Little did he know!

Some time before, I had purchased the best recorder available, a German-made Uher, which was widely used in the radio world at that time. Seven days before this symposium I had attended a professional marriage-counseling meeting in California and tried to record the various talks. Alas, I have no grain of mechanical or technological abilities (I am, in truth, a klutz) and so did not capture a word, because the four crucial buttons were not in their proper place. I don't recall doing much of anything to set the recorder correctly for this most important abortion symposium, but by the grace of God all four buttons worked, and I recorded every single word, even the notorious theologian Joseph S. Fletcher's incredible banquet address.

From the beginning of the abortion battle in the United States, baby-killers made abortion a religious issue, particularly a Catholic issue.[1] That ruse fooled many who did not know that abortion is not a primarily religious, sectarian issue but is concerned with natural law, with natural rights, with the basic right to life in which all other rights inhere. Just as no one should shoplift, whether he is a Lutheran, a Jew, a Catholic, or an atheist, so no one should kill innocent unborn babies. Even before this meeting was announced, I had received permission from my superior, Abbot John Eidenschenk, to wear civilian clothes whenever, as he said, I would find that helpful in the battle. Thus, I was nattily attired in a business suit as I took part in these unforgettable three days of hell.

Between four and five hundred would-be "implementers" from all parts of the country attended. I felt strange indeed, to say the least, sitting among so many evil people who were determined to change the law and the culture to allow the murder of unborn babies for their own convenience. I don't think I had ever felt so lonely in my life. Marching outside were about ten pickets. Of course I could not join them. As I walked in and out, most of them thought I was one of the

---

[1]   Bernard N. Nathanson, MD, *The Hand of God* (Washington: Regency 1996), pp. 86-90.

I had received permission from my superior, Abbot John Eidenschenk, to wear civilian clothes whenever, as he said, I would find that helpful in the battle. Here I am "undercover" over the years of the pro-life fight.

killers. But to one who recognized me I was secretly able to whisper that he and his colleagues would not believe what was going on inside the hotel. I recall the response: "Oh yes we would."

Of course, blatantly present and oppressively loud were numerous representatives of Planned Parenthood, the National Association for Repeal of Abortion Laws (NARAL), later changed to the National Abortion Rights Action League, and currently styling itself as the National Abortion and Reproductive Rights Action League, and other such groups that had sprung up to foment the war on the unborn.

Physicians and lawyers will recognize the names of such advertised lecturers as S. Leon Israel, MD; Robert E. Hall, MD; Sadja Goldsmith, MD (infamous for the concept of "outercourse"); George J. Langmyhr, MD, and Donald Minkler, MD (speaking on the role of private foundations); the Honorable Richard Lamm, who, as governor of Colorado, presided in 1967 over the first abortion bill

passed in this country; the very noisy and active medical professor
Edmund W. Overstreet, MD; J. Robert Bragonier, MD; Judge Ruth
Roemer; the notorious legal propagandist Roy Lucas, JD; Dr. Joseph
S. Fletcher, father of situation ethics; representatives of Blue Cross/Blue
Shield and other insurance companies; Prof. Irvin M. Cushner, MD;
and, of course, Oregon's now-disgraced Senator Robert Packwood.

The disreputable Packwood, who was unable to attend as scheduled, telephoned from Washington, D.C., and gave a forty-minute
speech, offering to answer questions. With remarkable frankness, he
literally coached the symposium on how to override restrictive abortion laws by challenging or breaking the law and/or bringing court
action. He even furnished details on how the abortionists could milk
the federal government and its agencies for maximum amounts of
money to promote baby-killing. The term "therapeutic abortion"
should be dumped immediately, he advised, and "legal abortion" sub-
stituted. He was confident that abortion would be legalized through
state-by-state legislation, or through court action, within two to five
years. Of course, he said, abortion was a woman's personal right, a
decision for her and her doctor alone to make.

The Supreme Court justices, the senator confided, felt much put
upon these days with pornography and other controversial issues.
They were keenly aware of public opinion and felt very hesitant about
becoming, possibly, the first Supreme Court to legalize abortion,
observed Packwood. How wrong he was! Packwood actually claimed
to have entertained several justices in his home and to have discussed
abortion with others. On these contacts he based his emphatic statement that he did not want to demean the institution of the Supreme
Court by nationalizing abortion-at-will. At the same time, Packwood
confided, most legislators, not least the members of Congress, wished
the Supreme Court would take them off the hook. Alas, seven justices
surely did!

In coaching his avid audience, the sinister Packwood suggested that
he might introduce a National Abortion Act, although he doubted it
would pass. The best thing to do in the situation was to have abortion
liberalized in the various states first, as legislators in Hawaii,
Colorado, and New York had already done, or as Washington had
done by referendum in 1970. The senator from Oregon proclaimed,

"It is going to take fifteen to twenty states to bring down the law, and possibly three or four years for Congress." To help launch the process, Packwood said he would introduce an abortion-liberalization bill in the District of Columbia. After the symposium, Packwood did indeed introduce his bill.

But he gave further advice: "Not going beyond what the federal government can do, we need to look at what the military establishment has done and can still do. The federal government has exclusive jurisdiction over military installations." Packwood confessed that he had been goading the Defense Department into allowing and promoting legal abortions for military personnel.

Packwood was relentless. He next commented that nothing had as yet been done for the Indian reservations and the Alaskan Eskimo settlements, which were "ripe for action." Here, too, Packwood had started the ball rolling by writing to the Bureau of Indian Affairs and to the Department of the Interior—without, however, receiving any reply. "They just have no policy," he moaned; "the federal government could see to it that they get one."

Packwood was appalled that the Tidings Family Planning and Population Act, which had allocated $382,000,000 for fiscal 1972- 73 for family-planning services and publication/research activities, excluded money for abortion. He gave detailed suggestions for by-passing that prohibition:

> If a national grant were made to Chicago's Planned
> Parenthood, for example, they could use the money for
> other purposes and expenses, while using the current
> monies to promote abortion. This would give every
> Congressman a way out if challenged by a constituent: he
> could say he voted against abortion.

Packwood had surely done his homework for his villainy: he proposed various health acts to funnel money to be used for abortion purposes. He went on:

> The Public Health Service Act likewise grants to states vari-
> ous monies, the purpose of which is to be decided by the
> states. For these various acts the federal government can

grant money to the states with liberal abortion laws, to be
used to implement abortion programs.

Packwood's thoroughness and frankness were truly amazing. For
example: "Section V of the Social Security Act, under the guise of
infant care and the like (in connection with low-income people), could
be used to make funds available for abortion services. Avoid using the
word 'abortion' in connection with these programs and monies." He
emphasized:

> The various agencies should not bug Congress unduly, but
> let the national agencies do what they can and want to do
> without undue pressures. Thus, we can talk about the wel-
> fare of maternal health when what we actually are doing is
> making possible abortion for these women. So far as the
> Hill-Burton monies are concerned, there is no problem. But
> what about hospitals' religious convictions as to abortion?
> The federal government will not push any state or hospital
> for two or three years. Too touchy. Years may go by.

Packwood admitted that last year he had not found a single sponsor for his bills among a hundred senators. "Abortion is simply political dynamite. Congressmen simply do not want to get involved with it
in any way—by deed, by vote, or by association," the senator
observed.

When the then-darling of Planned Parenthood Senator Packwood
had finished and the moderator had remarked that he had not thought
things were all that bad in Congress, because they did not even talk
about sex, Packwood responded, "They don't talk about it, they just
do it." That brought a burst of laughter.

In answer to a question, the abortion senator said that the only
national law in which money was forbidden for abortion was the
National Family Planning Act. He quoted the passage with emphasis
three times: "None of the funds appropriated under *this* [emphasis,
Packwood's] title shall be used in programs where abortion is a
method of family planning." To another question, he replied that in
his close relations with several Supreme Court justices (whom he
refused to name) he had learned that they really believed that the

From long before that momentous 1971 meeting in California to today, Planned Parenthood has always been my greatest enemy. Here Judge John Noonan and I picket in front of a Planned Parenthood abortion clinic in California several years later.

restrictive state abortion statutes were unconstitutional, but he sensed that these justices did not want to vote that way at this time if they could find a procedural way out.

The senator from Oregon held out little prospect that the Supreme Court would act for abortion repeal or that Congress would pass a national abortion act or even legalize abortion in the District of Columbia.

What were chances of funding sterilization programs that were now in committee? He thought that was possible in view of the tremendous change of attitudes, although abortion itself was still a "very dirty word." So much for Packwood's coaching the abortionists by phone from the nation's capital!

Now, one can only speculate whether this wicked senator, who had so frankly tutored these leaders in the abortion movement, was later punished by the Lord. At any rate, his troubles in Congress began with his legendary sexual activities and ended with his being relieved of his senatorial duties in great disgrace.

If I could designate a centerpiece of this whole outlandish meeting, it would probably be this astonishing statement by Professor Irvin Cushner, formerly deputy secretary of the Department of Health, Education and Welfare, also of UCLA's School of Medicine, later the

Abortion: the greatest exploitation of women. Here Dr. Garvin Kuskey held this sign at a HLI conference in Irvine, 1988.

head of Obstetrics and Gynecology and perhaps one of the country's most competent gynecologists:

> I suggest to you that for the individual, the role of abortion will be, as it has been, the second line of defense against harmful pregnancy and the unwanted child. These are contraceptive failures. The societal role will require that we see family planning in a true light; no matter how thinly you slice it, ladies and gentlemen, family planning is a euphemism. We don't intend or desire to prevent conception for conception's sake; we want to prevent conception because of what follows conception. Family planning is the prevention of births, and as birth is the end of a sequence which begins with the sexual urge, then family planning is anti-conception, anti-nidation [abortifacient], and the termination of the conceptus if implanted. This is the social role of abortion in the future.

I wish I could frame the above paragraph, put it on the wall in front of every Catholic priest's desk, and urge him to read it twice weekly.

In fact, how I wished, sitting through this three-day nightmare, that every bishop, priest, and religious were there to hear the many other candid acknowledgments that contraception was the logical prelude to legal abortion. Given the idiosyncracies of human sexual activity, as was stated again and again, no matter how successful the future development of foolproof contraception, abortion would always be necessary as a remedy for contraceptive failure!

The evidence is mountainous that contraception leads to abortion, and yet bishops and priests just do not seem to see the connection, if one may judge by the fact that they rarely (if ever) preach against it. I myself have preached in more than 600 parishes in the last thirty years, always telling it as it is and then going to the back of the church to absorb the flack of departing parishioners. In 95 percent of the parishes, people tell me I am the first priest to talk about contraception/sterilization from the pulpit. According to a 1990 U.S. census report, 47.6 percent of women and 20.8 percent of men in the United States had been sterilized by the age of 44 - 45.[2] Does any pulpit ring with condemnation of this gross violation of the human person, this "permanent contraception," as anti-lifers euphemize it?

The most well-known abortionist in the world, Dr. Malcolm Potts, openly admits what so many clergymen cannot see, or refuse to see. Potts, who once was the medical director of International Planned Parenthood Federation (IPPF) in London, said, "As people turn to contraception there will be a rise, not a fall, in the abortion rate."[3] An ace abortionist in England, Dr. Judith Bury, observed, "There is overwhelming evidence that contrary to what you might expect, the provision of contraception leads to an increase in the abortion rate."[4] I could cite forty abortionists who have admitted the same thing.

In connection with teaching family sociology, I have looked into the history of contraception and confirmed the fact that it has always led to abortion. Note this statement of the great Jesuit theologian, Father John Hardon:

---

[2] See U.S. Census *Advanced Data* #182, 20 March 1990, issued by the Vital and Health Statistics of the National Center for Health Statistics. See also pertinent sections in Brian Clowes' *The Facts of Life* (Front Royal: Human Life International, 1997.)

[3] *Cambridge Evening News*, 7 February 1973.

[4] *The Scotsman: Sex Education for Bureaucrats*, 29 June 1981.

THE **DEATH**
 PEDDLERS
WAR ON THE UNBORN
Paul Marx, O.S.B., Ph.D.

The Death Peddlers, *my first pro-life book. It sold 147,000 copies in English.*

I do not believe the pro-life movement will succeed unless those who are strongly pro-life are also defending the teaching of the Church from the first century—that contraception is a grave sin. For many years I have taught a course on the history of contraception. Now over 5,000 years of recorded history, all contraceptive societies became abortive societies. Contraception leads inevitably to abortion and abortion always leads to the destruction of society.[5]

And yet bishops and priests, by and large, seemingly do not believe this testimony; or they do believe it but are afraid to teach and preach it. Meanwhile, contraception, which most often is actually abortifacient nowadays, is destroying the Church and mankind.

At any rate, now I had captured on tape all the active abortion backers with their message of death for family and nation. Several articles I wrote concerning this meeting were published in a newsletter by my good friend John Harrington. Harrington urged, begged, and cajoled me to write a book to "expose these death promoters." "John," I pleaded, "I have no time for books. I have a full load of college courses to teach." He persisted. I did it. Five lawyers recommended to St. John's Abbey that my book not be published. Their fear: gigantic lawsuits, charging libel. It is to the substantial credit of the senior council of St. John's University/Abbey that they allowed its publication—given the good this little 191-page bestseller has done. Later, when I told the lawyer Robert Winn, a right-to-life leader in New Orleans, about the five lawyers who had objected to its publication, he pointed out that the infamous symposium was paid for in part by tax money. The taxpayer has a right to know how his money is spent. "Have them sue you; you can't win, but you'll get great publicity for the book, and you'll sell even more." So I demanded that the lawyers sue me.

---

[5]   One-page insert published by Eternal Life, P.O. Box 787, Bardstown, KY 40604.

The Death Peddlers: War on the Unborn was published in Spanish and Japanese as well as English. It sold 147,000 English-language copies and brought

Here stand the nine Justices who were sitting on the Supreme Court on that infamous day, 22 January 1973.

many into the pro-life movement—as so many have told me through the years. But it also made my life even more impossible. I had many TV and radio interviews as a result of that book. You see, I was a sociologist who opposed abortion. Sociologists usually favor abortion; hence, I was a "nut." Radio and TV like to showcase nuts of my kind. My experiences at being interviewed in this and other countries I shall tell in another chapter. Incidentally, the proceedings of this infamous meeting were published many months later. They were doctored. Honesty is not the long suit of abortionists.

In 1972 the abortionists, having been stymied after only eighteen states had legalized abortion, turned to referenda, choosing big Michigan and little North Dakota as their test sites. Thanks to a generous contributor, I poured 7,000 copies of *The Death Peddlers: War on the Unborn* into Michigan and 300 into North Dakota. One generous soul gave the two North Dakota bishops $100,000 to fight the abortionists. They wisely used some of the money to put under every household door a color folder showing preborn healthy babies and aborted ones at the same stage. In Michigan we won by sixty-two percent of the vote, and in North Dakota by seventy-nine percent. The leader of the pro-life movement in North Dakota was a Lutheran doctor.

Abortion promoters in the early days, as I have noted, charged that abortion was a "Catholic" issue. "Do you want the Catholic hierarchy to make all the moral rules?" they repeatedly asked. With this piece of dishonesty the baby-killers taunted the uninformed public, exploiting the latent anti-Catholic virus in the American culture. The abortionists are satanically clever. And Satan never sleeps. The psalmist calls Satan "a practiced deceiver." About one-fifth of North Dakota was Catholic, proving that not only Catholics had defeated the abortion referendum. Even so, on 22 January 1973 our nine Supreme Court justices voted seven to two in favor of baby-killing, virtually sanctioning abortion-on-demand during the nine months of pregnancy and thus inflicting on the United States the worst abortion law in the whole world, apart from China and Russia.

Phyllis Bowman, Mrs.
Pro-Life of England.

I was on a lecture-tour in England then, and upon hearing this most tragic of all Supreme Court decisions, I had two thoughts: 1) the United States has seen its best days; 2) from now on the quality of human/Christian life in the nation will decline rapidly. The moral fallout had begun; the moral meltdown was in progress. Everything that has happened since then indicates that the deterioration is proceeding almost unopposed. In many debates I confronted abortionists with, "Abortion today, euthanasia when?" I was laughed off scornfully. I countered by reminding my antagonists that the president of Planned Parenthood, Dr. Alan Guttmacher, was already sitting on the board of the American Euthanasia Education Council.

Today we are faced with legalized mercy killing. Nor should anyone be surprised. Human life is of one continuum, from conception to natural death. Either all are safe under one and the same law or no one is safe. Or, as a famous gynecologist observed after the Supreme Court justices wrote that there was no agreement as to the beginning of human life, human life begins at the beginning, with conception/fertilization, and is like a developing chain: if you break the chain before birth, you have abortion; if you break the chain after birth, you have euthanasia. How much deeper must Americans sink into infamy before they awaken to the truth? But nothing blinds like serious sin. And we have become a very sinful nation, using our money and influence to propel the contraception-sterilization-abortion-euthanasia movement all over the world. Would that all America could see what I have seen and experienced!

Seeing Pope Paul VI, four days after Roe v. Wade, 26 January 1973 in Rome. At that meeting, Pope Paul VI said to me: "You are a courageous fighta; never give up."

In 1970, three years before our Supreme Court's Black Monday Decision, one of Australia's six states—South Australia—legalized baby-killing. I went Down Under to give thirty-one lectures in thirty days in an effort to stave off further spread of abortion in that country. I left behind me a long manuscript to be printed as a warning of the imminent euthanasia. Reprinted multiple times, *The Mercy Killers* was revised and published in pamphlet form in several editions, the latest being *Death without Dignity: Killing for Mercy*. Well over a million copies were sold or distributed. It is still floating around.

On 26 January 1973, four days after the infamous U.S. Supreme Court decision was handed down, I went to Rome with Mrs. Pro-Life England, Phyllis Bowman, head of the Society for the Protection of Unborn Children. Our explicit intention was to start an international pro-life movement. We were waiting in Cardinal John Wright's office with his secretary, the kindly current bishop of Pittsburgh, Donald Wuerl, and were about to seek the cardinal's advice and assistance. Just then the ambassador of Japan walked in; out of courtesy we left, after telling Wuerl about our plans.

Cardinal Wright must have arranged for Mrs. Bowman and me to be in the front row when Pope Paul VI granted his next audience.

During that audience a certain priest, surprisingly well-informed of my pro-life activities, came over to tell me that the Pope would come down to talk to me. Judging from this priest's words, the Pope had been briefed about my pro-life activities in various countries, including appearances on radio and TV. The Pope had a medal intended for me; in his confusion he presented it to my dear friend Phyllis Bowman, who surely deserved it! Jewish by birth, she was one of twelve non-Catholics in England who in 1967 had founded the first right-to-life organization in the world, the Society for the Protection of Unborn Children. Because the English baby-killers, like those in America, had made abortion a "Catholic" hangup, the founders wanted no Catholics in their original group. Later, Mrs. Bowman became a devout Catholic. We often worked together, and I learned so much from her. She had been a noted journalist on Fleet Street and knew the world of journalism and lobbying inside out. She has used that insider's knowledge ever since.

When the Pope approached me, I informed him about the horrendous U.S. Supreme Court decision announced four days earlier. He already knew about it. I briefly told him how inclusive and disastrous it was. I don't know if he heard all I said, because he was straining to listen. But then he told me, "You are a courageous fighta; never give up!" That was all I needed to buoy up my spirits.

Alas, if only we could have started that international organization in 1973! The following year, 1974, I sat with medical personnel in Amsterdam organizing the World Federation of Doctors Who Respect Human Life. Although they have sponsored several important meetings in Europe, the organization has always limped because of lack of funds. Why does the enemy always have much money and friendly media, while pro-lifers attract little money and lots of hostility?

As I look back on that infamous abortion symposium of 1971, I ask whether these elite abortionists from the legal, medical, political, social-work, and academic professions were innocently naive or really knew what they were initiating. Did they realize that they were "implementing" the slaughter of helpless, innocent human beings, who just happened to obstruct the various ambitions of their elders? My opinion was and is that these death peddlers knew very well what they were doing—and therein lies the real horror.

Four months before the symposium convened, the editor of *California Medicine,* the official journal of the California Medical Association, published this brutally but refreshingly frank statement:

> Legal abortion will of necessity violate and ultimately destroy the traditional Western ethic with all that this portends. It will become necessary and acceptable to place relative rather than absolute values on such things as human lives, the use of scarce resources and the various elements which are to make up the quality of life or of living which is to be sought. This is quite distinctly at variance with the Judeo-Christian ethic and carries serious philosophical, social, economic, and political implications for Western society and perhaps for world society.[6]

The process of eroding the old ethic and substituting the new has already begun. It may be seen most clearly in changing attitudes towards human abortion. In defiance of the long-held Western ethic of intrinsic and equal value of every human life regardless of its stage, condition, or stages, abortion is becoming accepted by society as moral, right, and even necessary. It is worth noting that this shift in public attitude has affected the churches, the laws, and public policy rather than the reverse. Since the old ethic has not yet been fully displaced it has been necessary to separate the idea of abortion from the idea of killing, which continues to be socially abhorrent. The result has been a curious avoidance of the scientific fact, which everyone really knows, that human life begins at conception and is continuous whether intra- or extra-uterine until death. The very considerable semantic gymnastics which are required to rationalize abortion as anything but taking a human life would be ludicrous if they were not often put forth under socially impeccable auspices. It is suggested that this schizophrenic sort of subterfuge is necessary because while a new ethic is

---

[6] Vol. 113, no. 3 (September 1970).

being accepted the old one has not yet been rejected.

That statement said it all. The new barbarians were subtly at work. (See Appendix A for the whole editorial.)

CHAPTER 4

In Latin America

B efore 1970 I already knew that a worldwide movement to relax or remove all abortion laws was afoot, especially in the United States and Western Europe. So did the great pro-life Chicago lawyer Dennis Horan, whose premature death so deeply pained me. Also aware of the movement was the pro-life pioneer, my friend Dr. Joseph Stanton, and Dr. Bart Heffernan, who, with his wife Gloria (also a doctor), did so much to found Illinois Right to Life. I am sure there were others.

In 1952, the pernicious International Planned Parenthood Federation (IPPF) was founded, with headquarters in London. As pro-lifers have been pointing out, the backbone of the anti-life/anti-family movement is IPPF, internationally organized and funded by governments and foundations to promote contraception, sterilization, surgical abortion, abortifacients, euthanasia — and, not least, biological, explicit, value-free (or reality-based, as they now say) sex ed. Regionally organized into 140 affiliates around the world, IPPF claims within its influence 96 percent of mankind. The brain of this ruinous juggernaut is the Rockefeller-funded Population Council in New York.

The life-and-family-destroying IPPF has zealously infiltrated governments and the communications media, to say nothing of the legal and medical professions. With its further linkage to the United Nations Fund for Population Activities and other branches of the corrupted UN, it is, in my opinion, mankind's most dangerous enemy. At this writing fifty-eight nations have non-replacement birthrates of 2.1 or less, thanks to these nefarious organizations. (Nine nations are at 2.2.)

For years I had been tracking IPPF when, in 1972, I requested a year's sabbatical to spend several months in Latin America attempting to organize a pro-life resistance. I was thoroughly convinced that,

SYNTEX, the Pill manufacturer in Mexico, is part of the hideous American population control imperialism.

sooner or later, these death-promoters and family-destroyers would descend in full force on the only Catholic continent on earth.

In that same year the Family Planning International Association, a separately funded relative of Planned Parenthood Federation of America, began to "increase awareness of, and access to, family planning services in developing countries."[1] As always, they targeted teens with physical sex education, downplaying the influence of "old-fashioned parents," invading governmental health and education departments, and promoting contraceptives and abortifacients, even menstrual regulation, i.e., early suction abortion.

IPPF began spreading its tentacles by setting up "family-planning associations" (FPAs) in the British Commonwealth of Nations, often giving them different names in other countries to fit local situations. Thus, in Mexico, for example, they are known as MEXFAM, whose youth-oriented, sex-ed division, called *Centro de Orientacion para Adolescentes* (CORA), conducts totally explicit sex ed and distributes condoms and abortifacient pills to youth without parental knowledge

---

[1] PPFA 1987 Annual Report, p. 6. *Deadly Deception: International Planned Parenthood: Assault on Your Children, Your Family and Your Nation's Sovereignty* vol. 1, 1996. Robert Marshall and Charles Donovan, *Blessed Are the Barren* (San Francisco: Ignatius Press, 1991). See also Human Life International's Reprint 9: Gary Bergel, "The Monstrosity of Planned Parenthood" and Reprint 34: Jonah Dimaano, "Planned Parenthood: Wolf in Sheep's Clothing."

*Angelina Muñiz
— my interpreter
in Mexico.*

and consent. Founded on 15 May 1978 and now numbering 30,000 members, MEXFAM looks for leaders at educational, work, and rural centers, where it promotes unbridled "responsible" sex with a view toward luring the young away from what MEXFAM called the "outmoded" thinking and customs of parents. CORA spreads the idea that children between eleven and fifteen years have a right to sexual activity with contraception and sterilization, even without parental oversight. As in most developing countries, the Pill, Depo-Provera, and so on, are freely distributed without benefit of medical prescription.

In Brazil, Planned Parenthood calls itself BEMFAM, meaning "benefiting the family"; and in Germany, ProFamilia! In Germany and other Western countries, and more so in Third World nations, Planned Parenthood has encountered surprisingly little resistance.

Before advancing into Latin America, I knew one Spanish word— *caramba*! But loaded with films (no lightweight video cassettes then), slides, literature, and enough money to get back, I set out. I was brave then. The experience (lugging four bags!) was to cost me two hernias. But all in all, I can say it was indeed worth it. Over the years I had built up various contacts on which to construct eventual "beachheads." (By now, Human Life International has conducted more than thirty pro-life/pro-family seminars and symposia in Latin America and has set up an office in Miami with a staff of six working exclusively in Spanish-speaking countries.)

I began my tour in Mexico, where I knew several people and which I had already visited several times; I lectured in various locations,

My chauffer and ride in Mexico, 1987.

being assisted in 1972 and in subsequent years by Angelina Muñiz and her skillful interpretation. She helped me so often that she could have given my lecture—and, in fact, several times she did! (Eventually she began teaching natural family planning.) In Mexico I encountered MEXFAM and then proceeded to Costa Rica, Honduras, El Salvador, Guatemala, Panama, Ecuador, Peru, Bolivia, Chile, Uruguay, Argentina, Brazil, Venezuela, and finally Colombia. In addition to slide-lectures, I showed films whenever the opportunity presented itself. I distributed many copies of Father William Hogan's pioneer film *Abortion: A Woman's Decision*, in which appeared the eminent pro-life pediatrician Dr. Eugene Diamond. In El Salvador and other countries, medical professors and doctors sponsored me before their medical societies and groups of students, nurses, and others. In one of these Latin American medical schools I saw my first medical cadaver, and I remember how touched I was when a medical student asked me to offer a Mass for the cadaver he was carving up in order to learn anatomy.

I did an hour's program on Costa Rican TV, showing pictures of aborted babies at various stages and offering suitable commentary. When my interpreter and I got back to his home, the phone began to ring off the wall! I showed my set of slides and Hogan's film to many high-school students and other groups. The reaction of young and old was always total shock, even though illegal abortion was by no means rare. In fact, my biggest surprise during these months was learning the number of illegal abortions performed in Latin America.

Most of them were induced by the *comadrona,* unschooled midwives who would abort girls and woman in various ways, often leaving the victim bleeding and then telling her, "If this bleeding does not stop by tomorrow morning, rush to the hospital." Of course, the victimized woman thought for sure it would stop by noon; when she finally arrived at a hospital, the partial abortion had to be completed, and sometimes a hysterectomy ended her fertility permanently. Death of the mother, apparently, was a fairly rare complication. Doctors in El Salvador, with its six million people, told me that they estimated one hundred women died from illegal abortions yearly. That number is small compared with the propagandistic claims made by the abortionists promoting permissive abortion in Latin America and elsewhere today.[2]

In many subsequent returns to Mexico I gave a lot of speeches. I learned that so vast was the damage caused by the *comadrona*—so out of control was illegal aborting—that the Mexican government ran classes to teach them female anatomy so that they would do less damage and incur lower medical costs. Today the estimated number of illegal abortions is 800,000 in a population of eighty million. In 1984 I organized a large national symposium in Mexico City with the fine help of Angelina Muñiz, an auxiliary bishop, and several others. Mrs. Muñiz also headed our center there, which enjoyed the full cooperation of Cardinal Ahumada Corripio. The latter gave a truly outstanding address at our symposium; few cardinals have encouraged me more than he. I was to return often to Mexico, speaking in most of its large cities.

---

[2] See my books *Confessions of a Prolife Missionary, Fighting for Life, The Flying Monk,* and *The Warehouse Priest,* all published by Human Life International. See also frequent reports in Human Life International's monthly *Special Report* and in its *Population Research Institute Review.* Much information and data for this book came from my many diaries.

PERU AND BOLIVIA

A lasting memory of mine is the museum in Lima, Peru, that depicts the punishments generated by the Spanish Inquisition. In Lima I lectured to students in a medical school who were under the tender guidance of a highly concerned medical professor whose name I have long forgotten. I used to bring down the house by telling eager medical students to beware of the abortion-promoting "*imperialista gringo del Norte Americano.*" In the historic city of Cuzco I viewed the magnificent ruins of the Inca empire. Cuzco, the Incan capital, was hidden away from the Spanish invaders, high in the mountains; it was rediscovered by a Yale professor only in 1911.

Real troubles began for me in Puno, on the border of Peru and Bolivia. I had a ticket to cross overnight into Bolivia by ocean liner over Lake Titicaca, a huge, 100-mile-long lake at the top of a mountain—one of the great wonders of the world. Sections of a ship had been dragged up the mountain and reassembled there as a tourist attraction. For reasons I could not understand, the liner's conductors would not accept me, although my ticket had been purchased well in advance. A kindly ambassador's wife coached me on how to bribe an agent with American dollars, but even that did not help, although I tried several times. Finally a Cuban priest from the archdiocese of Washington, D.C., seeing my passport, discovered I was a priest and said I should have no trouble getting on the boat. "Give 'em a few bucks," he suggested. I did—only to lose more bucks! Well after midnight, shivering in the wintry cold of early morning, he and I, together with the deacon accompanying him, looked up the Maryknollers in town and rousted them out of bed at 2:00 a.m. They graciously gave us shelter.

One Maryknoller told us that when he first came to Chile a native priest invited him to dinner. While the pastor sat at the head of the table with three children in tow, the 'wife' served dinner. This Maryknoller was convinced that married priests were a future likelihood. I disagreed, saying Rome was not likely to approve. (Today I'm not quite so sure.) He predicted that, given the appalling shortage of priests, some bishop would force the issue by ordaining married men.

"Would a bishop be so rash as to risk excommunication?" I asked.

The next afternoon we followed the Maryknollers' instructions and proceeded by taxi, boat, and bus to La Paz, the capital of Bolivia and the highest city in the world. The airport is 14,000 feet and the city 12,000 feet above sea level. Instead of my checking into a cheap hotel—where I might have died, in the light of subsequent events—the good priest suggested that I join them at a parish mission conducted by a

Holding an Indian baby in Guatemala, 1972.

Maltese missionary-pastor with some nuns. The next day, while I was discussing the abortion movement with an American nun, she commented, "You look like death warmed over!"

Breathing ever faster for lack of oxygen, I soon found myself in a chilly bed in an unheated room. A bad head cold was making me even more uncomfortable. Eleven people were standing around my bed, wringing their hands and wondering what to do with this stupid monk who had come there in the winter and was gasping for air even as he worried about abortion. Indeed, they all tried to be helpful in their obvious helplessness.

In came the gentle, short Maltese missionary-pastor. He knew exactly what was happening to me. He had seen it many times before. It seems that some people actually die from altitude sickness; many missionaries periodically get out of La Paz for a time to recharge their systems at a lower altitude. Unfortunately, my travel agent had failed to warn me that I should have been taking certain pills to step up the production of red corpuscles per hour. So now I was desperately fighting for breath.

The good pastor quickly ordered all eleven people out of the room, brought in a Spanish doctor, and commandeered an oxygen tank—which, typically, did not work. The doctor, who could not speak English, did his thing; then he left the room to talk with the pastor. Back came the kindly pastor to relay the doctor's comments, saying in his gentle, broken English: "Fodder, Fodder: your wital signs are all

With the First Lady in Costa Rica.

gooood. You paanic. Don't paanic. I get you down by Saantiago. There's lots of air there. Don't worry. I take gooood care of you. Your wital signs are all gooood. Now I go to let you rest. But Fodder, I come baack in fifteen minutes. Fodder, don't paanic!"

True enough, every fifteen minutes, for more than two hours, he returned to assure me that although I *had* panicked, my "wital signs were all gooood." I continued to gasp. Meanwhile, he and others packed my things in my four bags, rearranged my ticket, threw the bags onto a beat-up pickup truck, and hauled me to the airport—2,000 feet higher! Alas, the President of Peru had just flown in, and we were faced with a long delay and a half-mile walk. The pastor kept reminding me that my "wital signs were all gooood."

After being checked again and again by a doctor as I lay waiting for Lufthansa, I was pushed to the plane in a wheelchair. Once I reached the pressurized cabin and had taken the pills the stewardess gave me, my "wital signs" and I were ready to lick every abortionist in the world!

Needless to say, I did not do much in Bolivia except to thank the good Lord profusely for the invention of oxygen. I witnessed appalling poverty in my travels through this immense, landlocked country, so rich in natural resources but the poorest in Latin America, known for its unstable governments. Only 7,156,591 people, eighty-seven percent of them Catholics, live on its 424,164 square miles. Sixty percent are descendants of pre-Colombian inhabitants, with more than thirty ethnic groups. Just recently I found out that an IPPF branch is making illegal abortions available to them.

What an experience! I learned, as nothing else could have taught me that, indeed, every breath is a gift from the Lord. I shall never forget this horrendous ordeal and the awful conviction that I was choking to death. I gained a total sympathy for asthma sufferers! Nor shall I ever forget the supreme kindness of that understanding little wisp of a Maltese missionary, whom I never saw again. He surely did me an enormous favor, literally saving my life. For that matter, if I had gotten onto that ocean liner at Lake Titicaca, I would have wound up in a cheap hotel and, overcome by altitude sickness and unable to communicate, may well have died. God has His ways. But I never want to go back to La Paz!

After hours of flying we finally arrived in Santiago, Chile, at four o'clock in the morning. Indeed, there was lots of air here, as the good pastor had predicted!

CHILE

Archbishop Roman Grieta of San José, Costa Rica, introducing me to his priests.

*W*aiting outside the airport were a number of taxis. One driver demanded an outlandish $16 to take me to the downtown hotel that the Maltese pastor had lined up for me. I bravely walked away, knowing another taxi driver would come along for further bargaining. Then one of those apparent miracles happened. (Keep in mind that I was dressed in my "professional" suit.) A small pick-up truck stopped; the grandmother driving it had come for her daughter and grandchild at the airport. In very broken English she asked me, "You downtown maybe go?" Indeed! I threw my four bags into the truck and gleefully jumped into the cab, asking my benefactors whether they always picked up bums like me. Mother and daughter looked at each other, perplexed;

they admitted that they never stopped for strangers. But then why did they pick me up? When I told them I was a missionary padre fighting abortion, they made me an instant hero.

It was the time during which the socialist Salvador Allende was trying to bring radical socialism to Chile. He had ruined the economy in the process, so that in my high-class hotel the waiter brought me gnarled apples and coffee for breakfast one morning. I showed my films and slides here and there. A thoughtful gentleman arranged my week and also gave me tours in and out of the city. One time I almost panicked when we reached an altitude of 7,000 feet, and he gently suggested turning back. To this day any altitude of 5,000 feet or more immediately alerts my alarm system—and memories.

Again, the week of laying foundations provided a base on which our great pro-life coordinator in Latin America, the incomparable Magaly Llaguno, could build. (In 1994, Human Life International conducted a large leadership conference and a symposium addressed by Cardinal Alfonso Lopez-Trujillo, president of the Pontifical Council for the Family. The symposium drew more than 5,000 participants from seventeen countries. More than 2,000 youth held their own meeting. The cardinal was surprised to learn that this was our eighth major meeting in Latin America.)

URUGUAY

*M*y next stop was Montevideo, Uruguay, where I was the guest of the zealous pro-lifer and priest, Father Pedro Richards, CP, who even to this day conducts a pro-family center with little money and lots of faith. Uruguay was in the throes of a socio-economic and political revolution, with not a few terrorists—the militant Tupamaros—doing their thing. I saw a great deal of this little country of 3.2 million people. They had the great misfortune of having their abortion law relaxed in 1938, with the usual consequences. I met officials of the Family Planning Association (*Associacion Uruguaya de Planificacion Familiar*—AUPF).

I also met a representative of the United States Agency for International Development (USAID) and asked him why his organization was engaged in international contraceptive imperialism. A bit annoyed, he insisted that population control was only a part of what they do—that they do only what developing nations request, all of which was untrue. Obviously he had never been faced with such rude questioning! He soon found out that I knew more about USAID than he had suspected. I gave the same treatment to a "Catholic" doctor bribed by IPPF to work with them, something I have often witnessed.

My greatest disappointment was the cancellation of a three-hour Saturday night session on the most popular program on nationwide TV. Thanks to Father Pedro's connections, I would have been allowed to show whatever I wished and say whatever I liked, with good Father Pedro coaching me and translating. Most unfortunately, a strike forced the abandonment of our carefully planned telecast. That was a sad blow to Father Pedro and me. Imagine: we could have had three hours on abortion over national TV in 1972! Thereafter we accomplished what we could with lectures here and there, and Father was often help-ful to me in my return visits to other Latin American countries.

Uruguay, slightly smaller than Washington State and sixty-six per-cent Roman Catholic, was once a wealthy country known as "the Venice of Latin America." But many wild political groups and enemies of the Church had plunged it into wretched poverty. I remember see-ing ancient cars, potholed streets, and buildings in shambles, like Cuba today. It came home to me again how much harm bad governments do; how important good governments are for the welfare of the peo-ple. Incidentally, that week I was asked what plane I had flown from Chile. My questioner said I was a very lucky man to be alive, because the airline I named was notorious for its crashes!

During my week in Uruguay I had the unusual experience of meeting some of the sixteen Andes survivors. You may remember the story. A Uruguay rugby team with family members and friends were heading to Santiago, Chile, by chartered plane. On their way, because of a series of downdrafts and a serious pilot error, the plane crashed in the vast, snowy wastes of the high Andes. One of the two pilots was killed instantly. The other, trapped in the crushed cabin with horribly painful wounds, begged for his revolver, but his companions refused to give it to him. The one doctor on the plane was instantly killed. After fourteen days, all official rescue efforts were abandoned, as the survivors learned from the reconstructed plane radio. Shortly thereafter an avalanche hit them. Without food, without medical supplies to ease the suffering of the dying, and without adequate clothing for the sub-zero temperatures, the young men and women who had set out from Montevideo endured a terrible ordeal. Let the author Piers Paul Read describe it:

> The Fairchild had carried five crewmen and forty passengers. Some were killed instantly. But those who survived clung to life with extraordinary tenacity and ingenuity. They formed themselves into an ordered society, distributing tasks according to individual skills and degrees of physical fitness. Leaders emerged who had never been leaders before.
>
> Realizing that what little chance they had to live lay in their own hands, they planned their escape. Rather than die of starvation, they made a difficult decision: they would use the bodies of their dead companions for food. They were still to endure unexpected and terrible hardships, and one unforeseen tragedy almost overwhelmed them with despair. Yet they refused to be demoralized, and their determination to save themselves increased by sheer strength of will.
>
> The hardiest were chosen as expeditionaries. A sleeping bag was sewn for them and snowshoes made from the seats of the airplane. They were given sunglasses made out of the dead pilot's plastic folder. Seventy days after the crash, two of the young men reached help. Their ten-day trek out of the majestic but hostile mountain range—an almost impossible feat for even a skilled mountaineer—saved the lives of their fourteen remaining friends.[3]

The sixteen survivors returned by plane to Montevideo, troubled by one overwhelming fear: what would people think—above all, their families—of their having survived on human flesh? A priest boarded the plane to reassure and calm them. The lads whom I met seemed thoroughly normal.

---

[3] Piers Paul Read. *Alive,* Philadelphia; Lippincott, 1974.

I shall never forget a remarkable postscript to the Andes tragedy. Some time later I was a guest in the home of the parents of one young passenger. Before learning of his survival, they had spent much money looking for their son in the high mountains for some four-teen days. The father, who was legal counsel to the Minnesota Mining and Manufacturing Company (headquartered in St. Paul, Minnesota),

With President Violeta Chamarro of Nicaragua.

remained almost silent as the mother calmly told me about the horri-ble anxieties they and the other parents had suffered during the long ordeal of not knowing what had happened to their children. Their son, she said, even as a first-year medical student, had already per-formed "surgical miracles." This couple had finally decided to have a funeral, in an attempt to bring their family back to normalcy. Just then, as she finished telling me their story, in walked the son who had been "buried!"

ARGENTINA

*F*ather Pedro Richards prepared the way for my talks and stay in Argentina, his native country; here he had a brother in religion and many other contacts. I spoke to various groups, showed films and slides, and promised to send more films, slides, and literature—a singsong routine by now. Again I was shocked at the number of illegal abortions; reputable doctors estimated some 250,000 illegal abortions for hardly thirty million people. Planned Parenthood propaganda, of course, was becoming solidly entrenched with little opposition. The Devil, "the Father of Lies," never advertises himself, but he is an expert in duplicity and infiltration—and murder. The "Practiced Deceiver," as Scripture calls Satan, surely knows how to put his best foot forward. So does his agent, IPPF.

On a later trip, an old archbishop, attired in a flowing white cas-sock, drove me all over his city in his old flivver, arranging talks for me here and there and seemingly everywhere to doctors, students, lawyers, his budding Catholic university, and even city officials. Once he stopped to buy something that looked somewhat like—but tasted very different from—a McDonald's hamburger. He must have noticed that I barely managed to survive the experience, because he solicitously remarked that my lecturing was more important than eating!

The great Archbishop Italo di Stefano of San Juan was also most helpful in getting the pro-life word out. On one occasion he brought out a special Easter cake his family had baked for him, and we duly demolished it. With me was Father Albert Salmon, who several times made lecture tours with me in Latin America. The archbishop was just building a large seminary. His zeal and understanding of the issues were very encouraging, as were those of other prelates. I recall making four lecturing excursions in this large and nearly empty country. Later I met this archbishop in the Miami airport where Magaly Llaguno fixed his tickets for some UN-sponsored meeting in Chattanooga, Tennessee. Wearing two overcoats because he was cold (air conditioning?), he would not allow this limping monk with a cane to carry his heavy bags.

BRAZIL

*M*y next destination was Sao Paulo and Rio de Janeiro. From my base in a large parish of the Oblates of Mary Immaculate and the guidance of Father Dan Meehan, OMI, I did what I could to alert the various groups and leaders to the coming onslaught of the abortionists. In Rio I visited a large monastery whose Benedictines ran a high-class secondary school for boys. When I showed one of the monks my pictures of aborted babies, he almost fainted. Then he delicately and fraternally informed me that I was not the man—though a fellow Benedictine—to speak to their students, most of whom came from wealthy families. I shook the dust from my shoes and left.

This monk was totally unaware of the secret activities of BEMFAM ("Benefit the Family"), the IPPF affiliate, in promoting contraception, sterilization, and explicit sex ed in the schools. This budding campaign, of course, was eventually to blossom into a full-blown effort to

Bishop Bosco Vivas from Nicaragua receiving "Precious Feet" from me.

legalize abortion. Illegal abortion was rampant, I became aware, but this monk did not know it. In a follow-up visit I met the Cardinal Archbishop of Rio, Eugenio de Araújo Sales, who was extremely cooperative. He called a large press conference, which others and I addressed, and spoke for one hour on abortion on his next Sunday television broadcast.

In subsequent visits to Brazil I discovered a great apostle for life, the late, saintly seminary professor

The enormous statue of the Risen Christ overshadows the city of Rio de Janeiro, Brazil.

Monsignor Ney Alfonso de sa Earp, whose activities we later financed. At my urging, Monsignor Ney introduced picketing and the rescue movement into Brazil. Through him we met the lawyer Humberto Vieira, who occupied a key position as advisor to the national government and once arranged for me to speak to the Brazilian Congress. Few attended. Later we did a seminar in Brasilia with the help of Vieira and others, and three hundred came. Now retired, Vieira uses his many talents to head Brazil's national right-to-life organization,

The Apostolic Nuncio in Panama, who presided over the opening Mass of the First International Conference for Life and Family in Panama. The three bishops to the right are Panamanians.

Providafamilia, which we also have financially supported.

In the late 1970's we conducted a pro-life seminar in Anapolis with the total support and most active participation of Bishop Manuel Pestaña, who linked us with many groups, including his seminary. When orthodox Bishop Pestaña took over the diocese, a number of priests left in protest. That, however, proved a blessing in disguise. With equal cooperation from Archbishop Pedro Marchetti Fedalto in Curitiba, in the state of Parana, we put on another weekend conference. With us was the active pro-lifer, Father Albert Salmon, who eventually became our Latin American coordinator.

No such luck with Cardinal Aloysius Lorscheider of Fortaleza! I informed him about the anti-life thrust gathering momentum in Brazil and warned him that Brazil could end up with massive legal abortion. He saw no danger! He assured me that if such a threat should arise, the bishops would surely resist it. "Now is the time to start this resistance," I mildly commented. "In fact, it may already be too late," I added, through teeth that heroically remained unclenched. Incidentally, this "fearless" cardinal was allegedly a dissenter to *Humanae Vitae*, according to his priests.

In 1973, according to several doctors well-qualified to make an estimate, there were probably 1,500,000 illegal abortions in Brazil, with its population of 150,000,000. A huge number of houses of ill repute

With Mother Teresa's nuns in Panama.

prosper in this "Catholic" country so lacking in seminarians, religious and priests. The rosary is not popular in pre-Lenten fiestas, but Mardi Gras is celebrated with a vengeance: two or three months later there is a noticeable increase in the number of babies aborted.

In the 1970s, nurse-nuns in Latin American countries, particularly in Brazil and Mexico, were already telling me about the policy of secretly sterilizing women or secretly inserting IUDs after childbirth, and about other abuses in public hospitals. I shall be surprised if the countries of Latin America can resist the eventual legalization of baby-killing. Brazil may be the second country to fall after Uruguay, the contraceptive imperialists having prepared the way through schools, media, entertainment, and government. October 4-6, 1997, will see a national pro-life/pro-family congress in Rio, with the Pope attending.

ECUADOR

*I*n Ecuador, my next stop in 1972, Dr. Olga Muñoz Reyes arranged for me to speak in various places and introduced me to a number of doctors, groups, and families. Her dynamic, tiny daughter Ojita organized fellow students on her Catholic university campus with the help of the pro-life Jesuit rector, Julio Teran Dutari, later to become auxiliary bishop of Quito. Today little Ojita is a solid pro-life lawyer and a great ally who has organized successful youth groups. To all these countries I returned later, lecturing, addressing doctors, and

Plotting in Latin America against Planned Parenthood.

Forever defending life (here in Santiago, Chile).

Addressing Peruvians in Lima, 1973.

Mass with Cardinal Alfonso Lopez Trujillo in Santiago, Chile at HLI's Symposium, 1994.

doing what I could to alert bishops, clergy, religious, and lay leaders to the real war on the unborn that was inevitably to descend on them in full force. We sponsored conferences in the hot and sultry city of Guayaquil and in Cuenca, which is cool, high up in the mountains, and graced with a gorgeous cathedral. With our help, Dr. Reyes set up a counseling center in Quito for pregnant women and girls considering abortion. Father Salmon and I also visited the alleged visionary about whom you may have been reading.

Pro-life Dr. Nestor Mario Gregorini from Argentina.

As early as the 1970s, doctors were being brought from various countries to four medical schools in the United States to be taught all about contraception, abortifacients, sterilization, and surgical abortion. Later I met some of these doctors personally. I shall never forget the anger shown by a young doctor who had gone through this program at the medical school in Denver. In the Mexico City home of his father, who was also a doctor, this young man told me that participants were introduced to every means of birth control, including "menstrual extraction," and then loaded down with equipment on their departure. All of this was paid for by the American taxpayer.

These young foreign doctors received the clear message that contraception and legalized abortion would be the remedy for back-street abortions and overpopulation. They were advised to exaggerate the number of botched illegal abortions and especially the number of deaths of illegally aborted women. This dishonesty would pave the way for legalized baby-killing. The tactic is still much used today. This young doctor told me with fiery Latin-American anger, "I come to your country, am wined and dined in a Hilton hotel and taught all these great evils that destroy family and society, and then loaded down with every kind of pills and contraceptives and the promise of more, all the while being taught to disobey our law by promoting abortion."

COLOMBIA

*B*ogota was my next stop. The secret anti-life movement and the social conditions were the same as everywhere else. Too often bishops, priests and religious did not seem to know their real enemies and thus did not know how to resist the force that would ultimately destroy State and Church. I am not blaming them. I am merely recording what became so obvious to me during all my Latin-American pro-life missions. Even so, we were able to present two weekend seminars,

Magaly Llaguno, Coordinator of HLI in Latin America, received HLI's annual award in 1995.

one in Bogota and the other in Medellin, with the pro-life leader of Colombia, Dr. Astrid Tamalyo de Bayer, who, despite fierce opposition and limited funds, has accomplished so much in her counseling centers to save babies from abortion.

I remember lecturing in a very fine Benedictine high school and in two international schools run by wealthy Catholic laity to make sure their children learned English. In the city of Barranquilla, I enjoyed speaking at a girls' school operated by American nuns; it was inspiring to behold the blend of American and Colombian heritage in these beautiful and intelligent girls so well educated in the faith. The nuns impressed me too.

To me it was as plain as the day in 1972 that the Church's greatest enemy was the well-financed, anti-life, anti-family, anti-Church, and anti-God IPPF, the collaborating UN, the Pathfinder Fund, USAID, and the many financing foundations and governments. These organized anti-lifers were spreading their poison everywhere, above all into the only Catholic continent on earth. Pitifully, the Church seemingly

Archbishop Juan Larrea Holgium, Guayaquil, Ecuador.

could never summon the resources, financial and otherwise, or the leadership to meet these powerful enemies head on and early on. Magaly Llaguno will remember our asking the Knights of Columbus for $500,000 to help stymie the early beginnings of IPPF in Latin America. We were refused, although we had successfully solicited the cooperation of bishops and cardinals to write to Knights' headquarters on our behalf. One thing I am proud of—it gives me deep satisfaction in my worst days—is that I did all I could to awaken leaders and ordinary citizens of all kinds.

VENEZUELA

*C*aracas in Venezuela was my last stop. The family with whom I stayed had been leaders in the family-life movement. They told me about the terrorist potential of the *favelas,* the fringe of dreadful slums surrounding virtually all the large cities in Latin America. My staunchly Catholic, intelligent hosts claimed that all that was needed was another Castro to ignite the angers of these people, who had been enslaved into utter poverty through the irresponsible and callous behavior of government and the rich. One thing caught my attention: The closer the Latin American country is to the United States, the more sterilizations there are. (Beyond supplying Hispanic literature, Human Life International has done little in this country, leaving it to the deVollmer family to fight Venezuela's pro-life battle.)

BACK HOME

*W*ith heavy heart I returned to St. John's Abbey/University to pick up my classes once more. I was all set to found the Human Life Center in 1972, which would produce pro-life literature and materials of all kinds to resist the horrendous advance of the gigantic anti-life/anti-family colossus. The facilities I had been promised were not available after all, although plans for the center had been hatched in 1970.

The then-president of St. John's University, Father Michael Blecker, OSB, had always displayed a good deal of reluctance and resistance toward the project. However, he suddenly became interested when I received a $50,000 grant from the De Rance Corporation in Milwaukee. I have always said that money doesn't talk: it screams! That check tipped the scales. The president found a large room immediately. Incidentally, Father Blecker once told me that using contraception was as harmless as taking a glass of wine. As president of Berkeley's Theological Union later, he died of AIDS on 11 September 1993 at fifty-seven years of age.

I began to build a staff and to take on the hardest task in my life: asking people for money in order to get launched. Some good monks at St. John's said that people financed my projects solely because they saw my great pain at having to ask! My distress, I am afraid, is genuine—even though I never ask for myself but rather for the greatest cause on earth, the defense of the voiceless, defenseless, voteless, and garmentless unborn children trapped in the human uterus, which is nowadays the most dangerous place on earth. The uterus, tragically, has become the pitiless slaughterhouse of our "progressive," hedonistic modern times.

I founded three publications to spread the pro-life message far and wide. Always interested in natural birth regulation, I began the quarterly *International Review of Natural Family Planning* in the spring of 1977 with the wise Virginia Gager as editor and Andy Scholberg as assistant editor. I have lectured in every state in the United States except Wyoming, and in every large Canadian city since the relaxation of their abortion law in 1969 there. More and more, I worked internationally, as the world became my parish.

CHAPTER 5

The Greatest Secret in the Church

Long before I was ordained on 15 June 1947, while as a seminarian I was working with married retreatants, I learned that birth control was an enormous problem in the Catholic Church. I also became convinced that, if God condemned contraception/sterilization as intrinsically evil, never to be used under any circumstances, then He must have provided some kind of alternative for couples who have legitimate reasons to regulate and control the number of their offspring.

If God had not done so, He would not be infinitely wise, all good, all provident. According to Vatican II's Pastoral Constitution *Gaudium et Spes* (n. 51), quoted by Pope Paul VI in *Humanae Vitae* (n. 24), " . . . [A] true contradiction cannot exist between the divine laws pertaining to the transmission of life and those pertaining to the fostering of authentic conjugal love." However, if through fifty years of active priesthood I have learned one thing, it is that there is no one single, simple, easy way of effective fertility control. That is why the British authority on natural birth regulation, Dr. John Marshall, could write after a lifetime of counseling experience that "a high proportion of couples abandon any method of avoiding conception after a short time."[1]

Fortunately, in the seminary (1942-1947) we were taught the latest methods of Natural Family Planning (NFP), even if we did not learn its history. It was in 1923 that the Japanese gynecological surgeon

---

[1]   *Love One Another: Psychological Aspects of Natural Family Planning* (London: Sheed and Ward, 1995), p. 16. Unfortunately, Marshall was a dissenter to *Humanae Vitae*.

Kyusaku Ogino of Niigata University published a classic scientific article in a Japanese medical journal[2] demonstrating that menstruation
follows ovulation, and that ovulation ordinarily takes place between
the *12th* and *16th* days before the onset of the next menstrual period.
If a woman had kept at least a year's record of her cycles, she could
determine the parameters within which she was most likely to get
pregnant, by calculating so many days off the longest cycle and so
many days off the shortest cycle. Between these parameters lay her fertility. This pioneering method was known as the Ogino Method,
Calendar Rhythm, or the Rhythm Method.

Of course, when a woman's cycle is extremely irregular in length,
abstinence would become formidable. Twenty-eight days is merely a statistical average; as Dr. Alan Treloar, one of the authorities on the menstrual cycle, wrote, "The only thing regular about the menstrual cycle is
its irregularity." As fertility declines with the woman's age, cycles may
become even more irregular, thus increasing the length of abstinence and
enhancing the possibility of pregnancy. How well I remember couples'
telling me that the problem was not so much abstinence as "the anxiety
of uncertainty." The inherent limitations, poor instruction, and faulty
application of this pioneer method gave NFP a lasting bad reputation.
Still, to this day I meet couples who used Calendar Rhythm successfully.
Properly understood and rigorously applied, the Calendar Method was
as good a means of fertility control as existed in the 1930s-1950s.
Ogino's trailblazing findings were confirmed, astonishingly, in an article
in the 7 December 1995 *New England Journal of Medicine*, to which I
shall refer again later in this chapter.

Dr. Ogino was truly a remarkable person. In 1934, Medical Arts
Publishing Company of Harrisburg, Pennsylvania, published his translated 94-page booklet, *Conception Period of Women*. Therein he says
that contraception is "quite unnatural," that the brief fertile period is
"holy time," that a woman's whole emotional-psychic life pivots
around her menstrual cycle.

In 1930 Dr. Ogino published his research results in German as
Sonderdruck aus dem Zentralblatt für Gynäkologie (Leipzig). Thus his

---

[2]   *Hokeutsu Medical Journal*, February 1923. See also *Japan
Gynecological Journal*, vol. 19, no. 6 (1924).

Speaking at the First National Convention on Natural Family Planning in the Philippines, May 1981.

discovery found its way into world medical literature. Upon reading Ogino's article in German, Dr. Hermann Knaus of Prague, a professor of gynecology, congratulated the Japanese pathfinder and assured him that he himself had

Discussing NFP with some Filipino bishops in the 1970s.

come to a similar conclusion by another route. This finding he had published in the *Münchener Medizinische Wochenschrift* of 12 July 1929—six years after Ogino's original publication. Strangely, however—and wrongly—Knaus maintained that the luteal (postovulatory) phase was always sixteen days. The Rhythm Method then became known officially as the "Ogino-Knaus Method." In the early 1930s, the American Dr. Leo Latz published a pioneering book, *The Rhythm*, for American users; it went through several editions, the last revision selling 60,000 copies.

Some uninformed cynics, overlooking the fact that contraceptive methods of that time—and even of today—have a high failure rate in

(l to r) Fr. Richard Welch, myself and Dr. Josef Rötzer. In 1951, Austrian Dr. Rötzer, an international authority on NFP, had begun his research into and development of the Sympto-Thermal Method.

actual use, pejoratively called NFP "Vatican Roulette." These cynics preferred to "get rigged to make love," as an American doctor observed, referring to condom and diaphragm.

They failed to recognize that the Rhythm Method reflected facts about human fertility that had long been noted. Some African tribes knew, long before scientists knew, that fertility and infertility could be assessed in terms of cyclic phenomena like cervical mucus. Justina Simon, an NFP teacher in Tanzania, related how, when her elder sister married, her mother explained that the fertile phase comes and goes with the cervical-mucus sign—seemingly a routine instruction for pre-marital preparation.[3] Even St. Augustine's writings (*The City of God*, XXII, 24) show that he was aware of the periodicity of human fertility.

The American physician Mary Putnam Jacobi in 1876 and the Dutch gynecologist Henry van de Velde in 1904 gave exact descriptions of the regularly returning temperature fluctuation in the human female.[4] However, they never related this advanced information to fertility control. The first one to do that was the German Catholic parish priest Wilhelm Hillebrand, who taught it to his parishioners in

---

[3] Oral communication and correspondence.

[4] Jacobi's 1876 publication is still available in the library of the New York Academy of Medicine.

Cologne. According to the German gynecologist Dr. Gerhard K. Döring, this pastor "developed the most reliable and successful abstinence form of birth control" of that time.[5]

Even before Ogino, it had been known for some time that at ovulation the woman's temperature rises slightly, usually at least 4/10 of a degree. Upon observing and charting three authentic higher temperatures following a lower five, properly measured by a basal body thermometer upon awakening in the morning, the couple could conclude that the egg, which has a lifespan of only 12-14 hours, was dead and that the remainder of the cycle was therefore infertile. This refinement was the next step in the development of NFP known as "Temperature Rhythm," to the clarification of which the Dutch gynecologist J. G. H. Holt contributed much in the 1950s with his book *Marriage and Periodic Abstinence*.[6] Temperature Rhythm is what we learned in the seminary in the 1940s. And this is what I taught students and couples for years into my priesthood.

The limitation of this method, however, was its failure to *anticipate* ovulation, since the required three-day temperature elevation is known only in retrospect, after ovulation has presumably already taken place; engaging in sexual relations on any of the five days immediately preceding ovulation, as well as on the actual day of ovulation, could possibly result in a pregnancy. In short, temperature rise does not predict ovulation but only implies that ovulation has already occurred. Later in the history of NFP, a new approach, combining the temperature rise with observations of preovulatory changes in cervical mucus (and several minor symptoms) became known as the Sympto-Thermal Method. By 1951, in fact, the Austrian Dr. Josef Rötzer, who was to become an international authority on NFP, had begun his research into the development of this method.

In 1953, the New York gynecologist Edward F. Keefe began recommending (in the booklet that accompanied his Ovulindex thermometer) the observation of cervical mucus along with daily waking temperatures. In 1962 he published his research on physical changes in the

---

[5]   Proceedings of a Research Conference on NFP (Washington, D.C.: The Human Life Foundation, 1972), pp. 170-171.

[6]   J. G. H. Holt, *Marriage and Periodic Abstinence*, 2d rev. ed. (London: Longmans, 1960).

Pro-abortion statistician Dr. Christopher Tietze waves to me at the 1985 Tietze Symposium.

cervix, a third major component of the Sympto-Thermal Method.

Dr. Christopher Tietze, an escapee from Hitler and a noted statistician who worked for Planned Parenthood and the Population Council in New York, once researched what the seven Catholic medical schools in Canada and the United States were teaching about natural family planning. He expressed his surprise that they presented virtually nothing. Knowing the failure rates associated with current contraceptive methods, he said that the method of analyzing the temperature rise and the history of cycles was not all that bad for those who were properly motivated to practice that method.

In 1953, Drs. John and Lyn Billings of Australia began to work out the indications of fertility in terms of cervical-mucus observation alone. This endeavor became known as the Ovulation or Billings Method. Dr. John Billings published his first book on the Ovulation Method in 1964.[7] In the ensuing years NFP has evolved to a point where, as a means of birth regulation, it has become as effective for the knowledgeable and motivated couple as any other means of birth control short of sterilization.[8]

---

[7] For background on Dr. Billings' work, see J. J. Billings, "Natural Family Planning," *National Catholic Register*, 17 March 1996, responding to Christopher Martinez, "Modern Medicine Catches Up with Church Teaching," *National Catholic Register*, 28 January 1996.

[8] M. C. Weissman, L. Foliaki and John and Evelyn Billings, *Lancet* (14 October 1972). R. E. J. Ryder, "Ovarian Ultrasonography Highlights Precision of Symptoms of Ovulation as Markers of Ovulation," *British Medical Journal*, vol. 292, 1562; "Natural Family Planning: Effective Birth Control Supported by the Catholic Church," *British Medical Journal*, vol. 307 (18 September 1993), 723-736. See also Ryder's and others' replies, *British Medical Journal*, vol. 307, (20 November 1993), 1357-1360. John Kelly, "NFP in the Developing World," "NFP—God's Plan for the Family," "Science and Natural

Drs. John and Lyn Billings of Australia began in 1953 to work out the indications of fertility, known as the Ovulation or the Billings Method of NFP.

For years the suitability of the term "Natural Family Planning" has been debated, because it seems to smack of the godless Planned Parenthood lingo—as if conception and gestation and birth were

------

Family Planning": three lectures given at Human Life International's International Symposium on Love, Life and the Family in Cincinnati, 1996, manuscripts in hand and on cassette. Allen J. Wilcox et al., "Timing of Sexual Intercourse in Relation to Ovulation," *New England Journal of Medicine*, vol. 333, no. 23 (7 December 1995), 1517-1521; see interesting critique of this report in the *National Catholic Reporter*, 28 January 1996. John Billings, "Good News from China," *Catholic Family*, no. 29 (1996), 11. Robert Ryder and Hubert Campbell, "Natural Family Planning," The Lancet, vol. 346, (July 1995). *Love, Life, Death Issues*, Newsletter of the Human Life Center, vol. 1, no. 3, (1 December 1975). Josef Rötzer, *Natural Family Planning* (Milwaukee: De Rance, Inc., 1980), 115-117. "Internationale Ärztevereinigung für Natürliche Familienplanung," *Medizin und Ideologie*, vol. 18, no. 3 (September 1996), 28-29. 12. Robert A. Hatcher, M.D. et al., *Contraceptive Technology 1994-1996*, Table 5-2, page 113. N.Y.: Irvington Publishers, Inc. 1996. See also Brian Clowes, *The Facts of Life* (Front Royal, VA: Human Life International, 1997), passim.

purely biological phenomena with no moral/spiritual components. That is why Rötzer and other leaders prefer the term *Natürliche Empfängisregelung* meaning "Natural Conception Regulation" in English, a rather awkward term. I am afraid we are stuck with "Natural Family Planning," and we shall use it in this book.

Predating both Billings and Rötzer was the greatest early authority on NFP, the German gynecologist Dr. Rudolf Vollman—Jewish by

birth, but an atheist—who had escaped from Hitler's Germany by swimming across the Rhine to Switzerland. Here, because Swiss citizens during World War II could not travel outside the country, he could assemble a stable group of some 691 women to do research directed toward helping them to regulate their fertility. His wife Emmi helped him to track 31,645 menstrual cycles. He told me several times that, given the way the Pill and the IUD had "so fouled up women," his study could never be duplicated. Using a combination of temperature rise, menstrual history, and his "Rule of the Mean" (three temperatures above the preceding month's average), he achieved a very high success rate with these women, in fact close to 100 percent effectiveness—seven unintended pregnancies, all from coitus in the postmenstrual (preovulatory) phase. Years later Dr. Carl G. Hartman, the famous researcher in reproduction, said of Vollman's work, "The world may never again see such willing collaboration between investigator and human subject."[9]

HLI's great friend, the great gynecologist, Dr. Rudolf Vollman of Switzerland.

Later, in 1977, Vollman wrote a scientific and theoretical book for scholars on his findings, but only after he had been in charge of gynecological research at the National Institutes of Health in Washington, D.C., for thirteen years. Dr. Vollman's book was a major contribution

---

[9]   C. G. Hartman, *Science and the Safe Period* (Baltimore: Williams and Wilkins, 1962), cited in R. F. Vollman's book, *The Menstrual Cycle* (Philadelphia: W. B. Saunders, 1977).

to medical literature about the
female reproductive system.[10]
Unfortunately, he died before he
could publish a practical manual. Incidentally, Vollman had
contacts with the German
priest-pioneer, Father Wilhelm
Hillebrand, mentioned earlier. In
1942 Hillebrand wrote Vollman
to thank him for confirming his
work, adding that the NFP
information came from heaven
and that it was a good sign that
both had discovered it separately.

*My great friends and foremost collaborators
Dr. and Mrs. Rudolf Vollman and Margaret
Nofziger during a visit to Collegeville, MN
during the '70s.*

Dr. Vollman became my great
friend and collaborator. He used to tell me about the horrendous
American experiments for the Pill foisted on Puerto Rican women in the
late 1950s. He always insisted that drugs would never be the solution to
the birth-control problem, out of which pharmaceutical companies and
Planned Parenthood have made many millions of dollars while exploiting
women with chemical warfare. What always amazed me is how this self-
described "atheistic Jew" recognized so clearly the evil of contraception
and Planned Parenthood. Whenever I was in Switzerland I would spend
days with the Vollmans, while he was still doing limited research for the
World Health Organization in Geneva. From both of them I learned so
very much.

In 1976 Margaret Nofziger, a member of a counter-cultural group
outside of Nashville known as "The Farm," issued *A Cooperative
Method of Natural Birth Control.* The first edition contained some
statements offensive to Catholic morality. (She had written the book for
a secular society.) I put her in touch with Dr. Vollman, who reviewed her
work and helped it methodologically; I myself worked with her to elimi-

---

[10] Vollman, *The Menstrual Cycle* (Philadelphia: W. B. Saunders,
1977).

Dr. Thomas Hilgers (a leader in the NFP movement) at HLI's Houston World Conference, 1993.

nate items objectionable to Catholics, whom she later met and twice addressed at my international symposia. Three corrected editions followed, and the four editions sold over 750,000 copies, including 105,000 in German. The book appeared in six languages.

Planned Parenthood, the recipient of millions of federal tax dollars from Title X to promote artificial methods, was forced to offer all options for fertility control; in presenting the natural methods, the organization chose Nofziger's book because it was ethically neutral while methodologically correct. In 1988, Nofziger's helpful reference book *Signs of Fertility: The Personal Science of Natural Birth Control* appeared; it sold some 9,000 copies.

Dr. Vollman never better demonstrated his brilliant mind and kind heart than in his many letters to Nofziger and me, as well as in the gentle counseling and meticulous articles he contributed to the *International Review of Natural Family Planning*. He was an unfailing guide.[11]

Drs. Billings, Rötzer, and Vollman were the mainstays who—together with a battery of other eminent speakers—manned the seven international symposia on NFP that I conducted at St. John's University each summer, beginning in 1976, under the sponsorship of my Human Life Center (HLC). This I had founded in 1972 at Minnesota's St. John's University, where I taught family sociology until 1974. Subsequently, as I'll describe in the next chapter, Human Life International, established in 1981 in Washington, D.C., continued the work of HLC.)

---

[11] I am deeply indebted to Margaret Nofziger for the many letters she sent me, long letters from Dr. Vollman to me and her, hers to him and mine to them, along with various pertinent documents.

In 1976 the Redemptorist Father Bernard Häring, a consistent and loud dissenter to *Humanae Vitae*, unexplainably published an obnoxious article in a German theological journal charging that the practice of periodic abstinence (such as that used in NFP) caused defective unborn babies, spontaneous abortions, and miscarriages.[12] He cited pseudo-scientific evidence. I invited him to defend his claims—now widely disseminated—before the faculty at my international symposium in Collegeville. I offered to pay his way. He was "too busy" to come. To refute Häring's false, but widely published views, the medical experts at my symposium composed a statement of total refutation. I scattered it throughout the world and published it as an international news release. There was no response from Häring.

My faculty members, Drs. Thomas Hilgers and Josef Rötzer, subsequently refuted Häring's scientific heresies in various theological and other publications. For instance, in March 1977, Dr. Hilgers thoroughly discredited Häring's thesis in an article published by *Theological Studies*.[13] This I reprinted in the summer 1977 issue of the *International Review of Natural Family Planning*.[14]

-----

[12] B. Häring, "Neue Dimensionen verantworteter Elternschaft," *Theologie der Gegenwart*, vol. 19, no. 1 (1976), also published as: "New Dimensions of Responsible Parenthood," *Theological Studies* vol. 37 (1976), 120-132.

[13] Thomas Hilgers, "Human Reproduction: Three Issues for the Moral Theologian," *Theological Studies*, vol. 38 (March 1977), 136-152, reprinted in the *International Review of Natural Family Planning*, vol. 1, no. 2 (summer 1977), 105-120. On page 117 Hilgers writes, "Are some early human losses ever secondary to aging gametes? I suspect that the answer. . .is yes, but I also think that this is most likely a rare occurrence, and then only when the normal, regularly occurring events in the female and/or the male reproductive tracts are disturbed for some reason. . . . For those using the [sympto-thermal and ovulation] methods to avoid pregnancy, the natural protective mechanisms should, as previously outlined, prohibit the union of aged sperm and aged ova."

[14] *International Review of Natural Family Planning*, vol. 1, no. 2 (summer 1977), 105-120.

Then Dr. Rötzer demolished Häring's errors even more pointedly in a 1978 article in *Die Neue Ordnung*,[15] referring to Häring as "thoughtless and carelessly uncritical" and observing, "Can spreading of falsehoods be reconciled with a priest's, a moral theologian's, particular duty to seek the truth?" This response of Rötzer's was translated and reprinted in the *International Review of Natural Family Planning*.[16]

The renowned New Zealand gynecologist Dr. H. P. Dunn also took on Häring's scientific aberrations, writing, "Who can prove the existence, let alone the loss, of the zygote?"[17]

In the summer of 1978, when I had a super faculty lined up at St. John's University for an international NFP symposium, we brought them, in collaboration with the University of Minnesota's adult-education program, to the campus of the University's prestigious medical school. I am confident in saying that this was the only such co-sponsored seminar on any university campus in the world up to that time. (Much later, similar sessions took place at Sacred Heart University in Rome.)

Heading the University's Department of Obstetrics and Gynecology at that time was the well-known gynecologist Dr. John McKelvey, a mentor of my college classmate Dr. Konald Prem, who was an early expert on NFP on McKelvey's staff. Dr. Prem at times served as a member of the faculty of some twenty-five weekend conferences on NFP that HLC sponsored across the country. Prem eventually became head of the Department of Obstetrics and Gynecology at the University of Minnesota Medical School, but only after he had been mercilessly picketed because he was a Catholic who spoke out against abortion. Here he taught his medical students NFP.

A Presbyterian, Dr. McKelvey assured a generation of doctors that the only reason to do an abortion was to save the mother's life; he told

---

[15] Die Neue Ordnung, vol. 1 (1978), pp. 1-15.

[16] Josef Rötzer, "Responsible Parenthood: Is Rhythm So Great a Problem?" *International Review of Natural Family Planning*, vol. 2, no. 3 (fall 1978), 191-202.

[17] "The Gynecologist and the Encyclical," *International Review of Natural Family Planning*, vol. 1, no. 1 (spring 1977), 20-21.

his students that they would most likely go through a lifetime of medical practice without having to perform a single abortion. He thundered, his students told me: "To the extent that I hear you are doing abortions, I will know you have not learned your lessons."

McKelvey was a man of extraordinary competence, integrity, and dedication. When I was invited to speak on abortion to the Olmstead County Medical Society at its meeting at the Mayo Clinic, McKelvey—by that time an old man and retired—drove across the Twin Cities in ice and snow to help me prepare my lecture. (I was on weekend assignment at Incarnation Parish in south Minneapolis.)

When abortion first came up for a hearing in the Minnesota legislature in the 1960s, he eloquently defended the unborn with his commentary on four bottled fetuses at different stages of development, and then dared legislators who favored abortion legalization to prove to him that these small babies were not human. McKelvey's long tenure at the University of Minnesota Medical School is the chief explanation of how Minnesota became one of the most pro-life states and in 1967 generated the first state right-to-life group in the United States, Minnesota Citizens Concerned for Life (incorporated 1968), with whose founders (the late Alice Hartle, Father William Hunt, and Marge Mecklenburg) and officers I worked for years. (I had just missed the organizational first meeting.)

At Prem's request, McKelvey allowed me to attend special updating medical conferences that pertained to birth control and allied subjects, "provided that [I] ask no questions." At one of these meetings he introduced Dr. Prem's lecture on NFP by saying, "Now we'll have the gospel according to Prem."

It was at one of these sessions at the University of Minnesota Medical School, in the 1960s, that I first witnessed the world-famous, pioneering fetologist, A. W. Liley of New Zealand, demonstrating intrauterine blood exchange in the case of RH incompatibility. When Liley told the young doctors to needle-stab the baby in the buttocks or the flesh of the leg and to do the exchange as quickly as possible because "he/she is hurting," I became keenly aware that babies in the uterus indeed are demonstrably alive, reacting to stimuli and even feeling pain.

Liley was the first scientist to "personalize" the young unborn child, showing how, when he sweetened the amniotic fluid, the baby would drink more, and when he gave the fluid "a foul taste" the little one would cease to swallow it. To facilitate blood-exchange for RH babies, Liley developed the technique of amniocentesis that was subsequently used to facilitate abortion. That misuse of his technique by the March of Dimes and others became the great pain of his later life. In the 1970s I sponsored the shy and generous Liley on a lecture tour throughout the United States to demonstrate to Americans the humanity of the unborn child and the enormity of abortion. With Dr. Patrick (H. P.) Dunn he founded the Society for the Protection of the Unborn Child in New Zealand, where the two attracted their own enemies, the abortionists.

Here allow a digression. Sometime in the late 1970s I visited Belgium. My collaborator, the Belgian law professor and pro-life pioneer Dr. Charles Convent, insisted, together with others, that I attend a seminar on the new triphasic birth-control Pill at Louvain University. The seminar was sponsored by various Pill companies that, I sensed, secretly gloated that they could promote their dirty product at a prestigious "Catholic" institution. And promote it they did! Their pitch: Because the triphasic Pill mimics the menstrual cycle, using it is more healthful, more "natural," and more effective than other Pills. (They lied!)

At a news conference, with four medical "experts" and the Catholic head of the Louvain Medical School available for answers to questions, I asked about the abortifacient character of their new product. There followed immediate, obvious consternation and evasion, if not an outright denial that their new Pill was abortion-causing. One panel member, a female English doctor, reacted immediately to my question, clearly if reluctantly betraying the fact that I had hit upon an embarrassing reality.

Even more embarrassing to the panel was a gentleman who confronted the Catholic chairman about how the latter, a Catholic doctor at a Catholic university, could sponsor a seminar on a type of birth control totally forbidden by the Catholic Church. After some uncomfortable hesitation, the chairman mumbled the platitude that we have so often heard from heads of "Catholic" institutions: "Louvain is a university, and we look at all aspects of human life and learning." He then promised something he never carried out: a future one-day seminar on NFP. After the news conference, I offered to help him assemble an expert NFP faculty, since I knew the authorities from having sponsored such international meetings. At his request I listed the experts' names, addresses, and competencies. I never heard from him. I submitted a written account of Louvain's disgraceful Pill-promoting conference—which surely would have been news to American Catholics—to the American bishops' National Catholic News Service. Typically, it was not distributed.

In 1964 the National Federation of Catholic Physicians Guilds unanimously approved a resolution calling for extensive educational programs to promote "the rhythm method of family planning." Monsignor Christopher Knott, director of the American bishops' Family Life Bureau, then suggested that this Bureau and the National Federation sponsor a pioneer symposium. When this meeting took place 21-22 October 1964 in Washington, D.C., I was in attendance. Out of this event grew a conjoint committee of seven from each group to promote the Rhythm Method. After several meetings, the committee broke up because several priest members had begun to waffle as to the intrinsic evil of contraception in these pre-*Humanae Vitae* times. The Catholic doctors continued to meet as the National Commission on Human Life, Reproduction and Rhythm. This commission sponsored five significant national symposia.

In the winter of 1968, after publication of *Humanae Vitae*, Cardinal Patrick O'Boyle and constitutional lawyer William Bentley Ball founded the Human Life Foundation to promote NFP. Soon thereafter they hired Larry Kane as director. Cardinal O'Boyle succeeded in raising about $1,000,000 with the help of several American bishops. Another $250,000 was collected from various foundations while the Knights of Columbus paid for large printing bills, with the Catholic Foresters also contributing.

In 1972 the Human Life Foundation sponsored the first scientific meeting on NFP, and it eventually published some thirty books, including a thirty-minute film on NFP. Because various other groups were now promoting NFP, in 1983 the Foundation's board decided to dismantle the Foundation while it was still solvent. Earlier, Larry Kane had worked out a diocesan plan that was adopted by the bishops' Committee on Pro-Life Activities in 1981.

In my annual two-week seminars on Marriage and Family Life at Collegeville, which began in the 1960s, I always included lectures on

Fr. Anthony Zimmerman and me. Thanks to the avant-garde work of Fr. Zimmerman and collaborating Japanese scientists, a device called *L'Sophia* has been produced to record pertinent events of the menstrual cycle.

NFP and, in the early 1970s, side courses for potential teachers of NFP. However, as I'll describe later in this chapter, by the 1970s the promotion of NFP had all but collapsed because of some well-publicized theological dissent to *Humanae Vitae* and the half-hearted or nonexistent support that document earned in 1968 from the American hierarchy as a whole.

In 1967, before *Humanae Vitae* was issued, the Rockefeller Foundation sponsored and paid for a meeting on birth control for prominent Catholic doctors at the Jesuit Creighton University in Omaha. There Dr. Jack Willke proposed a resolution favored by a large number and asked for a unanimous vote that the Catholic Church should cease opposition to contraception. (The Willkes have since then been very orthodox theologically through the years.) The resolution was turned down on a close vote, to the disappointment of John D. Rockefeller. Rockefeller had offered to write a birth-control encyclical for the Pope. The president of Notre Dame, Father Theodore Hesburgh, subsequently arranged a meeting between Pope Paul VI and Rockefeller. The multi-millionaire Rockefeller told the Pope that if he did not change the Church's teaching it would be swept away by history. The whole sordid affair, along with the Hesburghization of higher Catholic education in the United States, is described in Dr. E. M. Jones's classic biography of Cardinal John Krol.[18]

The joint meeting of the Human Life Center and the University of Minnesota Medical School in 1978 inspired *Natural Family Planning:*

---

[18] E. M. Jones, *John Cardinal Krol and the Cultural Revolution* (South Bend, IN: Fidelity Press, 1995).

Here with Theo Stearns, leader of Catholics United for Life. This group went from being Catholic hippies in the mountains of California to Third Order Dominicans in New Hope, Kentucky. I gave an NFP seminar to their group in the California mountains back in the late 1970s.

God's Way, Nature's Way, a reader edited by my faculty member Father Anthony Zimmerman, SVD, and published and financed by Milwaukee's De Rance Corporation. Father Zimmerman, my graduate-school classmate, is a native Iowan who became a fine demographer and a great missionary to the Japanese. He arranged for 90,000 copies of the reader to be printed in Japan and sent by container to the Human Life Center in Collegeville. From here they were distributed to every pastor and bishop in the United States and to many Catholic institutions in the whole English-speaking world. This reader became a favorite teaching aid at a time when few such aids were available.

The Collegeville NFP international symposia produced vast results in many countries. The 1976 conference was attended by 210 participants from thirty-six U.S. states and ten countries. I recall that one year a group of thirty-four participants arrived from Japan, where, Father Zimmerman maintains, the symposia inspired widespread, effective teaching. Hardly a week goes by, in fact, without my meeting someone still teaching or promoting NFP who got his/her start or instruction from these symposia and the many seminars we sponsored.

To boast a little, Zimmerman attributes his own interest and work in NFP largely to my prodding him to do something.

Today Japan, with only 400,000 Catholics in a nation of 125 million, has proportionally more couples practicing NFP than does the United States, with some 50 million Catholics. Extrapolation of figures from the *Mainichi* newspaper's biennial surveys allows one to believe that roughly 1,000,000 couples in Japan practice pure NFP, that is, without supplementary condoms. Undoubtedly one reason for that dif-

Here I am with the late Bishop Thomas Stewart of Chun-Cheon, Korea, and Dr. Meng, both experts on NFP. Bishop Stewart taught NFP to his whole diocese.

ference is the early findings of the Japanese pioneer researcher Dr. Kyusaku Ogino, already mentioned. A contributing factor may be the serious preparation for marriage in Japan. There parents intensely investigate the background of a son's or daughter's future spouse. But another reason unquestionably is the trailblazing work of Father Zimmerman. I was astonished at the large crowds attracted to his Japanese seminars, supported by the De Rance Corporation. Of course, Mother Teresa's presence and lectures always helped much.

Again thanks to the avant-garde work of Father Zimmerman and collaborating Japanese scientists, a device called *L'Sophia* has been produced to record the pertinent events of the menstrual cycle. It seems to have real potential of easing and advancing considerably the practice of NFP and is already widely used in Japan. Sales have started in Europe and the United States.

Looming large in the history of NFP in the United States are Drs. Herb Ratner, Clement P. Cunningham, William A. Lynch, Edward F. Keefe, John Brennan, John G. Boutselis, John F. Hillabrand, and Konald Prem; Larry Kane; and Cardinal Patrick O'Boyle. Active early in Canada with the organization SERENA (*Service de Regulation de Naissance*) were Drs. Claude Lanctot, Suzanne Parenteau, and Gilles Breault; and Rita Henry-Breault.

Special mention must be made of Sheila and John Kippley, the heroic pioneers and founders of the Couple to Couple League, the largest and most effective NFP organization teaching the Sympto-Thermal Method in the United States. Their enterprise began with

Sheila's *Breast-Feeding and Natural Child Spacing*, first written on instruction sheets in 1967, then printed by mimeograph in 1969, and finally published by Harper & Row in 1974. In 1970 Alba House published John Kippley's *Covenant, Christ and Contraception*, a comprehensive defense of *Humanae Vitae*.

In 1972 the Kippleys produced *The Art of Natural Family Planning*, the League's basic manual, published in its fourth revised edition in 1996. The League's apostolate has spilled over into seventeen countries, along with its publications, including the CCL Home School Study Course.

From the beginning, their consistent silent encourager was Dr. Konald Prem. The Kippleys and Dr. Prem had seen that one-night stands presented by orthodox doctors in parish halls (with which programs they had plenty of experience, as did I) were not the answer. What they had observed led them to believe that NFP clinics or hospital-based centers teaching NFP eventually failed. The apparent solution: a cadre of well-trained couples who were themselves using NFP and could share their knowledge and experience with others, and counsel them as needed.

Fr. Marc Calegari, the late, great Jesuit promoter of NFP.

The Couple to Couple League has been offering this solution since 1971, working today out of Cincinnati, Ohio (P.O. Box 111184, Cincinnati, Ohio 45211-1184; phone: 513/661-7612).

In the 1970s I introduced Dr. Thomas Hilgers to Dr. John Billings at our seminar in Collegeville. Out of this relationship eventually grew Omaha's Paul VI Institute for the Study of Human Reproduction, the largest NFP research and professional teaching operation in the world. Hilgers's program aims at training medical personnel in the Creighton model of NFP—an indispensable contribution (Pope Paul VI Institute,

6901 Mercy Road, Omaha, Nebraska 68106-2621; phone: 402/390-6600).

Many participants learned NFP from the Collegeville international symposia on NFP that began in 1976, the two-week seminars on Marriage and Family Life that began in the early 1960s, and about twenty-five weekend seminars HLC subsequently sponsored in various parts of the country. Some participants became teachers, and some of these teachers are still active, like Anne Fitch-Dececchi (6214 Rose Lake Avenue, San Diego, California 92119-3343; phone: 619/466-1507).

In sponsoring seminars and workshops on NFP, I once encountered a certain bishop (who shall go unnamed) who told me that he had never read *Humanae Vitae*; but he allowed us to present a weekend seminar in his diocese, every session of which he attended; thereafter he told me, "I learned a lot." Incidentally, Bishop (now Cardinal) Bernard Law was one of five bishops who sent delegations to my NFP symposia at Collegeville from his diocese of Springfield-Cape Girardeau in Missouri.

I had been a priest for at least a decade before I met another priest who knew the latest methods of NFP. He was the late and greatly lamented Jesuit Father Marc Calegari, who helped me very much in propagating NFP in the United States and Canada. At St. John's Abbey/University/Seminary I knew only one professor (a priest-biologist) who had a viable grasp of NFP: this reflected the situation, I dare say, in intellectual circles elsewhere.

A great helper also was Bonnie Manion, with whom I founded the Northwest Natural Family Planning Center at St. Vincent's Hospital in Portland, Oregon, still functioning today under Rose and Michael Fuller with their chaplain Father Richard J. Huneger.[19] In 1974 we organized there what was the first seminar on NFP ever held in this country, with an excellent international faculty. Over two hundred participated; some fifty were turned away. Mrs. Manion and I conducted a number of weekend conferences in various parts of the nation; she did much to spread NFP throughout the Northwest. Also very active in teaching the Ovulation Method have been Mercedes

---

[19] They produce an excellent NFP newsletter, *Stepping Stones*. Write to Northwest Family Services, 4805 NE Glisan Street, Portland, OR 97213. Phone: (503) 215-6377.

Wilson of the Family of the Americas Foundation and Father Denis St. Marie, both of whom also worked in other countries, including China. There were and are many others.

In the mid 1960s, during Vatican II, Bishop Peter Bartholome of St. Cloud, Minnesota, then moderator for the American bishops of the National Family Life Bureau in Washington, D.C., wrote to my superior, Abbot Baldwin Dworschak, asking that I be ordered to cease teaching and promoting NFP. Thankfully, the late Abbot Baldwin faced him down and, in fact, even encouraged me to go on. And I "went on" so much that at St. John's Abbey they used to call me "Father Rhythm"; when some bright economist learned that the temperature of a woman rises with ovulation, they renamed me "Father Temp"; and I have been secretly praying that I shall never be known as "Father Mucus"!

In 1951, Pope Pius XII twice addressed the subject of natural fertility control. In his first address (to midwives) he said, "There are serious motives . . . that can exempt for a long time, perhaps even the whole duration of the marriage, from the positive and obligatory carrying out of the act. From this it follows that observing the non-fertile periods alone can be lawful only under a moral aspect" (Address to Midwives, 29 October 1951, n. 36). He studiously refused to use the term "birth control," which implies that babies are a kind of product to be manufactured through the whim and will of the individual couple. In that first address, Pius XII showed himself quite aware of what had developed and was still developing in the field of NFP. He therefore admonished the midwives to base their advice not on popular publications but on scientific objectivity and the authoritative judgment of specialists in medicine and biology (n. 30).

Note that he recognized the possibility that some couples would find themselves in such a difficult situation that they could legitimately avoid all births; they would place their sexual relations in the infertile phase of the cycle exclusively. The rule that couples consult a priest before practicing NFP was the unfortunate invention of theologians, not of Pope or Church. This Pope once told a confidant that he would give his right arm if he could solve the problem of the regulation of births.

I recall theologians of that era who thought that the conservative Pius XII had become rather liberal about the control of fertility through use of only the infertile phase of the cycle. Apparently their opinion was reported to him. Less than a month later, on 26 November 1951, he spoke as follows to the Congress of the Family Front. He did not hesitate to affirm a wide latitude in the legitimacy of regulating births by using infertile times only: "Therefore, in our last allocution on conjugal morality, we affirmed the legitimacy and at the same time, the limits—in truth very wide—of a regulation of offspring, which unlike so-called 'birth control' is compatible with the law of God" (n. 21).

In still another address, titled "The Large Family," January 1958, the same Pope congratulated and thanked couples for having the courage and goodness to raise large families: "You are and represent large families, those most blessed by God and specially loved and prized by the Church as its most precious treasures. . . . Wherever you find large families in great numbers, they point to: the physical and moral health of a Christian people; a living faith in God and trust in His Providence; the fruitful and joyful holiness of Catholic marriage."[20]

The Catholic Church has never been "hung up" about sex, as is so often charged; surely Pius XII was not. Sexual intercourse is a gift from the Lord to the married, not to be abused and played with outside of marriage. God, he said, made the act pleasurable, and couples may accept the pleasure with gratitude: "The Creator . . . has ordained also that in performing this function, husband and wife should experience pleasure and happiness both in body and soul. In seeking and enjoying this pleasure, therefore, couples do nothing wrong. They accept that which the Creator has given them" (To Midwives, n. 59). Human sexuality is a blessing from God, and as Pope John Paul says so beautifully, "When God gives life, He gives it forever."

The present Pope has been at great pains to explain the teachings of the Catholic Church in connection with sexuality, preparation for marriage, true married love, and above all responsible family planning; the last teaching, he laments, is greatly misunderstood. Long before he became Pope, he had written much and pleaded often for "responsible love and procreation," for "conscious parenthood," resulting from a

---

[20] Compare Pope John Paul's book *Love and Responsibility*, where the same principles are stressed.

truly personal, committed, mutual love defined as the "self-giving" of committed, loving persons.[20] As auxiliary bishop in Cracow he had initiated a parish center for pre- and post-marital education that eventually spread throughout Poland. Long before *Humanae Vitae*, the Pope had come to the realization from theological meetings and studies that, if contraception were to be morally sanctioned by the Church, sexual morality would more or less disappear. Unfortunately, we have no time to go into these matters here.

For Pope John Paul II's best comments on the immorality of contraception, see Appendix A to this book. No other Pope or bishop has fostered NFP as Pope John Paul II has. Appendix B is a typical sample of his promotion of NFP as Pope. Appendix C provides more examples of his understanding of the subject.

In 1987, while speaking to the American hierarchy in California, the Pope showed an astonishing familiarity with the inner dynamics of conjugal life—so too in his classic *Love and Responsibility*. No doubt this familiarity is the fruit of his long experience in promoting marriage preparation, conjugal love, and NFP in Poland. On this occasion, too, he made an astonishing statement to the whole American hierarchy (imagine yourself a bishop):

> It is sometimes reported that a large number of Catholics today do not adhere to the teaching of the Church on a number of questions, notably sexual and conjugal morality, divorce and remarriage. Some are reported as not accepting the Church's clear position on abortion. It has also been noted that there is a tendency on the part of some Catholics to be selective in their adherence to the Church's moral teachings. It is sometimes claimed that dissent from the Magisterium is totally compatible with being a "good Catholic" and poses no obstacle to the reception of the Sacraments. This is a grave error that challenges the teaching office of the bishops of the United States and elsewhere. I wish to encourage you in the love of Christ to address this situation courageously in your pastoral ministry, relying on

---

[20] *Love and Responsibility*.

the power of God's truth to attract assent and on the grace
of the Holy Spirit which is given both to those who proclaim the message and to those to whom it is addressed.

What the Pope was talking about everybody knew, including the
reporters in the back of the room. The Pope, of course, was referring
to those many Catholics who, while contracepting during the week
and rarely, if ever, going to Confession, stumble over each other to
receive Communion on Sunday. At the news conference that followed
almost immediately, one reporter asked the president of the American
hierarchy what the bishops would now do about birth control. The
president's response was to the effect that "What will we do? I suggest
we'll do this evening what we did this morning—perhaps with more
fervor."

Most unfortunately, there is no seminary known to me in the
United States—or in the world, for that matter—that offers an adequate informational and training program in the latest developments
in NFP. St. Charles Borromeo Seminary in Philadelphia does give some
training on this vital subject. I have always maintained that the priest
should have a working knowledge of current methods and above all
familiarity with the best theology of married love and life—the "theology of the body," as the Pope calls it. Today there is an enormous clerical ignorance about NFP—even worse today, it seems to me, than
when I was ordained in 1947.

In 1980 Father Zimmerman and I made a courtesy call to Cardinal
Terence Cooke at the North American College in Rome. Cardinal
Cooke was the archbishop of New York and head of the national
Bishops' Committee on Pro-life Activities. As we met, the cardinal
pointed to me and said, "There's the real pioneer of natural family
planning." I was totally startled. After all, I had had no correspondence
with the Cardinal; we had never conversed; we had never met. The
next year, in 1981, Cardinal Cooke as chairman of pro-life activities for
the National Conference of Catholic Bishops (NCCB) launched the
episcopal effort to promote NFP—a wee little bit too late.

NFP has never caught on in the United States, for many reasons.
I cannot suppress the thought that, if the bishops and seminaries had
taught all we knew, from the implicit acceptance of Ogino-Knaus

Rhythm by Pope Pius XI in his encyclical *Casti Connubii* in 1930 to Pius XII's strong request and encouragement in his two addresses in 1951, and had kept promoting NFP as it developed, along with a theology of the body and the true integral married love so well expounded by the present Pope, we would have a different family-life situation today.

Would more than sixty percent of today's married couples in their forties in the United States be sterilized?[21] Would some ninety percent of Catholic "family planners" be

Dr. Herb Ratner, Ilinois pro-life leader and early promoter of NFP.

mired in sinful birth control? Would so many have fallen for the unhealthful and sometimes abortifacient Pill, the IUD, Depo-Provera, Norplant, Cytotec, the morning-after Pill (also now known as "emergency contraception"), and so on? Perhaps by now, if we had carried out the wishes of Pius XII fortified by the writings of this present Pope, we would have many more families whose size was generously and naturally controlled, and many more religious and priestly vocations fostered by unselfish parents in the friendly environment of the large family. Perhaps by now the example of healthy, happy, holy Catholic families would have inspired serious Protestants to make the same generous choice, returning to their own tradition of more than 400 years—a tradition that opposed contraception until 1930, when the Anglicans decided to accept it, after a two-decade debate. This change is already happening in some instances: I can think of the Scott Hahns, the Steve Woods, the Gerry Matatics. More than fifty Protestant ministers have converted to Catholicism in the last decade,

---

[21] Consult the current U.S. Census.

a number of these because of their admiration for *Humanae Vitae* and their respect for Catholic theological orthodoxy.

It is ironic that the Anglicans gave up more than 400 years of anti-contraceptive doctrine in 1930, just when NFP came to be known.

In Milwaukee there is a center called "Protestants against Birth Control." Again, it is most encouraging to meet more and more Protestants—people like Randy Terry—especially in the pro-life movement, who are beginning to see the wickedness and consequences of artificial birth control, with its multiple evils stemming from the abuse of sex in and out of marriage.

At the Third International Pro-life Leaders' Meeting in Rome, 3-5 October 1995, James Bopp, counsel to the National Right to Life Committee, lobbied that non-abortifacient contraception (that is, true contraception) not be condemned in the final document. He should more carefully analyze what contraception and "permanent contraception" (sterilization) have done to the modern youth, family, Church, and world.

I do not have time here to record the historical evidence showing that past cultures have rotted from within largely because of their abuse of sex and have thus experienced the subsequent destruction of both family and society. Today, for those who will look, the evidence is all around us: The whole Western world is dying out, given the heightened, irresponsible sexual activity engendered by and facilitated by contraception, sterilization, abortifacients, and surgical abortion.

"Sex leads to most infections," reported the Center for Disease Control and Prevention in 1995. Of the nine infectious diseases researched, chlamydia, gonorrhea, and AIDS ranked as the top three and in that order. As an ancient wise man once said, "God always forgives, men sometimes, Nature, never"; she is jealous of her fertility; she strikes back. And no generation should know that better than today's people. Widespread legal euthanasia is threatening. Daily the line between contraception and abortion becomes ever thinner, while new chemical abortifacients are being added to the arsenal of death and may soon obscure the high visibility of surgical abortion.

Theologians who dissented to *Humanae Vitae* do not realize how heavily they contributed to the unleashing of the sexual instinct; to the destruction of youth and family; to the proliferation of out-of-wedlock births; to the increased number of single-parent families; and to the massive escalation of venereal (now sanitized as "sexually transmitted") disease, divorce, that "alternative lifestyle" we used to call "shacking up," marital unhappiness, and a host of other evils, including child and spousal abuse.

You will recall that my older brother Joseph became a Benedictine monk (Father Michael) at St. John's Abbey. Roman-trained, he taught theology and Scripture for years there. He died 5 May 1993. He and three confreres, Fathers Godfrey Diekmann, Aelred Tegels, and Kieran Nolan, joined Father Charles Curran in officially dissenting to *Humanae Vitae* in 1968, a subject Father Michael and I could hardly ever discuss thereafter; he persisted in his false view to the end. From all four I learned from what flimsy grounds and inexperience this sad dissent stemmed. To militantly reject *Humanae Vitae* is really to reject the Church's moral authority, and such rejection, I have noticed, colors a priest's whole theological outlook and performance. In the first twenty-five years of my priesthood, whenever I met a priest for the first time I could sense an immediate rapport, because we were in total theological agreement. Today the same kinship is felt only when one learns that the newly met priest accepts *Humanae Vitae*.

Humanae Vitae was issued by Paul VI on 25 July 1968. I did not sleep that night. After having tried to help so many couples with the then-available methods of NFP, I yielded to my doubts about the encyclical; I took the dissenting theologians too seriously; I even sponsored some of them. But before long I saw the consequences of contraception and how far they would extend—that contraception, with its abortifacient tentacles, was already devastating Church and society. I sensed, too, from an abundance of NFP counseling, teaching, and promotion, what a tragedy the rejection and contradiction of that encyclical would induce.

But we now know that the prophetic Pope Paul VI in *Humanae Vitae* was entirely right in making his amazing three predictions: that the practice of contraception would lower general morality; cause men to use and abuse women; and put a weapon into the hands of government, which then would enter the sanctuary of the home and there dictate to the couple how many children they may have. All of these predictions have subsequently been fully verified in the estimation of all who have eyes to see. Every day the message of that controversial document resounds more convincingly. After all, *Humanae Vitae* means "Of Human Life," and you cannot defend human life unless you defend its source, which is God's great gift of human sexuality, whereby He invites the truly loving married couple to intimately cooperate with Him in the mysterious act of creation.

It is astonishing that no more than approximately five percent of American Catholic couples practice natural birth regulation. It is astonishing as well that priests and bishops--given the dimensions and ramifications of the birth-control problem--have done so pitifully little to recommend and promote NFP. I have been waiting for our bishops to write a national pastoral addressing chastity *in* and *out* of marriage; certainly NFP, and loving abstinence where necessary, would be a part of this pastoral.

It is more than astonishing to me that parish priests rarely, if ever, preach on contraception and even less on sterilization, the fastest growing means of birth control on earth. The first line of attack on fertile women was chemical warfare by Pill; nowadays the weapon of choice is permanent neutering by mutilation. Female sterilization has become the most common means of fertility control in the world, and women are more and more becoming the always-available playthings of men, as the Pope predicted. Meanwhile, we have the radical feminist Germaine Greer telling us that "most of the pleasure in the world is still provided by children and not by genital dabbling."[22]

It is perhaps even more remarkable, to say it again, that so many Catholic bishops and priests and laity to this day do not recognize sinful birth control as a basic cause of marital/sexual infidelity, divorce, family destruction, fornication, the emptying of the seminaries and religious orders, etc., etc., etc. And I will keep saying, with Father John Hardon, that a right-to-life movement that does not oppose contraception and abortifacients will never win the battle for the protection of the unborn.

That, in fact, is why I founded the Human Life Center at St. John's University in 1972 and launched the *International Review of Natural*

---

[22] *Sex & Destiny, The Politics of Human Fertility* (New York: Harper & Row, 1984), p. 257.

Family Planning in the spring of 1977. It is gratifying to note that in 1995 the *New England Journal of Medicine*[23] recorded the results of a study made by the National Institutes of Health in which researchers found that pregnancies in 221 women were initiated in the five days before ovulation or on the day of ovulation itself—something that had been known for years by all veteran NFP teachers and practitioners. The pioneer medical researcher William Harvey could no longer say today that conception is "indeed an obscure business." And remember our friend Father Bernard Häring and his assertion that NFP might cause fetal defects and miscarriages? The scientists who conducted this study found again no evidence for the theory that fertilization by older sperm may be associated with a higher rate of spontaneous abortions.

All of this research reminds me of what the Stanford University chemistry professor Carl Djerassi, one of the developers of the Pill, wrote three years ago: that scientists have gone as far as they can with contraception; he foresees the solution as some kind of well-timed intercourse.[24] Pope Pius XII said this very thing in 1951. Rome and NFP proponents have been saying it for a long time.

Given the current disintegration of the family; the confused youth; the empty seminaries, monasteries, and convents; the increasing number of divorces; the scandalous neutering of couples by sterilization; and the host of other connected evils, *Humanae Vitae* looks better every day. The great Catholic geneticist Dr. Jerome Lejeune observed that *Humanae Vitae* may prove to be the most significant encyclical of all time. Some time before his death he told me that this encyclical seemed to manifest the Holy Spirit's taking the beleaguered Pope by the neck and saying, "Go this way."

In *Humanae Vitae* Pope Paul VI gave an anguished plea for bishops and priests to teach and to preach the truth about the evil of contraception. In the equally binding 1930 encyclical *Casti Connubii*—Pius XI's response to the Anglican betrayal of twenty centuries of Christian teaching—that Pope was even stronger:

---

[23] Vol. 333, no. 23 (7 December 1995).

[24] This Djerassi referred to as a "jet-age rhythm method." On Djerassi, see Brian Clowes, *The Facts of Life* (Front Royal, VA Human Life International, 1997), pp. 100-101.

We admonish, therefore, priests who hear confessions and others who have the care of souls, in virtue of Our supreme authority and in Our solicitude for the salvation of souls, not to allow the faithful entrusted to them to err regarding this most grave law of God; much more, that they keep themselves immune from such false opinions, in no way conniving in them. If any confessor or pastor of souls, which may God forbid, leads the faithful entrusted to him into these errors or should at least confirm them by approval or by guilty silence, let him be mindful of the fact that he must render a strict account to God, the Supreme Judge, for the betrayal of his sacred trust, and let him take to himself the words of Christ: "They are blind and leaders of the blind: and if the blind lead the blind, both fall into the pit" (n. 57).[25]

---

[25] *Christian Marriage*, p. 29.

CHAPTER 6

From Collegeville to Washington, D.C.

*I*n 1980 I was invited to attend the International Synod on the Family in Rome. San Francisco's Archbishop John R. Quinn opened the discussions by asking for a re-evaluation of *Humanae Vitae.*[1] Some cardinal-canonist pounced on him, saying that the whole issue had been decided, let us not waste time, let us move on. It was strongly rumored that the Benedictine archbishop of Westminster, Cardinal George Basil Hume, who appeared next, had planned to speak the way Quinn had; if so, he quickly changed his tune.

At this synod various delegate-bishops and cardinals gave ten-minute presentations. I was pleased to hear Cardinal William Baum, then archbishop of Washington, D.C., citing the Human Life Center as an example of good apostolic action on behalf of life and the family. Not all bishops were happy at being told to accept *Humanae Vitae* as a finished issue. Among the unhappy was Archbishop Denis Hurley of Durban, South Africa, who was a fan of the dissenting German theologian Father Bernard Häring, whom he often quoted in his writings. I was surprised at the number of bishops who wanted to allow Communion to divorced and remarried Catholics. This proposal was, however, quietly rejected. Here is neither room nor place to report fully on this synod. Suffice it to say that out of this meeting came Pope John Paul II's magnificent document *Familiaris Consortio (The Role of*

---

[1] Apparently Quinn has not changed his mind. See George Weigel's "The Quinn Proposals," *Crisis*, vol. 14, no. 10 (November 1996), 16-19.

the Christian Family in the Modern World). Some thought of this as the completion of *Humanae Vitae.* Unfortunately, its appearance was delayed by the attempted assassination of the Pope in 1981.

While I was in Rome a decision was made by abbey/university authorities to force me to take a year's sabbatical, ostensibly to rest. In my absence they delegated various close friends and collaborators of mine to plead with me upon my return to step back for a year. Meetings were held to explain to my friends and various associates that I needed a year off. My removal would also be a good thing, these authorities claimed, for the Human Life Center. The fact is that HLC was then flourishing with a $1,000,000 annual budget, twenty-four workers, and a recently founded pro-life monthly newspaper, *Family Life News,* edited by Dan Lyons, to which we were receiving twenty-five subscriptions per day.

Sometime before, the president of St. John's University, Father Michael Blecker, OSB, had appointed a guiding board for HLC— two of whose members had been on the Pill. Also, Father Blecker had appointed a supervisor over me, a brilliant former student and later monk-friend, Father Paul Siebenand, OSB. Father Siebenand removed my personal correspondence from my files and used it against me in the Minneapolis meetings of the friends and collabo-rators who were being primed to persuade me to take a sabbatical. (He later left St. John's Abbey and today is pastor of St. Catherine of Alexandria on Santa Catalina Island in the Archdiocese of Los Angeles.) It is only fair to say that he knew next to nothing about pro-life matters, and the young, inexperienced layman, John Boyle, whom Siebenand chose to actively manage the operation, knew even less. Obviously I was to remain merely the goose that laid the golden egg.

The decisions and actions of the board convinced me, as nothing else could, of what I already knew, that good pro-life work does not get done by a large committee or board. I do not know a single flour-ishing pro-life effort in the whole world that is conducted by a large administrative board. Doing pro-life/pro-family work in a materialis-tic, anti-life, anti-God culture demands certain quick decisions almost daily, and emergencies appear often, especially when you are involved internationally.

I should emphasize that, so far as I know, my removal from HLC was really the work and decision of only three people, Abbot Jerome Theisen, OSB (only recently elected), President Michael Blecker, OSB, and the canonist Father Daniel Ward, OSB.

The Blecker-appointed board/committee met shortly after my return from Rome and went into executive session. They rubber-stamped the decision that I was to take a year's sabbatical, giving no reasons except that I needed a rest.

In early November, Father Siebenand released a memo to the HLC staff directing that I was not to use HLC stationery or car, not to set foot in HLC offices, not to speak for HLC, and not to occupy my office after December 1. I would have an office, but not in HLC, which had been built out of a $168,000 grant I had solicited from the De Rance Corporation; I would be given a secretary, and I could still use what was then the best pro-life library in the world. Meanwhile, all the locks were changed, and my new office turned out to be a small room in an out-of-the-way building in an obscure area. Again, I was offered no clear, sensible reasons for this strange procedure. (Father Berthold Ricker, OSB, who then was prior and who always encouraged me, read this chapter before it was published. He assured me that he knew nothing about the secret meetings and machinations going on behind the scenes.)

In about mid-November, Dan Lyons and Andrew Scholberg, both key HLC employees, were fired by mail, with two days' notice. Lyons, as I have mentioned, was the editor of the Center's *Family Life News*, and Scholberg was the editor of *Human Life Issues* and the assistant editor of the *International Review of Natural Family Planning*. Mr. and Mrs. Scholberg were expecting a baby within a month.

Later guidelines instructed me not to associate in any way with Lyons and Scholberg, not to say anything "volatile" to the press, not to disturb the workings of HLC, and to show mercy and kindness to any fellow monk whose views differed from my pro-life stance.

Taking over the direction of HLC was my friend Rita Marker, whom I had known for years. She had wide experience in pro-life work as head of Washington State's pro-life group, Human Life. She soon encountered difficulties similar to mine and, in addition, experienced financial problems with HLC, as I had predicted. In 1986 she

At a meeting in Rome in 1983 with my great friends Judie and Paul Brown.

moved HLC to Steubenville University in Ohio, along with my precious library. Rita Marker became an authority on euthanasia and
eventually, having left HLC, founded the International Anti-
Euthanasia Task Force.

On the HLC committee/board appointed by Father Blecker were
two very dear and brilliant former students and later friends of mine.
One was the chairman, John Kidwell, who was then the president of
7-Up in St. Louis; the other was Norb Berg, an executive officer with
Control Data in Minneapolis. I hope it is correct to say that they were
misled by the authorities to believe that I definitely needed a rest and a
change; I have never had any doubt about their good intentions. But
the whole affair ended two very dear friendships, for I never talked to
either of them again—and that was not by my choice.

Having come to the conclusion that St. John's Abbey/ University
was not the place where HLC's apostolate could continue to flourish,
I immediately began making plans for continuing my international
pro-life/pro-family work elsewhere. Paul and Judie Brown invited me
to re-establish in Washington, D.C. Dr. Edmund Pellegrino, then president of the Catholic University of America, invited me to re-start on
the campus of the Catholic University. To this day I cannot help won-

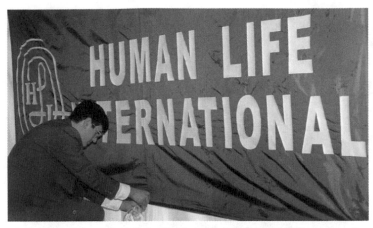

My pro-life work began in 1963; in 1970 I conceived the Human Life Center (formally organized in 1972); and in 1980 I founded Human Life International, which continued the mission of HLC.

dering about the reason—was it to add a conservative influence to a liberal campus or to acquire a new source of financing? After visiting there, I declined. There were other invitations. President Warren Carroll kindly invited me to re-establish a pro-life center at Christendom College at Front Royal, Virginia, but I thought it was too far from Washington, D.C., the political capital of the world. Ironically, today our international headquarters is in Front Royal!

I started Human Life International in 1980 to continue the mission I'd begun at the Human Life Center. Of course, to do this I had to receive permission from my abbot; and, as I shall later recount, I ultimately received a five-year leave.

Never did I gain the slightest impression that Abbot Jerome knew the nature and extent of what I was doing with HLC all over the world. Perhaps his ignorance was my fault. Nor had he any awareness of the budding anti-life/anti-family movement. But what superior did at that time? Never did he ask me about my work. I know he was surprised at the multitude of phone calls and letters received when the public learned that the board had given me an enforced sabbatical. (True-blue active and experienced pro-lifers knew exactly and immediately what had happened, for if there is one thing they understand, it is opposition and persecution, often arising even from their own nominal comrades.)

I was back in Washington, D.C., the political capital of the world.

Once, after I had collected a million dollars a year for my worldwide pro-life ministry, Abbot Jerome asked me, "Do you have any friends?" Again, in the recreation room he once asked me to attend a special meal in the monastery. (I have forgotten the occasion.) To my shame, I must admit I ignored his request: on my mind were two pro-life leaders from a distant city awaiting me in the guest quarters. Phone calls, correspondence, and "drop-in" visitors were my cross then—and still are!

My year of hibernating, praying, and suffering in limbo at St. John's Abbey was very, very painful, although I kept on furiously writing, editing, publishing, fund-raising, advising, and lecturing both inside and outside the United States. Suddenly the world had become my monastery, my parish, my responsibility. My life indeed was impossible. Despite tenure, I had been rudely and unnecessarily fired as professor of sociology through an insulting letter from Father Daniel Ward, to whom Abbot Jerome had made me responsible. In dismissing

The entrance to the head-quarters of Human Life International when we were in Washington, D.C.

me, the HLC board had innocently asked me to travel and rest, for which Father Daniel allowed me only $1,000. I did not accept it, because I traveled only to fight the family destroyers. Father Daniel also wanted me off the HLC board, but chairman John Kidwell thought that was rude and uncalled for.

In such distressing circumstances you find out who your friends are. For a typical reaction, eloquently phrased, see Judie Brown's letter, originally published in *Orthodoxy* (January-March 1981), and reprinted in Appendix E. This is a board member's frank, inside view of what really transpired behind the scenes.

Painful rumors and accusations fly fast and furious at a time like this. I was accused of being on an ego trip; Minneapolis papers called to ask whether I would leave the Benedictine Order and even the priesthood. I was accused of neglecting pro-life needs in the United States (!); of centering HLC around "the cult of one person" (!); of being unable to get along with others; of working the staff too hard (perhaps true!!); of having a hard time relinquishing control; etc., etc.

I was never told what the grievances against me really were. I still don't know the full motivation and reasons for the year's sabbatical forced on me, supposedly for a rest that I did not need, and about which I was not consulted beforehand. I do know that one attack I

made on Planned Parenthood on a Twin City talk show brought rever-
berations. Some good monks speculated that I had said and written too
much about contraception and had defended *Humanae Vitae* too eloquently and that this candor would make it hard for the university to
get government grants. (I was one of the first—if not *the* first—to consistently point out in many articles and lectures the connection between
contraception and abortion seen by me in every country I visited.)

Others said that contracepting alumni and faculty members
objected to my pro-life/pro-family work at HLC, along with the promotion of Natural Family Planning (NFP). Whenever Father Don
Talefous, OSB, long-time chaplain to students, downgraded the
authority of *Humanae Vitae* in his otherwise excellent weekly
"Chaplain's Letter," saying that contraception was a matter they could
decide in conscience, I would tangle with him in in-house publications.
Few faculty persons would come to my defense, but then it's likely
that many of the lay members were no fans of *Humanae Vitae* and
possibly were already contraceptors. Four priest-monk theologians on
the seminary faculty were formal dissenters. As I mentioned in the previous chapter, they were Fathers Godfrey Diekmann, Aelred Tegels,
Kieran Nolan, and Michael Marx (my brother). No doubt my work
through HLC—the symposia, the seminars and publications fostering
NFP—were uncomfortable reminders of their defection—and uncomfortable reminders to contracepting faculty members.

At this point a few words are in order with regard to the faculty's
general attitude toward abortion and contraception. Shortly after the
Roe v. Wade disaster in 1973, Robert Joyce, a member of the philosophy department of St. John's University, and his wife Mary—my close
collaborators—proposed that we get the university faculty to pass a
resolution decrying the Supreme Court decision and pleading for an
immediate restoration of protection for the unborn, whether by law or
by constitutional amendment. The Joyces, by the way, wrote one of
the first books in the United States opposing abortion, *Let Us Be
Born*, with the subtitle *The Inhumanity of Abortion*. I suggested to my
good friend Bob Joyce that offering the resolution was a bad idea
because it would never pass, given the local university climate, and
then we would be worse off.

I proved to be a prophet. But I shall never forget the faculty discus-

sion. Rabbi Nahum Schulman, who
taught Jewish studies, thought the resolution was very "unecumenical"; he
conceded, however, that the Court's
decision was tragic. One professor of
accounting and allied subjects stood
up and said that we do not know
when life begins—and even after it
begins, who knows when and whether
it is human? A biology professor,
Father Bertram Niggeman, OSB, then
explained to him the facts of life.
Others got up but didn't make much
sense. The discussion betrayed an
enormous ignorance of pro-life issues,
that is, of what was really at stake in
the light of the *Roe v. Wade* tragedy.

Here I am in 1984 in my office at HLI's Washington, D.C. headquarters.

I cited data to demonstrate that the
"intelligentsia" did not resist the abortion/euthanasia movement of
Hitler's Germany; in fact, some noted professors fostered it, only to be
blamed later for their activity. Surely we would not want to be similarly viewed by a later generation. As Albert Einstein complained, the
press, media, and universities—and even some church groups—did little to turn aside the Nazi onslaught. My friend and fellow abortion-
fighter the Episcopalian priest Father Charles Carroll, who had been a
witness at the Nuremberg trials, kept reminding me, "Do not expect
salvation from intellectuals."

Bob Joyce, who had called several meetings (poorly attended) to
arouse the faculty, pointed out that the faculty's moral credibility
would be at stake if it did not denounce *Roe v. Wade*; that "this egre-
gious violation of civilized humanity is surely the most important issue
this faculty has ever discussed in my years here."

A prominent liturgist and dissenter to *Humanae Vitae*, Father
Godfrey Diekmann, OSB, quoted theologian Karl Rahner to the effect
that life may not be human in the first stages of pregnancy and
warned that we might look foolish at some future date for having said
that all human life should be protected from conception to natural

death.[2] Incidentally, on 13 July 1988, Father Godfrey was given the Virgil Michel award; in his acceptance remarks he pleaded for the sanctioning of women-priests.

Here is the Resolution Concerning Human Life:

> We, the undersigned members of the Faculty of Saint John's University, affirm that:
>
> 1. Individual human life begins at conception and continues, whether intra- or extra-uterine, until natural physical death.
>
> 2. This living human individual deserves the basic protection accorded to persons under public and civil law, at

---

[2]   Here is a summary of Rahner's false views on which Father Godfrey relied: it was written by Frau Elisabet Backhaus and published in her *Recht und Gesetz*, pp. 31-32, distributed by two of Germany's strongest pro-life groups (Aktion Leben, e.V. and Europäische Ärzteakion, e.V.: "Nach Karl Rahner tritt die geistige Seele erst in einem späteren Stadium der embryonalen Entwicklung und nicht schon bei der Zeugung in Existenz. Zwischen dem befruchteten Ei und dem geistbeseelten Organismus gebe es mehrere biologische Stufen, die noch nicht Mensch sind. Ein noch-nicht-menschlicher biologischer Organismus steuere auf eine Zuständlichkeit zu, in der die Entstehung einer Geistseele ihr genügendes biologisches Substrat hat." (Karl Rahner: Zur Erschaffung der Geistigen Seele, in P. Overhage, K. Rahner: *Das Problem der Hominisation*, Freiburg, 1963, S. 79).
Karl Rahner doubted whether even the born child already had a soul: "Karl Rahner bezweifelt sogar, dass das schon geborene Kind eine Seele hat: Ich jedenfalls setze lieber hinter das Schicksal der unmündig sterbenden Kinder, wenn es diese geben sollte, ein Fragezeichen des Nichtwissens, als dass ich von ihnen aus schliesse, es könne auch ohne Freiheit eine selige Vollendung geben. . . . Ich kann dann mindestens immer noch fragen, ob ich vom christlichen Dogma her sicher verpflichtet sei, an die Unsterblichkeit dieser Seele zu glauben. . . ." (K. Rahner, Karl-Heinz Weger: Was sollen wir noch glauben?, Herderbücherei Nr. 700, 1979, s.96).

every stage of growth and development, and no matter how socially dependent he or she becomes in the course of natural life.

3. The only decent and human position for anyone who doubts whether the person exists at any particular stage of growth and development or condition of social dependency is to give the person the benefit of the doubt.

4. All persons in our society should do whatever they can to protect and enhance human life and to alleviate or eradicate the social evils that inevitably perpetrate the deliberate destruction of innocent and defenseless human beings.[3]

This pro-life resolution was rejected by secret ballot: For—24; Opposed—47; Abstaining—14.

I can still see Bob Joyce sitting stunned after the meeting. I recall walking up to him and tapping him on the shoulder: "Bob, it's maddening to be told you were told, but I did tell you." As a result of this faculty meeting, Joyce took a survey of faculty opinion; as he recalls, "The silence was deafening." With the help of my classmate the sociology professor Dr. Lee Blaske and Sisters Ellen Cotone and Renée Domeier of the neighboring College of St. Benedict where I was also teaching, Joyce later founded "Educators for Life"—which, however, given the anti-life climate, died a quick death.

The university faculty dialogue I described was typical of how most intellectuals thought or failed to think at that time. Pro-life issues were not in the general consciousness, despite the fact that in 1959 the American Law Institute had already proposed to the state legislators a model bill allowing virtually abortion-on-request; also despite the fact that by 1972 eighteen states had already legalized baby-killing. Actually, by October 1972 alert pro-life people defeated 57 pro-abortion bills in 30 states.[4] Even so, most people did not know about these

---

[3] From the minutes of the St. John's University Faculty Meeting, 27 March 1973.

[4] *The Confrere*, 26 Oct. 1972. Propaganda for legal abortion began in the early 1960s; the first state to legalize pre-born baby-killing was Colorado in 1967.

developments unless they were fighting the battle for life, and they were all too few.

But why such obtuseness among the intellectual elite? And to this day, with notable exceptions like Notre Dame's Dr. Charles Rice, a collaborator with Human Life International (HLI) for years, and like the Franciscan University of Steubenville, Ohio, intellectuals by and large, and their universities, have not been prominent in the pro-life battle. Remember, it was president of Notre Dame University, Father Theodore Hesburgh, who said "all too often they [pro-lifers] are crude and mindless zealots." Remember, too, it was Notre Dame University that allowed Planned Parenthood to sponsor a national meeting on its campus. From my observations over the last thirty years I can tell you that the financial support given to my pro-life endeavors by intellectuals, including professors, is minimal.

Where did Abbot Jerome stand on *Humanae Vitae*? He did not formally dissent, like some of his theologian-monks. But he surely did not support it. On the contrary, he allowed my confrere and friend Father Philip S. Kaufman, OSB, to attack *Humanae Vitae* in various publications,[5] among them his dissenting book, *Why You Can Disagree and Remain a Faithful Catholic* (1989).[6] This went through several printings, including an expanded and revised edition (1995).

Father Philip was a convert from Judaism. In the abbey the monks used to say that he was a "convert who never became a Catholic." I believe that his writings and lectures reflect this shortcoming. He and I had an ongoing theological dialogue in the seminary, often disagreeing. Strangely—or perhaps not so strangely—the Jesuit Father Richard McCormick contributed a laudatory foreword to this dissident book that has done so much harm. Father Andrew Greeley recommended the book, which, typically, bears no *imprimatur*. Besides disparaging *Humanae Vitae*, Father Kaufman assaults the indissolubility of marriage, advocates the right to divorce and remarry (contrary to

---

[5] "Autocracy Isn't the Catholic Style," *Commonweal*, vol. 26, no. 4 (27 February 1989), 110-114; "Abortion: Catholic Pluralism and the Potential for Dialogue," *Cross Comments*, vol. 1, no. 37 (Spring 1987), 76-86.

[6] New York: Crossroad Publishing Company, 1989.

to *Gaudium et Spes*, 49), and calls for democracy in the Church through the election of bishops. No wonder he was invited to lecture at the notorious Call to Action conferences![7]

The essence of his book is that only the teaching that the Extraordinary Magisterium has explicitly and officially declared to be infallible need bind the conscience in all circumstances. In this erroneous view, the decrees of the Ordinary Magisterium of Pope and council, even those (like *Humanae Vitae*) that have achieved the status of infallibility through constant teaching, reiteration, and promulgation of the Church throughout all her centuries, do not bind one's conscience in the same way that *ex cathedra* papal pronouncements do. In other words, all papal/episcopal teaching and decrees apart from those few statements of the Pope expressly declared to be infallible may be filtered through the individual conscience. This false understanding, of course, overlooks many decrees of the Church to the contrary, for example, Vatican II's decree in *Lumen Gentium*:

> This religious submission of will and of mind must be shown in a special way to the authentic teaching authority of the Roman Pontiff, even when he is not speaking *ex cathedra*. That is, it must be shown in such a way that his supreme Magisterium [teaching authority] is acknowledged with reverence, [and] the judgments made by him are sincerely adhered to. . . . (n. 25)

Here there is no space to fully critique Kaufman's thesis, but the reader is invited to read a blistering review of his book by the canonist/theologian Monsignor Vincent Foy, published in the *Homiletic and Pastoral Review*.[8]

Abbot Jerome Theisen allowed Kaufman to propagate his errors in lectures to various audiences throughout the country, for whom he would approvingly play a tape of Bernard Häring's shrill dissent to

---

[7]   As to CTA's notoriety see Human Life International's *Special Report* nos. 143 and 145.

[8]   *Homiletic and Pastoral Review*, "A Damaging Attack," vol. 91, no. 5 (February 1991), 73-76.

Humanae Vitae, which he also used in training deacons at St. John's. Two Canadian archbishops (names withheld) telephoned Abbot Jerome to tell him that Kaufman was not welcome in their archdioceses; the abbot still did not recall him.

Now, to reject *Humanae Vitae*—which taught nothing new but merely reaffirmed constant teaching throughout twenty centuries—is to reject Church authority, causing a ripple of doubt and rebellion in virtually all other theological areas, surely in the whole body of moral theology and ethics. Thus, the acceptance or rejection of *Humanae Vitae* truly creates a watershed. Given also the dissenting statements of some ten national hierarchies (out of some 120), today we find a tragic and enormous international theological confusion at all levels of Catholic education and catechesis. Pope John Paul II, who has repeatedly begged bishops to abide by the authentic teaching and to promote NFP, made it clear as early as 1987 that the morality of contraception was not in the area of legitimate theological questioning and discussion. This sexual confusion and immorality is also at the bottom of the tragic sex-ed predicament.

Now, I don't wish to downgrade the institution that nurtured me, the university where I taught for years. After all, faculty member Bob Joyce (with wife Mary) produced one of the first books against abortion. Further, St. John's University published my controversial *The Death Peddlers*, against the legal advice of its five lawyers. Remember, too, that university authorities allowed HLC to start and flourish, releasing me to direct it full-time in 1974. In several ways, St. John's University—through my international symposia and seminars throughout the country and beyond—pioneered natural family planning in the United States. Finally, I do not know any Catholic university on whose campus the future Human Life International (HLI) could have functioned and flourished. Ironically, some time before my troubles began I was invited to become president of Newman College in St. Louis. I told them that I had more important work to do at St. John's University with HLC.

Back now to the details of my ouster from HLC and its aftermath. Months before the proposed sabbatical, Abbot Jerome left a note in my mailbox saying that he had made arrangements for me to undergo a psychological evaluation at a Catholic institute in St. Louis. I was stunned. He gave no reasons. I called the psychiatrist Conrad W. Baars, whom I knew well as a friend. He was adamant in telling me not to go to that institute; it was not a competent one; I might get into some kind of argument with a homosexual, he told me, and then the record of this encounter would go to my superior and be used against me. I guess I was an early "papist priest." In the climate of that time— and it has worsened since then—some good and creative priests had already been destroyed in just this way, Baars reminded me. After discussing the matter with my spiritual director and other highly competent people, I informed Abbot Jerome that I could not in conscience accept his directive. I begged him to tell me what he perceived my problem to be. No response.

Shortly thereafter—I recall the incident as if it happened yesterday—within fifteen minutes after I had returned from a brutal seventeen-day winter lecture tour in icy, cold Canada, Abbot Jerome phoned me to insist I go to a psychiatrist of his choice. "Why?" I impatiently demanded to know. No answer. "Am I a homosexual or what?" No answer.

Later he called me in to tell me that if I did not go to a psychiatrist of his choosing he would suspend me within twenty-four hours! I was more than stunned. I had never had any trouble with my superiors. I once specifically asked Abbot Jerome's predecessor, Abbot John Eidenschenk, OSB, whether he had received any complaints about me, since I was carrying on a difficult and sensitive apostolate. He said no. I had spoken with Abbot Baldwin Dworschak only about five times, briefly, during the twenty-one years of his tenure. I must have behaved myself! In any case, I begged Abbot Jerome for forty-eight hours instead of twenty-four, and he reluctantly granted this request.

Faced with my forty-eight-hour deadline, I consulted canon lawyers and other legal experts; I also called Father John Hardon, the great Jesuit theologian who has indeed been a very good friend and guide of HLI for years. He advised: "Whatever you do, don't get suspended, because then you'd lose your credibility."

Father Hardon asked me to call the Congregation for Religious Institutes in Rome to present my case and to seek advice. He gave me his credit card and charitably said I could use it as much as necessary. (I never did.) From a top canonist and legal expert I learned that no superior can canonically or legally send a subject to a specific psychiatrist, or even to any specific doctor. In the forty-seventh hour I walked into Abbot Jerome's office and said that what he was asking me to do was illegal and not canonical; I had consulted proper authorities. He backed off immediately—for a time.

Meanwhile, I made the tenacious Abbot Jerome an offer to have myself evaluated by a noted clinical psychologist, Dr. Loyal Marsh, who had worked for years with priests in Portland, Oregon, and elsewhere. Abbot Jerome grudgingly consented. I was personally evaluated by Dr. Marsh after taking every psychological test under the sun, or so it seemed, including the Minnesota Multiphasic Personality Inventory; after conducting more interviews, Marsh wrote a favorable report measuring my personal strengths and weaknesses and delivered it to Abbot Jerome, giving a copy to me. But clearance from Dr. Marsh was not enough; I still had to see a psychiatrist!

Sometime thereafter I was summoned to the abbot's office. In the presence of the canonist Father Daniel Ward, OSB, and the then-acting president of St. John's University, Father Alberic Culhane, OSB, Abbot Jerome read to me ten reasons why he could suspend me! This time I was too numb to be stunned. I asked him for a copy, since I could not remember all the reasons. He refused, and I asked why. Said he, "I know what you might do with it." The next morning I met the abbot in the corridor; again I asked him for that list. He said that the only important points were that I could not write, publish, or meet the press, and I could not leave campus without his express, written permission. I still cannot remember the other reasons he read to me in his office. The prohibitions were never enforced. Nor could I find in the archives the document alleging ten reasons why I could have been suspended.

About then my spiritual director, who knew ecclesiastical politics, was a personal friend of fellow Croatian Cardinal Franjo Seper and had many connections in Rome, suggested I take my case to the apostolic nuncio, Archbishop (now Cardinal) Pio Laghi in Washington, D.C. He had only recently arrived from serving as nuncio in Argentina. "Write to Laghi with a copy to the abbot. Then the abbot will know you mean business," was the practical advice given me. This time the abbot was dumbfounded; he called all kinds of meetings.

I phoned Archbishop Laghi for an appointment. He graciously granted it. Archbishop Laghi was very busy; he said he had only ten minutes, but he kindly gave me a half-hour. I told him that I was befuddled by the way I had been handled; that my trusted confreres, spiritual director, and several canonists had told me it was a sheer case of injustice and persecution; and that my spiritual director had asked me to appeal to the apostolic nuncio for advice and possible decision. He suggested I take the sabbatical, go to Rome and elsewhere to do research, and above all write the definitive paper on euthanasia that Cardinal Franjo Seper, then head of the Holy Office (now Congregation for the Doctrine of the Faith), had asked me to do during an earlier interview with him in Rome. This request by a major Church official, by the way, was the only one I was never able to honor—the result of my harassment.

Archbishop Laghi promised to write to the abbot. He did, as Abbot Jerome admitted to me, even telling me the content of the letter. Abbot Jerome told the nuncio that I should first have presented my case to the usual Benedictine grievance committee—exactly what I had been advised to avoid. Besides, this hearing would have dragged on interminably while babies were being killed all over the world. The abbot told me he had written to Laghi in response, citing prior consultation with Archbishop John R. Roach of St. Paul-Minneapolis and Bishop George H. Speltz of St. Cloud, the local ordinary.

I then wrote to Archbishop Laghi that Archbishop Roach had waffled on *Humanae Vitae* in his first speech as president (from 1980 to 1983) of the American hierarchy, and that Bishop Speltz had tolerated the presence on his seminary faculty of the four St. John's theologians who were formal dissenters to *Humanae Vitae*. For all I know, Bishop Speltz did what he could about the latter situation, as he did about a dissenting student chaplain. But how can a bishop of a small diocese stand up against the world's largest, most powerful Benedictine monastery, whose resources included three schools on campus, a publishing house, and twice as many priests as the diocese?

Bishop Speltz, incidentally, was thoroughly pro-life and gave me nothing but encouragement through the years; he appreciated my NFP work, both in his diocese and nationally. Late in the ongoing turmoil Bishop Speltz sent me a half-page, hand-written letter asking me to

reconsider my decision to leave and to continue with HLC at
St. John's University. I clearly recall his kindly suggestion that I might
be destroying what I had worked so hard to build over so many years
with HLC. He also asked to see me personally before I left to thank
me. He even invited me to dinner with him, during which he gave me
a donation and thanked me for all my pro-life work. But it was too
late for second thoughts: the funding had been ruined.

Once, when the Australian NFP expert Dr. John Billings was at St.
John's University, Bishop Speltz invited (I composed the invitation) all
Catholic doctors in St. Cloud (more than forty) to a dinner featuring a
Billings lecture on NFP. Only five showed up. Bishop Speltz told me
later that he would gladly do it again, so convinced was he of the
importance of NFP and the evil of contraception. To this day, St.
Cloud's NFP program, headed by Kay Ek, may be one of the best
diocesan programs in the country.

Sometime after our conference regarding the correspondence with
Archbishop Laghi, I was again surprised when Abbot Jerome faced me
with a document that unhappy priests sign before leaving for a supposed one-year sabbatical and then walking out of their religious
order, everything canonically approved. I told the abbot that my faith
had never been stronger, that I loved my priesthood and the
Benedictine Order, that I felt God was calling me to do pro-life/pro-
family work: I could not possibly sign this document.

All along I had been asking for a five-year leave of absence to start
pro-life work elsewhere, because I was thoroughly convinced that the
board had destroyed HLC and by now—given the publicity—ruined
the prospects for fundraising: at St. John's Abbey/University I could
no longer do what needed to be done. Abbot Jerome was very reluctant; the overabundance of bad publicity already generated for St.
John's by this whole affair had given him much to ponder, I am confident, and of course, it did not help seminary attendance. (As one
bishop told me confidentially, if there is no room for HLC at St. John's
University, then there is no room there for his seminarians.)

Finally Abbot Jerome granted the leave, and HLI was born in
Washington, D.C., in 1980, after many labor pains, with the help of
Judie and Paul Brown, and incorporated in 1981. I shall be forever
grateful to the Browns for giving me a desk in their office, housing me

for a while and then finding me a place to stay.

The super-kind Dominican Prior Raymond Smith, who was head of St. Dominic's Friary in Washington, D.C., and a reader of HLC's newsletter, *Love, Life, Death Issues*, took me in and said that I would have to pay nothing, in the light of what had happened. Four years later his successor, Father Edward Gaffney, OP, turned me out after I exposed the wild theology of the Dutch Dominican Father Edward Schillebeeckx.

Back to my departure from the Abbey: After my teaching for thirty-two years at St. John's, collecting several million dollars for HLC, and writing the pioneer anti-euthanasia piece *The Mercy Killers* (1970) and the best-seller *The Death Peddlers* (1971), on which the Abbey made a good deal of money, the treasurer, Gordon Tavis, offered me $7,000 and a used Ford Escort; when I protested, I received a new mid-sized car, a Chevrolet Citation. I was denied my mailing list of supporters, my health insurance, and the quarterly *International Review of Natural Family Planning*. (The latter followed HLC to Steubenville, Ohio, and within a year or two had its name shortened to *The International Review*, even as its content broadened to include human-life issues in general. It died a gentle death.)

It was like starting all over again from scratch. Would the Lord of Love and Life help me to re-establish the mission?

Upon my leaving, Abbot Jerome graciously gave me his blessing and the requested document affirming that I was indeed a priest in good standing. In friendly conversations years later, he told me, without elaborating, that he had made mistakes. At the age of sixty-seven he died suddenly of a heart attack in Rome on 11 September 1995 as abbot president of all Benedictine congregations. There can be no doubt that Abbot Jerome was interested in promoting Benedictine monasticism. He was largely responsible for setting up an M.A. program of monastic studies at St. John's Abbey.

It was with leaden heart and many doubts that I left St. John's Abbey/University. But never have I seen the hand of God more in my life than since that departure and the incorporation of HLI in 1981. I now regard the whole painful affair as providential. As I commented earlier, at no university could there have been done what HLI has accomplished with the grace of God. It is a little miracle that the work even survived, given the many enemies who hoped to dance on its grave.

From a measly beginning, by 1997 HLI has grown to have a more than eight-million-dollar domestic budget, seven national offices, seventy-five branches in fifty-seven countries, ten newsletters in various languages, eleven distinct pro-life/pro-family programs (mostly international), ninety-eight paid workers, and many volunteers all over the world. We ship pro-life material to more than eighty countries and publish in several. Without HLI, there would be no pro-life ministry in many developing nations.

I attribute whatever good HLI has accomplished to God's grace and guidance, and to the very many people who believe deeply in HLI's work and support it with their prayers and financial offerings. We have an international prayer network. Indeed, the Lord has blessed HLI with many competent people who conduct the largest pro-life/pro-family ministry in the world. The future I leave to God.

Let it be known to all who read this: I have always believed that life is too short for grudges, and I bear no hard feelings against anyone. By the way, after the five years of my leave of absence were up, Abbot Jerome generously gave me another three years (all he could offer me under the rules); when that additional leave had expired, he suggested that I appeal to the Holy See for another five years. My request was duly granted. Today I am a happy member of St. John's Abbey, and my sympathetic Abbot Father Timothy Kelly is my encouraging superior.

CHAPTER 7

Interesting Personalities Along the Way

One blessing in doing pro-life/pro-family work around the world is that you meet the greatest human beings and Christians. In many ways they are all alike in their convictions, their opposition, their persecution, their problems, and, I might say, their consolations. I find that there are no more committed Christians than those who are truly pro-life/pro-family; they see their work as quintessentially necessary for humanity and Church, since they are always dealing with the origins and development of both. Further, as Pope John Paul II wrote in his *Letter to Families*, virtually all social problems have their origin in a disordered family life. Indeed, as he said in another context, the history of mankind runs through the family.

DOCTORS

Among the significant people I have worked with is **Dr./Prof. Jerome Lejeune**, the great geneticist who discovered the cause of Down's Syndrome. This famous Frenchman loved to quote St. Vincent de Paul, who said that it is the care of the ugly, the rejected, the dispossessed—those who cannot reward us in any way—that keeps us human and makes us charitable. So the least and the sickliest in society also have their vocation and mission from God!

Dr. Lejeune often spoke at my conferences all over the world. And never did he speak only once, for he was always in demand in every city and country and he gave of himself most generously. He winced only slightly when in Houston, for example, at our symposium there in 1993, he had to get up at 6:00 a.m. to address a group of doctors at 7:00 a.m. some miles away. But that was typical of the man—never to miss an opportunity, especially if he could foster the welfare of the little ones, and it was to their defense that he came with all his engaging personality, wisdom, and charity. The great German pro-lifer Dr. Siegfried Ernst once whispered to me after a typically brilliant Lejeune lecture in the Netherlands, "We heard a great scientist and saint."

Lejeune spoke English well, although slowly. Now and then he got stuck, paused for a moment, and then, like a true Frenchman, invented a word. So you hoped he would get stuck and give you a new word! It happened once in Sydney, Australia, when he spoke to a prestigious medical faculty, amongst whom were notorious abortionists. He was aware of their presence and did not lose the opportunity to teach them a pointed, gentle lesson. Said he, slowly, "The kangaroo is the only animal in the world that aborts its young. [Pause] But mudder kangaroo allows the little one to crawl between her legs, into her pouch in front, where are the breasts to complete the pregnancy. [Pause] Now, now: If mudder kangaroo can sense the [gets stuck; invents a word], the . . . 'kangarooity' of her offspring, why is it that the human mudder cannot sense the humanity of her offspring?" [Long pause while the knife sinks in.] Facing his own peers, Lejeune never knew any fears. He didn't have to. Armed with the truth, scientific and religious, he was totally competent.

His brilliant defense of the seven frozen embryos in a Tennessee court, where he was faced with the abortionists' best legal and scientific talent, was truly a classic.[1] Several observers have said that the sharp courtroom encounter with pro-abortion scientists and lawyers should be made into a motion picture. But, by controlling the media and the entertainment industry, the enemies of life will make sure that never happens.

---

[1]   Professor Lejeune's testimony, along with court documents, can be ordered from the Center for Law and Religious Freedom, 4208 Evergreen Lane, Suite 222, Annandale, VA 22003.

While I was lecturing with him in New Zealand, Lejeune was always sought out in every city by reporters who knew of his accomplishments.[2]
I recall that in Wellington a reporter asked him whether he would ever do an amniocentesis. "No," came the gentle but pointed reply. "Why not?" "Well,"

The late great Dr. Jerome Lejeune (from France).

responded Lejeune slowly, "you see, if I do an amniocentesis, I might find a handicapped baby; and being an honest doctor, I would have to tell the mudder; but if I tell the mudder she may very likely abort—and I would be responsible." Then came the inevitable clincher of which he was the

---

[2]　Thus Dr. H. P. Dunn of New Zealand wrote me on 5 October 1996: "In 1975, as a result of public pressure, the Government set up a Royal Commission on Contraception, Sterilization and Abortion. It was to this Commission that you and Prof. Lejeune so generously gave evidence but your advice and warnings were ignored. The people and the politicians wanted free access to abortion and that is what they got. The Contraception, Sterilization and Abortion Act was passed in 1977 and the number of abortions has steadily increased every year since then. Unwittingly the politicians acknowledged through the title of their Act the inseparable connection, which at that time you alone used to stress, that there is between contraception and the other two facets of the anti-life triad. Now we can see that the same philosophy leads on inevitably to euthanasia and—we ought to have the courage to say it—homosexuality. Obviously they are all aspects of being anti-Christ. And that is the fundamental explanation of the anti-life Satanic campaign, as you well know."

Dr. Hymie Gordon.

master: "I refuse to make myself part of a human disposal system."

Once on French TV he debated Dr. Etienne-Emile Beaulieu, the developer of RU-486, the abortion drug. Beaulieu asked Lejeune a question he soon wished he had not, something like, "You so-called pro-lifers are a strange lot. Since you believe that embryos are human beings, why don't you baptize miscarriages?" [As a matter of fact, the Church requires the baptism of such infants whenever possible.] Shot back Lejeune, "I thought you and I would engage in a scientific discussion. I'm a scientist, and I like to think that you are too. But if you wish to discuss theology, we can do that also." So the debate went, and of course the jury voted Lejeune the winner. Obviously, he was not someone you took on a second time for debate.

In 1988 Lejeune, speaking on "Ethics and Genetics" at a congress in Brussels, told his rapt audience, "Chemical contraception is really like making love without making a baby; *in vitro* fertilization is making a child without making love; abortion is undoing the child; pornography is undoing love—all of these are contrary to the true nature of human love and life." In the context Lejeune quoted a woman who had undergone *in vitro* fertilization as saying she "made love with a syringe."

So famed was Dr. Lejeune that he could go on London's BBC almost on request, and he used this network at times to serve his purpose of defending the unborn. While Lejeune won numerous awards, it may be true, as rumored, that he was never given the Nobel Prize precisely because he was too Catholic and pro-life. But knowing his humility, deep spiritual life, and love of Catholicism, I am certain he never lost one wink of sleep over that possible deprivation. What hurt him most, I am sure, was the French government's and foundations' denying him—reducing or cutting off—grants for genetic research. In this regard Randy Engel helped somewhat with her Michael Fund.

At the end he was working on a solution for Down's Syndrome and was optimistic he could find it in terms of diet. He often said that if the medical profession had always killed when faced with a problem, science and the art of medicine would never have advanced. He died in Paris on Good Friday in 1994. He was buried from Notre Dame Cathedral with Cardinal Jean-Marie Lustiger officiating and Pope John Paul II, a friend with whom he and his wife had had dinner shortly before, sending a special message. The Pope had only recently appointed him President of the Pontifical Academy of Life.

Another fine defender of the unborn, and again someone you did not challenge a second time for debate, was the late **Dr. Hymie Gordon**, HLI's great Jewish friend. As a much-published young geneticist he founded the Mayo Clinic's Department of Genetics and was its head until he retired in 1989. Dr. Gordon hailed from South Africa; there he fought apartheid and befriended the Catholic bishops. He once told me that he did as much as he possibly could for the blacks there without making it impossible for him to return to visit his dear mother.

I got to know Dr. Gordon early in the abortion fight in Minnesota. Like Dr. Lejeune, he was always most generous in responding to the needs of pro-lifers and to invitations to speak to audiences large and small. Totally articulate and supremely intelligent, he was a fierce debater. For example, one evening in a Minnesota debate on abortion he tangled with an abortionist who spoke first, boasting about all the abortions he had performed in so-and-so-many cities and states.

When his opponent had finished, Dr. Gordon rose slowly, walked to the podium, and let go in his beautiful, enchanting English/South African accent. Speaking deliberately, he began, "I didn't know that I was to be confronted tonight by an itinerant death peddler." Alas, this abortionist was described every few sentences, as "this itinerant death peddler"; he left early. Hymie could be ruthless when the occasion called for it.

His testimony was just as devastating after Senator John East of North Carolina had called eleven experts, mostly gynecologists, to Washington, D.C., to give witness to the origins of human life. Among them were Drs. Lejeune and Gordon. The latter, typically, opened his address by stating, "I never wasted more time in my life than by flying 1,200 miles from Minnesota to Washington to say what every beginning student in biology knows, that human life begins when ovum and sperm merge—at conception/fertilization." By the way, of the eleven experts, a Harvard professor, the gynecologist and notorious abortionist Dr. Kenneth Ryan, was the only one to waffle. He claimed that the origin of human life was a philosophical/theological question and, as such, could not be settled scientifically.

As mentioned, Dr. Gordon was magnanimous in sharing his talent, experience, and expertise. As you know, from the early sixties I sponsored two-week seminars on marriage and family life at Minnesota's St. John's University. One of the highlights each summer was Dr. Gordon's lecturing all Saturday morning—always with endless questions, some of them going unanswered for lack of time. Hymie was one of those rare individuals who always flowed with thought, precisely and effortlessly expressed. I recall my staff's debating whether Hymie in a three-hour lecture/discussion would make a slip of the tongue. I do not recall that he ever made one, as often as I heard him. He was always thoroughly prepared, truly a perfectionist, to the point where he insisted on moving his own slides, because a slide had to coincide with split-second accuracy with a certain word or phrase. One of his Mayo Clinic colleagues once told me that the greatest demonstration of genius he had ever witnessed was Hymie Gordon at the piano, commenting on Beethoven's life while playing excerpts from his nine symphonies.

Hymie would come to Collegeville on a Friday night and leave Sunday afternoon. He was fascinated with and informed about monastic life. He knew that in the Benedictine monastic setting he was witnessing a historical/cultural development of fifteen centuries. Widely read, he seemed a master in so many fields—not least, Jewish, Christian, and medical history. His reward for a three-hour lecture: three loaves of "Johnny bread," a local product allegedly made by the monks—who ate it, to be sure, but did not make it. When Hymie retired, the Mayo Clinic asked him to make sixty hour-long videos on the history of medicine. At least one of these was truly a masterpiece: "How Medicine Became a Science," in which he typically drew from all fields of knowledge. Dr. Gordon each year gave this lecture to incoming medical students. The reader can find these videos in the library of the Mayo Clinic. Once more they demonstrate Dr. Gordon's true genius.

In the end, he was deeply involved in bio-ethics. One of his last

lectures at Collegeville dealt with "The Genetic Auschwitz," wherein
he described the horrendous future possibilities and consequences of
genetic engineering. In 1988 he co-founded with the philosopher John
Dolan the Program in Human Rights and Medicine at the University
of Minnesota; at this university, as well as at the Mayo Clinic, Dr.
Gordon gave many lectures to appreciative medical audiences. The
program's foremost aim was and is to promote medical ethics.

Hymie commanded a professional lecture fee of $5,000-$10,000 and
was always in demand worldwide. Yet he often spoke *gratis* to the
smallest groups where he could deliver the pro-life message. Several
times he told me how shocked he was to find Jesuit priests, whom he
encountered in debates and discussions here and there, betraying their
vocation by ineptly discussing pro-life issues. It was a sad day when I
learned he had died of a heart attack at sixty-eight on 5 February 1995
in South Africa. He was buried in his beloved Jerusalem. With him a
great scientific, human, and religious light went out on this earth.

Dr. Jerome Lejeune and Dr. Hymie Gordon were the only world-
famous pro-life geneticists. What a loss!

Let me digress at this point to note that deception and lying characterize abortionists and the abortion movement. In fact, the whole
movement is based on falsehoods: they say we don't know when life
begins; they insist that what is aborted is not human; they are experts
in verbal engineering, which is always the forerunner of social engineering.[3] They call abortion the "termination of pregnancy," conve-
niently forgetting that all pregnancies "terminate," usually in nine
months. They deceive, claiming that early abortion amounts to remov-
ing a little, jelly-like glob of protoplasm. They euphemize, referring to
abortion as post-conceptive family planning and the removal of the
products of conception—and so on and on. Some few abortionists,
once they can no longer rationally defend the assertion that we do not
know when life begins, then assert—and I have heard it said—"Oh
well, so it's human; who needs it? Who wants it? The woman must
have freedom of choice. Besides, she needs abortion for her health and
life." Minnesota's ace abortionist, Dr. Mildred Hanson, once asked

---

[3]   William Brennan, *Dehumanizing the Vulnerable* (Chicago: Loyola
University Press, 1995).

"what would be a medical reason for abortion?" retorted, "Any woman who wants an abortion has a medical reason." And so on *ad nauseam.* One is reminded of Our Lord describing the devil as a liar and a murderer from the beginning.

And now, back to the personalities. Knowing **Dr. Bernard Nathanson** has been a great boon. Here is another generous pro-lifer. After presiding over the deaths of some 60,000 preborn babies and in addition killing 15,000 by his own hand, including his own child, he has gone to many parts of the world to defend the unborn, asking only that his expenses be paid. In 1983, when the Irish were about to relax the abortion law, I invited him to tell them the whole story of how the abortion movement began in the United States. He gave a magnificent address to a full house, truly the inside story, relating how he and three others—Betty Friedan, a certain Mr. Wright, and the master abortion-propagandist Lawrence Lader—successfully worked, wrote, lied, lobbied, and propagandized for legal abortion.[4]

Their deception paved the way for the *Roe v. Wade* Supreme Court decision of 22 January 1973, which gave the United States abortion-on-request, at that time the worst law in the world except for Russia's and China's. They did their damage by doctoring polls, manipulating the press, lying with statistics, falsely claiming that abortion was only a "Catholic" issue, and so on and so forth. The 1,000 Irish sat on the edge of their seats. We won the referendum. Nathanson's superb lecture is still available on audio-cassette at HLI.[5]

Before we left, we contacted the super-liberal Gay Byrne, the Johnny Carson of Ireland. He agreed to interview Nathanson, first on his morning radio hour and then on his TV talk show on Saturday night, watched by more than two out of three adult Irishmen. But when Byrne realized from his radio interview that he could not manipulate Nathanson, he typically and abruptly canceled him for Saturday

---

[4] Nathanson tells all in his fascinating autobiography, *The Hand of God* (Washington: Regnery, 1996).

[5] Cassette: "What Nathanson Told the Irish about How Abortion Came to America."

Dr. Bernard Nathanson and me.

night. I personally know the unscrupulous Byrne from my own two appearances on his program.

Many times Dr. Nathanson spoke at our conferences and symposia in and out of the United States, always drawing a crowd. He is one who comes prepared with a great message based on his wide reading of not only medical literature but many classics, as is evident from his autobiography, *The Hand of God*. In fact, his autobiography grew out of a magnificent lecture— "off the cuff," he said, revealing to his audience his whole family and educational background. When an editor for Regnery Publishing Company heard the tape in his car, he asked Nathanson to write a book on his life.

In *The Hand of God* he is thoroughly frank in telling the story of his sad life and then of his discovery of the Lord Jesus. He was baptized and confirmed at St. Patrick's Cathedral by Cardinal John O'Connor at 7:30 in the morning of 9 December 1996. I prayerfully and thankfully witnessed Nathanson's reception of these sacraments, the fruit of the prayers of many pro-lifers worldwide. The cardinal remarked that "Bernie" had told him that the love and friendship of Catholics really got to him.

In reading *The Hand of God*, I was reminded of St. Augustine's *Confessions*. It is brutally candid, personal, and honest. Dr. Nathanson's two films, "The Silent Scream" and "The Eclipse of Reason," have brought home the evil and cruelty of abortion to thousands, perhaps millions, of people. HLI scattered these films worldwide, hundreds in Latin America, South Korea and the Philippines alone, as we shall see. We soon withdrew "The Silent Scream" from Russia because the Russian doctors, in their admiration of all things American, thought "the nice, clean way" of doing abortion was the way to go, and showing the film became counterproductive.

I truly admire this generous, intelligent, converted pro-lifer who has done so much and will do so much more to defend the unborn, now that he has found, through baptism, peace of mind, God's forgiveness, and grace in the Catholic Church. Baptism wiped away all his sins, and now this learned Christian doctor with a Jewish background and upbringing will be able to tell the pro-life/pro-family truth as never before, above all as it applies to bio-ethics, his latest interest. I am flattered to read the inscription on the front page of *The Hand of God*: "For all those who have prayed for me—especially Fr. Paul Marx (that saintly man). . ." (Would that it were so! But thanks, Dr. Nathanson.)

You don't work long in the pro-life and NFP movements without meeting a lot of stalwart doctors. Too little known is the work of **Drs. John and Lyn Billings**. Starting their research in 1953, as we have seen, they developed the Ovulation Method of NFP and have literally gone all over the world—even to China—to promote it, starting in the 1960s. These Australians are heroic in their dedication, untiring in their work, and unstinting in their perseverance; they have been a real godsend to have known and sponsored.

One can say the same for **Dr. Josef Rötzer**, the great Austrian NFP pioneer who has done so much since the early 1950s in the German-speaking countries and whose NFP organization is flourishing with a success rate better than that of the abortifacient Pill. Often Rötzer spoke at my seminars and international symposia on NFP; I was privileged to have put him in touch, through these symposia, with the whole NFP movement worldwide. His *Natürliche Empfangnisregelung* is, in my opinion, the best methodological book on NFP.

Also a frequent lecturer at my seven international symposia on NFP was **Dr. Rudolf Vollman**, whose innovative work with NFP is described in Chapter 5. Long after Dr. Vollman retired, he did part-time research for the World Health Organization at Geneva, Switzerland. One of his last projects was to establish the median age of the menarche (onset of menstruation) in European girls: 12.8 years. Rudi had assembled in his Swiss home the largest collection of gynecological periodicals in the world.

A classmate and lifelong friend and collaborator, the dentist **Dr. Aelred C. Fonder,** has been very helpful in a number of ways.

His degrees speak for themselves: D.D.S., F.A.P.P., F.A.F.P., F.A.C.S., and F.I.D.S. To rebuild faces scarred in accidents of various kinds, he founded the Rehabilitation Institute of Chicago and developed the Maxillofacial Prosthetic Dental-Medical

Dr. Siegfried Ernst of Germany receiving HLI's annual award in 1991.

Specialty. Like few others he has considerably advanced the science of dentistry and dental care, on which he has lectured worldwide. His *The Oral Physician* is a classic. His superior skills repaired my mouth after a horrendous car accident in the 1970s. His never charging me was only one way of expressing his total dedication to the cause of saving the unborn. You may soon hear more about Dr. Fonder's organization, The March of Pennies.

No doctor in Europe did more to oppose abortion than the Lutheran surgeon **Dr. Siegfried Ernst** of Ulm, Germany. Invited to join the medical staff of Adolf Hitler, Ernst refused, serving the German Armed Forces as a surgeon instead. His parents sent him as a young man to England, where he learned English and discovered the Moral Rearmament Movement. The basic principle of the Moral Rearmament Movement is that members should be totally honest, totally chaste, totally unselfish, and totally charitable. When these virtues are fully practiced, one is in total contact with God, Who then will use one's life in the promotion of His kingdom in this world. Dr. Ernst became a lifelong, dedicated promoter of Moral Rearmament and, in accepting its beliefs, lived a life protected from many accidents and tragedies. Ernst was doing surgery in the basement of a private home in Warsaw when the Russian armies overran that city. How to get out? Asking God to guide him, and practicing the precepts of the Moral Rearmament Movement, he carefully walked his way through many mine fields back into Germany.

I met him for the first time in Germany in 1972. Thereafter our paths crossed often. As we traveled and lectured together, he recounted his fascinating war experiences in Poland and Russia and his convictions about Christian life and living. I remember that one evening I helped him carry pro-life literature through the back door of the German Parliament in Bonn, where we left this literature on the desk of every parliamentarian. In many letters, articles, books, memoranda and visits, he would beg bishops and other leaders to educate and organize the people to withstand the coming abortion monster.

The battle in Germany, propaganda-wise, was no different from that of other countries, as I learned when I sat for two days in the Parliament in Bonn in 1975 listening to the fierce debates of the pro- and anti-abortion factions. I was with Dr. Ernst and others in Amsterdam in 1974 when they founded the World Federation of Doctors Who Respect Human Life. Ernst and I attended medical and Lutheran church meetings together. With Walter Ramm, founder in 1979 and still leader of Germany's largest pro-life group, *Aktion Leben*, we planned the large pro-life conference in Dresden, East Germany, in 1990—a first in that country. In the end, Dr. Ernst did all the organizing and made all the financial arrangements. *Bewegung für das Leben* is a loosely organized group of pro-life groups headed by Father Otto Maier, SAC.

A true intellectual, Ernst confronted many wild theologians, both Catholic and Lutheran; he warned them of their grave errors and did all he could to push Catholic and Lutheran bishops into mounting an intelligent resistance to the approaching legalization of abortion. In his battle for life, Christianity, and personal moral rectitude, he refuted Catholic theologians like Hans Küng, Franz Bökle, and other German dissenters, as well as the French atheist-existentialist Jean-Paul Sartre. He worked hard to win over the leaders of the German Medical Association; he is a frequent contributor to the high-class *Medizin und Ideologie*, edited by the prolific **Dr. Alfred Häussler** . (Häussler is my great friend and an early exposer of the abortifacient character of the Pill, which the blunt Germans rightly call "die Anti-baby Pille.") As a

Dr. Alfred Häussler of Germany.

leader in the Württemberg Lutheran Synod, the largest in Germany, Dr. Ernst won the synod over to a pro-life stance—for a time. He wrote endlessly to defend the unborn and to refute the modern hedonistic paganism. His written and oral condemnation of pornography and explicit sex education has no equal. His translated book promoting chastity, *Man, the Greatest of Miracles*, published by the Liturgical Press, went through two printings.

In 1964 Dr. Ernst was the chief author of a remarkable brief sent to the government pointing out the future consequences of sex education and propagation of the Pill. The brief, remarkably, made ten predictions, all of which were later verified. While it was signed by forty-five university professors, twenty-four noted gynecologists, and 350 doctors, few of these persons would sign it today, given the moral decline in Germany, says Dr. Ernst.

He had several chats with Pope Paul VI, whose encyclical *Humanae Vitae* he staunchly defended against Germany's most prominent waffling theologians and bishops, never satisfied that the German hierarchy and Lutheran church leaders were doing all they could to prevent the legal slaughter of preborn babies.[6] Like all true-blue, militant pro-lifers, he was and still is mercilessly persecuted.

Dr. Ernst once invited me to accompany him to the German hierarchy's episcopal semi-annual meeting in Fulda. Having an American priest with him, he thought, would enhance his efforts to lobby the

---

[6] *Is Humanae Vitae Outdated?* (Gaithersburg, MD: Human Life International, 1993).

bishops to take a stronger position against abortion. I can still see him talking to them and giving them pertinent literature—seemingly to little avail. I still see him pleading with the president of the German hierarchy and his friend, Cardinal Julius Döpfner, while the latter was placidly dipping his *Kuchen* (a German pastry) into coffee.

Incidentally, soon after orchestrating the subtle German dissent to *Humanae Vitae* Döpfner saw his mistake, and on national TV said something like, "When everything is said and done, I think the Pope was right about *Humanae Vitae*." But it was too late. Soon thereafter, he died suddenly. Today Germany is a dying country that uses more coffins than cradles, as the blunt Germans say, numbering 600,000 fewer Germans every year. Who knows what Cardinal Döpfner would have done had he not died prematurely?

During the West German episcopal debate over the dissent to *Humanae Vitae* in 1968, Cardinal Georg Bengsch of isolated Berlin, head of the Catholic hierarchy in Eastern Germany, eloquently pleaded with Cardinal Döpfner not to dissent, pointing out the inevitable consequences and enormities of doing so.[7] It is little known that—thanks to Bengsch—the East German hierarchy stood firm on *Humanae Vitae*. Too bad he was trapped in Berlin and could not get to the West German hierarchy debating and eventually dissenting to the encyclical. His eloquent defense of *Humanae Vitae* was late in reaching Pope Paul VI.

The German hierarchy today, despite the pleadings of the Pope, are directly involved in the abortion process by participating in the government-paid counseling required to make abortion, although still illegal, not punishable in the first three months of pregnancy. (The full story is too long to tell.) Refusing to go along with this participation is the great German Archbishop Johannes Dyba of Fulda, whose volunteer centers offer counseling that is strictly in defense of the unborn child. It is very telling that Catholic Chancellor Helmut Kohl and Pro Familia (Planned Parenthood) want the Church involved in the government's curious counseling business, apparently to lend it respectability. Strange that Chancellor Kohl should ask the Pope in

---

[7]   The whole story is told in the German Catholic newspaper, *Deutsche Tagespost*: no. 48 (22 April 1995); a copy of the manuscript is in HLI archives.

Fridolin Huber, Dr. Siegfried Ernst, Dr. Jack Willke and yours truly. We were all together for a conference in Belgium.

1996 on the Pope's visit to Germany, to give in on contraception when his country is a dying one.

Sadly, Dr. Ernst incurred stomach cancer in 1977. After surgery, the best medics in Germany had no hope of saving his life; Dr. Ernst put his condition under the intercession of Blessed Rupert Meyer, to whom he had a great devotion. By the grace of God he has survived now for nineteen years without a stomach, while continuing to work as before, every day, in an incredible fashion. Rome has taken note of the possibility of a miraculous healing. Already more Catholic than most Catholics, he once told me that if he became a Catholic he could not continue to defend the Pope as a Lutheran! Dr. Ernst and Mrs. Ernst, a relative of Copernicus, have six children, of whom four are doctors and three are Catholic. He is truly one of the most remarkable persons with whom I have had the privilege of collaborating. Let me add that he is the only human being with whom I worked who did not tire before I did. I shall never forget his telling me that the Protestants made their greatest mistake in 1930, when they allowed contraception, the first such concession in twenty centuries of Christendom. He explained that contraception unleashes the powerful sexual drive, is inhuman and unnatural, is a bad parental example for the children, obviously opposes God's design and plan, and destroys youth, family, and ultimately church and society.

Fr. Charles Fiore published the first slide-cassette program "The Face of Abortion" in the early 1970s, in both English and Spanish. Thousands of copies were sold and used. Active through the years, he also founded the first national pro-life Political Action Committee (PAC) in Chicago in 1978. Other PACs founded by others followed. Fr. Fiore has written much and often worked successfully behind the scenes to protect pre-born babies.

In 1970 **Dr. Jack and Barbara Willke** and I attended the meeting of the California State Marriage Counselors Association. Let Jack tell about our encounter:

Martin Humer (from Austria), Albin Rhomberg and Dr. Herb Ratner.

Our memory of that encounter is very clear because it was one of the things that ultimately pushed us into writing *Handbook on Abortion*. While eating, you asked us what we were doing on abortion. With some mock surprise, I told you, "Nothing, Paul, and we're not going to."

You went on to explain why we should be involved—we were accomplished speakers; we had the medical background, the knowledge, etc., and that this was very important; we should get into it. My memorable words to you were, "Paul, if we get started on abortion, it will swallow us up." Truer words were never spoken.

John Hillabrand, an indefatigible pro-lifer.

Swallowed up they were. The first edition of their *Handbook on Abortion* appeared in June 1971, went into ten languages, and sold more than a million copies. Besides the *Handbook*, the Willkes created

much pro-life litera-
ture through the
Hayes Publishing
Company, some of
which HLI spread far
and wide. The
American pro-life
movement owes the
Willkes very much.

Dr. Edward Keefe.

Another wonderful
medical authority
who crossed my path
was the Anglican
pro-lifer **Dr. Ian
Donald**, the famed British gynecologist who wrote the classic *Practical
Obstetric Problems*, still used in medical schools today. During World
War II, the British had learned to track German submarines by ultra-
sound. After the war, Dr. Donald designed a machine using this technique to observe the unborn baby riding in the fluid of the amniotic
sac in the uterus.

In Glasgow, one evening in 1973, he showed and explained the
whole apparatus to me, a fascinating, unforgettable experience. Over
dinner and late into the night, we had a long discussion about many
mutual interests. I learned a lot. His understanding of the Bible made
me feel ashamed. I shall never forget what he told me that evening:
"As one lives, so one thinks." E. Michael Jones makes that aphorism
crystal clear in his *Degenerate Moderns*, summarizing Dr. Donald's
insights: Truth and morality are one. Living a moral life is a prerequi-
site for grasping the truth—scientific, philosophical, and theological.
Conversely, living an immoral life will lead one into error, deception
and intellectual perversity.

A brilliant lecturer in demand all over the world, Dr. Donald fascinated my conference audiences at St. John's University. To the
Anglican Dr. Donald, the British 1967 abortion law was the nation's
greatest tragedy. Nor was he surprised the following year when a bill
authorizing euthanasia appeared—and was defeated— in Parliament.
"It all hangs together," he told me, "this bundle of anti-life evils."

Dr. Patrick Dunn, New Zealand's pioneer pro-lifer.

Other superb doctors I worked with and remember well, real pro-life pioneers, were **Drs. Herb Ratner,** his classmate **John Hillabrand, Edward Keefe** and **Konald Prem,** all of whom made significant contributions to the pro-life movement in the early days and to the NFP apostolate particularly. A convert from Judaism, Ratner had a remarkable talent for one-liners, e.g.: "The Pill is chemical warfare on women"; speaking of euthanasia: "We doctors kill off enough patients unintentionally without being asked to do it intentionally." The gynecologist Hillabrand was one of the founders of Alternatives to Abortion in 1971 (now known as Heartbeat International). I too was deeply involved from its beginning with this baby-saving enterprise. In 1974 I sponsored with Alice Brown and Dr. Hillebrand the first national training conference for emergency pregnancy counselors at Collegeville, attended by 280. In Chapter 5 we noted Dr. Prem's sterling contributions to NFP.

Then there were the gynecologist and author **Dr. Pat Dunn** of New Zealand and **Dr. A. W. Liley,** the great fetologist of New Zealand. Dr. Liley, as you will remember from Chapter 5, developed the medical procedure of amniocentesis, only to see it used later—to his great pain—as a prelude to abortion. No one could describe the tiny unborn more elegantly than Dr. Liley, and HLI spread his colored pictures of these little persons all over the world. Drs. Dunn and Liley never failed to impress participants at my conferences. But let Dr. Dunn say what I have forgotten:

The first time I met Fr. Marx was in 1970. I had had a call from Archbishop Liston, of Auckland, New Zealand, saying: "There's an American priest here who wants to speak to the Catholic doctors. Would you please arrange a meeting for tomorrow night. Thank you. Goodbye." So, with a bad grace I must confess, I got a small meeting together and then promptly fell under the spell of this remarkable man who was to have such an influence in my life and such an impact on the pro-life battle.

At that time abortion was still illegal in New Zealand, but we sensed the chill under the dark cloud that was irresistibly moving over our country. England had passed its Abortion Act in 1967; the abortion rate immediately soared. In 1970 Professor Sir William Liley and I launched the Society for the Protection of the Unborn Child with good publicity; we fondly thought that that would be sufficient to control the abortion monster. Fr. Marx soon disillusioned us. After his whirlwind tour of Australia in 1970, and his visit here, we all realized what a disaster lay ahead. I had had a major article published in our national medical journal entitled "Therapeutic Abortion in New Zealand" (NZMed J. 1968, 68: 253—8) setting out all the spurious reasons for abortion and the troubles it would cause, but it was all to no purpose.

In subsequent years Fr. Marx invited me to speak on the faculty at St. John's University, Collegeville, Minnesota, on two occasions; and on others in Philadelphia, Los Angeles, Mexico City and other cities. In 1974 I joined his team at the first World Population Congress in Bucharest, Romania, where I presented a paper on "Population Optimism." It was only a small audience but it provided a handy point of reference, and it demonstrated how the anti-life forces must espouse population control through their usual hysteria.

In my practice as an obstetrician-gynecologist I delivered personally some 15,000 babies, with no recourse to abor-

(l to r) Dr. Joseph Stanton and his wife, Mary, (from New York) and Drs. John and Lyn Billings (from Australia).

tion, sterilization or contraception. There were three maternal deaths, which gave a rate that was much the same as the national average. One patient died suddenly from a ruptured aortic aneurysm. Another was getting dressed to go home after a Cesarean and dropped dead on the floor. She had a major pulmonary embolism. The third had high blood pressure made worse by toxemia. She died from a cerebral hemorrhage. My perinatal death rate was also equal to everyone else's.

Of the patients referred to above, some 200 were unmarried mothers whose ages ranged from 12 to 17. I had no problem with managing labor in these very young patients. My philosophy was that, if they were mature enough to conceive, they must necessarily be mature enough to deliver. There was no medical indication for abortion either in them or older women.

Fr. Marx was a man with courage and vision. Before most national and church leaders could see it, he realized the holocaust that was going to destroy Western countries. With determination and tenacity he set about developing a pro-life organization that is without equal in the world. How he managed to finance it remains a mystery to me, but he seemed able to charm money out of stones. Throughout all these years in the pro-life battle, he has demonstrated with great clarity that the Church's stand on

(l to r) Joseph Scheidler with Glenys and Dr. Claude Newbury (of South Africa).

sexuality and marriage is the right one and the only one. Pope Paul's *Humanae Vitae* in 1968 was the event that showed brilliance and prophetic perception. Along with the Pope, Fr. Marx was one of the first to stress that contraception is the key issue—once contraception is accepted, abortion will inevitably follow.

Many people attempt to analyze the causes of abortion and hence mount some rational attack on it, but the fundamental explanation for the evil, as Fr. Marx so clearly realized, is that it is a diabolical phenomenon. Who stands for life? Christ does. "I am the way, the truth and the life." "I come that you may have life and have it to the full." "I am the bread of life. . . ." Who stands for death? Satan does, and he is a reality. "The wages of sin is death." Abortion— physical death, spiritual death.[8]

Dr. Joseph Stanton was an indefatigable worker, scholar and pioneer; his brilliant lectures at my symposia were always greatly appreciated. Who would have thought that he, after coming out of an iron lung in 1935 at the age of fifteen, would do battle for the unwanted unborn and the unwanted elderly for sixty-two-plus years! In 1970, he founded the Value of Life Committee in Boston. He has been a highly intelligent fighter for life with pen and tongue. I recall that he arranged for Dr. Mildred Jefferson and me to appear on a large

---

[8]   Letter: Dunn to me, 12 May 1996.

Boston radio talk-show in 1972. I performed quite badly, but the eloquent Mildred performed splendidly. Dr. Stanton is a good example of
what an indomitable spirit and keen mind can do even in a very weakened body—and he has done much! In later years he contributed
mightily to the revival of the Hippocratic tradition in medicine; he has
produced a cogent, updated Hippocratic Oath.

Dr. Claude Newbury and his wife Glenys are the marvelous pro-life
apostles of South Africa. I met them for the first time in South Africa in
1982 and with them organized three pro-life seminars there. A persecuted and fierce debater on TV, Dr. Newbury gives HLI credit for
defeating the abortionists twice in South Africa, in 1972 and in 1976.
Nathanson's "The Silent Scream" videocassette came into my hands
early; I immediately air-mailed a copy to Dr. Newbury, who was in the
midst of the abortion battle. He succeeded in having it screened in South
Africa's Parliament, and that seemed to have won the battle at that time.

There were years when both Glenys and Claude gave three hundred
lectures in their country yearly, often meeting no small resistance from
doctors, priests, religious, media, and bishops. They have been truly
heroic in their pro-life work and witness. Only God knows how many
babies they have saved, not only in South Africa but also in neighboring countries. Glenys founded Victims of Choice, an organization that
does post-abortion counseling. Were it not for the abortion battle, they
could be a wealthy, carefree family. Today Dr. Newbury heads up our
huge pro-life/pro-family African project. But let Dr. Newbury tell his
own story:

> The establishment of HLI-Africa can be traced to the South
> African government's passage of the Abortion and
> Sterilization Act of 1975. The Act permitted abortion only
> for the various so-called "hard cases," as nearly every such
> law does initially. It was then that Mrs. Louise Summerhill
> (foundress of Birthright) visited Cape Town.
>
> On 24 January 1976, after a public meeting, a small group
> (promoted by Mr. Graham McIntosh, a member of parlia-
> ment), together with Mrs. Elena Moore, Mrs. Sheila
> Cowburn, Mr. Frank Sokolic and Mr. Bobby Bertrand,
> founded Pro-Life. The members agreed to work together,

having as their chief priority to prevent the new abortion
law from becoming more permissive. This small group
effectively managed to keep the issue of abortion in the
public eye mainly by means of public talks, newspapers and
the wireless (we had no TV here then).

Things really got moving in a totally "pro-life" way when a
radio program brought dynamic young schoolmaster Mr.
Peter Doherty into the group. He soon brought in a physician, Dr. Norma Wardle, whose emigration from the UK
had been partly prompted by the abortion situation there.
Increased pro-life activity spread information in many
Catholic parishes and surrounding Christian communities
in the Western Cape area.

Soon it was thought necessary to cooperate with other
pro-life groups. Pro-Life contacted the Society for the
Protection of Unborn Children (SPUC), LIFE in the UK,
and Dr. Philippe Schepens of the World Federation of
Doctors Who Respect Human Life.

We also began working with Professor Sir Albert William
Liley of New Zealand, Professor Jerome Lejeune of France
and Fr. Paul Marx. The contacts with these organizations
and individuals provided the essential encouragement, information and access to pro-life materials and resources, all of
which were put to effective use by Pro-Life South Africa.

Meanwhile, in 1979, I attended a so-called "abortion
debate" at the University of the Witwatersrand in
Johannesburg, at which all the "debaters" faithfully pro-
moted abortion. Inspired and assisted by our parish priest
Fr. Cedric Myerscough, S.J., and his assistant Fr. John
Berrell, S.J., I invited several people to a meeting with the
objective of starting an anti-abortion movement. This meet-
ing was held in the basement of the Holy Trinity Catholic
Church, sited on the boundary of the University Campus.
During the meeting Dr. Koos van der Wat, a famous
Johannesburg obstetrician and gynecologist, suggested that

rather than "re-invent the wheel" we should join forces with Pro-Life of Cape Town (sited 1,000 miles away at the extreme tip of Africa). Fr. Myerscough used the parish telephone to contact Pro-Life Cape Town, and Pro-Life Johannesburg was officially formed.

Pro-Life South Africa's first conference, held 4-6 February 1982, was a great success. Fr. Marx gave four inspirational talks on abortion, euthanasia, Planned Parenthood, NFP and Christian Sexuality. Both before and after the Conference, Fr. Marx trained the Cape Town Pro-Life group by showing slides projected onto the wall of Dr. Norma Wardle's lounge.

These training sessions form only one of the many blessed and treasured moments of our first encounter with the world's greatest pro-life missionary. Those memories are fresh even years later in the souls of the remaining members of that first small and valiant Pro-Life group.

On his way home from Cape Town, Fr. Marx spent several days in Pretoria and Johannesburg; the local pro-lifers were privileged to hear him speak at several meetings. It was at the Newbury home that the local pro-life members really got to know and love this valiant fighter for life. This admiration and love for Fr. Marx has grown steadily over the years, and we were delighted and privileged to have him visit us in South Africa on three subsequent occasions.

Pro-Life, assisted in every way possible by Fr. Marx, has succeeded in defeating all efforts, repeated almost annually, to liberalize the 1975 abortion law. We have done this through our regular public education efforts, as well as providing help and alternatives to abortion. Most effective were two letter writing and petition campaigns demonstrating to the government the truly overwhelming opposition to abortion among all races and creeds in South Africa.

On one memorable occasion—by the grace of God the day before an attempt in Parliament to introduce abortion-on-demand—the very first copy of "The Silent Scream" was urgently air-freighted to us by Fr. Marx and then shown to members of South Africa's Parliament. This showing was the cornerstone of our success in frustrating the murderous intentions of the abortionists.

Our pro-life apostolate has also involved detailed submissions to the South African government on such pro-life matters as abortion, euthanasia, test-tube babies, surrogate motherhood, artificial insemination and value-free sex education.

In fact, Pro-Life South Africa was actually the first to alert the government in 1988 to the impending AIDS catastrophe. Unfortunately, our warnings were not only disregarded but were ridiculed by official state epidemiologists as mere scare-mongering. Today the same bureaucracy declares fifteen percent of sexually mature citizens are infected with HIV!

We have also submitted written and oral reports to the South African Catholic Bishops' Conference on such topics as abortion, Natural Family Planning, the abortifacient nature of many "contraceptives," marriage preparation courses and others. These activities were substantially assisted by Fr. Marx through his inspiration, the steady and plentiful stream of information and pro-life educational material that he shipped to us, as well as the opportunity he afforded us through his international conferences to meet and hear pro-life leaders from all parts of the world.

In September 1995, we were again privileged to have Fr. Marx and a magnificent team of pro-life activists that he gathered and brought with him—Rev. Johnny Hunter, Mr. Joe Scheidler and Dr. Brian Clowes—for two Pro-Life conferences in Cape Town and Johannesburg. Rev. Hunter returned to South Africa in April with three other members of his organization Life Education and Resource Network, bringing a mound of materials supplied by HLI. Rev.

Louvain professor Fr. Michel Schooyans (of Belgium) and Dr. Peggy Norris, founder of ALERT (of United Kingdom).

Hunter and his team again spread the "Gospel of Life" in Cape Town and Johannesburg.

Our contacts with HLI over the years have not only proved to be an inspiration to Pro-Life South Africa but also have provided tremendous help. Tons of pro-life material sent to us by Fr. Marx and his tireless staff have enabled us to activate and stimulate the almost instinctive abhorrence for abortion that is typical of African peoples.

This fact makes a mockery of our now "democratic" government's determination to impose abortion-on-demand—in the name of our new "Bill of Human Rights"—and the usual litany of "politically correct" trends. If the Termination of Pregnancy Bill approved by Mr. Mandela's Cabinet on 3 July becomes law, it will be the worst abortion law in the entire world outside Red China. [That bill was passed in 1996.]

During my work-visits in South Africa, I also collaborated with a Schönstadt nun, Sister Magdalene Mertz, deeply involved in promoting NFP. She arranged lecture opportunities and valuable contacts for me. So did Pat McGregor, who monitored NFP for the South African

Catholic Bishops' Conference. One day we drove far into apartheid territory until we came to a boarding Catholic high school in the middle of nowhere, conducted by eleven aging Belgian sisters. The 600 black girls were totally attentive and well mannered. The local bishop sat in the front row along with some priests. At a little party after the lecture, I told the nuns how much their work and their girls impressed me. They sadly told me how they could not carry on any longer than five years since they were getting no replacements from Belgium, and local vocations were still too few. The next day we visited a medical center overflowing with mostly women patients. When the English doctor saw me, he came to tell me about his work. When I told him the intra-uterine device (IUD) was an abortifacient, he told me, "I know all that, but the IUD is the only thing you can stick into dumb women." I often wished radical feminists could have heard him.

Thanks to **Phyllis Bowman,** in 1972 I met the indefatigable **Dr. Peggy Norris and her husband James,** also a doctor in Liverpool. Together we presented "pro-life evenings" to alert the British to the

Here I am with Pope John XXIII.

developing abortion slaughter and the inevitable euthanasia to follow.
Dr. Peggy is the co-founder of ALERT, opposing euthanasia in
England. She seems to be forever on radio and TV, or otherwise
responding to the anti-life media. An international lecturer, she has
often enlightened our symposia audiences and has written many
pro-life tracts; she heads the British branch of the World Federation of
Doctors Who Respect Human Life.

Sharing some intimate words with Pope Paul VI.

POPES

*M*y life spans that of five popes, three of whom I have met. In 1959 I was part of a small tour group in Rome when the roly-poly, short, wide **John XXIII** waddled into the room with his huge smile and a large hand graciously extended to each one. He seemed as broad as he was tall. Told that I was a Benedictine, he wanted to know what abbey I belonged to and what Benedictine congregation. In a very brief conversation, he told me that as a Benedictine with an historic monastic tradition I had an important mission in an increasingly unbelieving world.

Standing next to me was a young, budding actress, a member of my group. For good reasons the Pope spent about five minutes telling her what a significant mission her very delicate profession had handed her. He had a kind word for everyone. This Pope obviously loved people, and he had a hard time tearing himself away from any group, disarming all with his enormous hand and smiling face as he toddled along

Providential words uttered by Pope John Paul II to me: "You are doing the most important work on earth" (1979).

from person to person.

When President and Mrs. Jack Kennedy came to see him, it is said, there was debate beforehand as to how the Pope should address the President's wife. Allegedly he was given many suggestions; he ignored them all and, on meeting her, greeted her with, "Hi, Jackie." His English was shaky at best. When the Eisenhowers visited him he had a prepared English text from which to read. But in the first line he made a big blooper. Turning to President Eisenhower, he calmly said, "Ike, this is going to be quite a show." The reader may remember the President's doubling up with laughter.

Earlier in this account I described the papal audience that Phyllis Bowman and I attended in January 1973, a few days after the U.S. Supreme Court had handed down its ignominious Black Monday Decisions. The words **Pope Paul VI** addressed to me—"You are a courageous fighter. Never give up"—have consoled me many times since.

On 17 November 1979, I met **Pope John Paul II**. He stunned me by saying, "I know you." I had been giving lectures against abortion in the previous five years, now and then in Europe, especially in German-speaking countries. I remember that the superb pornography fighter Martin Humer guided me all over Austria to lecture in 1974 and 1975—I spoke sixty-eight times, claims Herr Humer.

In Vienna I said the right thing for a change one night in 1974; a large Viennese paper subsequently published a photo of me holding up a banner depicting an unborn child, with the caption "Never to smile, never to laugh." The accompanying article bore a headline quoting

Pictured here with Pope John Paul II and a group of prolifers from around the world. (l to r) Dr. Wanda Poltawska (Poland), myself (USA), Dr. Josef Rötzer (Austria), Dr. Herbert Ratner (USA), Pope John Paul II, Cardinal Josef Tompko (Rome), Fr. Chars Corcoran, O.P. (USA), Unknown Man, Mgsr. Martin (Rome), Fr. Pedro Richards (Hungary), Fr. Anthony Zimmerman, SVD (Japan), Msgr. Gerhard Fittkau (Germany), Dr. François Guy (France) and Pat Riley (USA).

me, "Third World War: Abortion."

John Paul II was then the Cardinal Archbishop of Cracow; occasionally he would read about a certain "Marx" who was flailing away against abortionists on the other side of the Iron Curtain. Fighting Marxists every day, he may have thought that perhaps there was at least one decent Marx in the world after all—and it happened to be me.

At any rate, the Pope now said, "I know you. Is there a little bit of Karl in you?" I responded, "Only through Adam and Eve." The Pope chuckled. I had a further comment on my tongue but didn't manage to get it off: "Now that these wild theologians and so-called Scripture scholars have removed Adam and Eve from the Bible, there could be no connection whatsoever." The Pope had just returned from his first visit to the United States, where, speaking in Chicago to the American Catholic hierarchy, he had roundly condemned contraception. I thanked him for that. I told the Pope that I had been in forty-eight (today ninety-one) countries of the world and had always found that contraception inevitably led to abortion, that I could find no excep-

Pope John Paul II, in a brief encounter in 1991, called me "the Apostle of Life."

tion, that no one had ever been able to point out an exception to me. That lit him up, because he was thoroughly convinced of the same relationship, as evidenced from his promotion of NFP and marriage-preparation work in Polish parish centers, and also from his very many subsequent writings and lectures. I spelled out for him my conviction not only that contraception always leads to abortion but also that the legalization of abortion increases fornication and sexual recklessness, leading to ever more venereal disease, infertility, single-parent families, illegitimate births, and divorce. The legalization of abortion, I continued, dries up the adoption services, prostitutes the medical and legal professions, and inevitably ends in euthanasia. The Pope, in his very bad English (he has improved a lot since then), said, after a long pause, "You haf lots of experience. You must bring dis pro-life movement all over dee world; if you do dat, you will be doin dee most important work on ert. Surely dee Americans will help you."

I don't always catch on right away, nor did I in this instance. It was not until a couple of hours later that it occurred to me that, if there is no replacement birthrate in a particular country and in the Church, country and Church obviously have no future. Every worthy cause in

the world assumes the reproductive progression of human life, ideally
the fruit of generous husbands and wives in the loving commitment of
marriage. I was, and am, thoroughly convinced that the pro-life/pro-
family movement is quintessential, that nothing is more important,
and that all depends on it—above all, Church, State, and humanity. As
if to sum up my own experience-tested convictions, the Pope, in a brief
encounter in 1991, called me "the Apostle of Life."

It continues to astonish me that few people see this truth, even some
pro-lifers. Surely, by and large, priests and bishops do not seem to see
it, because if they did they would make the pro-life/pro-family movement a true priority, using every means, every resource, every opportunity to promote chastity in and out of marriage; to defend the unborn;
and to foster healthy, happy, holy families, above all by insisting on an
intensive preparation for marriage. And surely they would not
embrace the seamless-garment theory of the late Cardinal Joseph
Bernardin who derailed the pro-life movement with his 1982 Fordham
speech suggesting that abortion is on a par with poverty, capital punishment, and a whole catalog of social ills.[9] And because contraception
is the source of so many evils, not least abortion, no Catholic couple
should start their married life without knowing the beautiful, mysterious, unique, holy, human reproductive system. If there is one thing a
married couple should understand on their wedding day, and even
before, as Pope John Paul II has made clear in *Familiaris Consortio*
and earlier writings, it is how to control their fertility responsibly, lov-
ingly, generously. As an early promoter of the Natural Family Planning
(NFP) movement in the United States and Canada, let me repeat that
we are worse off today than when I was ordained in 1947, when it
comes to marriage preparation and perhaps even to the teaching of
NFP. But that's another story, already told in Chapter 5.

PRIESTS

*A*bbot Alcuin Deutsch, OSB, was a great religious leader who was
given all too little credit—credit being the last thing he would

---

[9]   Professor James Hitchcock, "The Bishops Seek Peace on Abortion,"
Human Life Review, Winter 1984, pp. 27-35.

ever have wanted. He presided over the largest Benedictine monastery in the world, St. John's Abbey, which I entered in July 1941. Every year he had interviews with all students studying for the priesthood. I remember him for many things. After my ordination, for example, I recall that every fall when I would seek permission to travel with the high-school football team for which I was line coach, he would give me a lecture. He was opposed to football on Sunday: shaking his head, he would admonish me, "If it rains and the field is muddy, your players will roll in the mud. How does that honor God? Wouldn't it be much better if they were at Vespers?"

After his exhortation—and I learned to be very patient, because I got the same one every year—he would give me his blessing and wish me well. And I would ask him to pray to hold off the rain.

Abbot Alcuin did not believe that vacations were a part of monastic life. His view surely confirmed my own workaholism. He forbade radios in monastic rooms. What would he have done with TV? Every Saturday after Night Office, he would proceed to "death row" where lived the old, retired monks waiting for eternity; to one of them he would go to Confession. He was always most mellow after Confession, and that was a good time to see him for whatever you wanted.

Abbot Alcuin restored a number of failing Benedictine abbeys. I have already mentioned the very influential San Beda in Manila, to which at a crucial time before World War II he sent seven monks and thousands of dollars. Owning considerable land, San Beda recovered after the war and today conducts the best law school, as well as several other schools, in that city.

During World War II, two of Abbot Alcuin's monks were interred with many other priests and religious in a concentration camp run by the Japanese. Every day they secretly offered Mass with drops of wine and bits of hosts they managed to sneak in and preserve. A very highly trained team of marines eventually rescued them, breaking in one day amidst plenty of commotion and shooting. When a sergeant demanded, "Are there any goddam Japs here?" the interred religious and priests thanked the Lord, knowing that the intruders were Americans.

Among the abbeys Abbot Alcuin restored were St. Gregory's in Shawnee, Oklahoma; Immaculate Conception in Richardson, North Dakota; and others in various countries. He financially helped very many after the war. While he was tough and strict, he was always sensitive and fair. He showed great foresight in allowing Father Virgil Michel to establish the Liturgical Press, and *Orate Fratres* (now called *Worship*) in organizing the liturgical movement in the English-speaking world. He defended him from the attacks that always plague pioneers.

If any seminarian had a serious, persistent problem with sex, he was sure to be gently invited out of the seminary/monastery. No one would ever accuse Abbot Alcuin of hiding away priests accused of pedophilia or reappointing them to other parishes—the price for which folly in the United States at this writing is estimated at more than 600 million dollars, good Catholic money that could so well have been used in so many worthy projects.

Fr. Virgil Michel, OSB in 1936.

Abbot Alcuin also founded a biracial priory in South Union, Kentucky, as a living example of black monks and white monks living together in racial justice and harmony. It is worth repeating that, under him, St. John's University and Abbey were among the first to accept black students and novices. He was fond of pioneering the missions in the Bahamas, where the monks conduct what is today considered one of the best Catholic high schools in the islands, St. Augustine's. Having many vocations to work with, he was always afraid that if the abbey became unmanageably large, "St. John's University would become the dog and the abbey the tail," as he once put it.

When everything is said and done, Abbot Alcuin Deutsch was a farsighted Benedictine missionary who, again, would be embarrassed if anyone gave him credit for the abundance of good he did for the Benedictine order and the Church itself.

In reading twenty-two years of correspondence by **Father Virgil Michel, OSB**, for my doctoral dissertation—*Virgil Michel and the Liturgical Movement*—I ran across the names of two marvelous lay apostles, Dorothy Day and Catherine De Hueck, among others. Father Michel had a great fondness for the work of both and encouraged them, and others like them, even if he did not agree with everything they said, wrote, or did. He possessed the enviable virtue of respecting the good that people could do, even if certain activities were affected by limitations or facets that others thought detrimental.

He literally went looking for lay apostles. Thus, he walked into Catherine De Hueck's outpost in a Toronto slum in 1934, finding her and her helpers thoroughly discouraged in this time of communist/socialist threat. Sitting on an orange crate, he asked them whether they went to Mass every day. "No," said Catherine, "but we go every Sunday and sometimes during the week." "Why not go every day?" Father Virgil asked. "Between two Masses you can bear everything." That was a line he often used with discouraged laymen who knew what they should be doing but met nothing but resistance from churchmen who should have known better. It is good advice today for discouraged or defeated pro-lifers.

He was a staunch defender of Dorothy Day. In general, Father Virgil was an unexcitable intellectual. But when someone once severely criticized Dorothy Day, he would not stand for it. Perhaps for the first and only time, he came close to losing his temper, saying in her defense, "I don't worry about the eternal salvation of people like Dorothy Day, but I perhaps should worry about people like you who should know better."[10]

He was a great promoter of the so-called Catholic Action for which Pius XI had so often pleaded. Knowing the liturgy and appreciating as he did the Mystical Body of Christ and the mission of every baptized Christian therein, Father Virgil believed that Catholic social action would flow naturally from an active liturgical life properly understood and thoroughly lived. At St. John's University he founded the Catholic Social Institute in the 1930s, a truly pioneering effort to disseminate the Church's social doctrine. In 1937 he wrote *Christian Social Reconstruction*, a commentary on Pope Pius XI's social encyclical, *Quadragesimo Anno*. On that subject, too, he wrote a whole series of pamphlets.

He was really a philosopher who hoped to rewrite St. Thomas Aquinas for the modern world. This project would entail not only the

---

[10] See Dorothy Day's tribute and interesting comments after Fr. Virgil's death in *Orate Fratres*, vol. 13, no. 3 (22 January 1939), 139–141.

knowledge of St. Thomas's thought but also an understanding of modern culture—just as Aquinas had understood the world of his time. Unhappy with religion texts at grade and high-school levels, he pioneered with the Dominican Sisters of Grand Rapids, Michigan, a set of primary-school texts for each grade. He himself wrote two preliminary texts for high school. Critics maintained that with these he was far ahead of his time. His confreres, not altogether admiringly, said that he suffered "from constipation of ideas and diarrhea of the pen." In writing my thesis on his life and work, I had to deal with fourteen pages of mere titles of his books, booklets, reviews, pamphlets, articles, and twenty-two years of correspondence. A personal friend of Mortimer J. Adler and deeply interested in the Great Books Movement, he had plans to revamp the curriculum at St. John's University.[11] But he died prematurely at forty-eight on 26 November 1938. Writing up his life and work really affected me, to what extent I am still not sure.

An unforgettable priest-collaborator was **Father Aloysius Schwartz.** Almost single-handedly this little American priest, originally a member of the archdiocese of Washington, set up in South Korea, the Philippines, and Mexico six orphanages providing care and education for thousands of "throw-away" kids; a huge hospital in Pusan, Korea, and two charity hospitals for the poorest of the poor there; a home for abandoned old men; two tuberculosis-convalescent homes for about 900 bed patients and 1,000 out-patients; two expectant-mother homes serving 90 young women; a village of life for 2,000 Catholic men; and a village of life for 400 severely retarded children; as well as a religious order of nuns, the Sisters of Mary, to work in these various institutions. He accomplished much more, including the founding of Korean Relief, which became Asian Relief. In a display of fund-raising genius, he collected with his assistant William Vita, many millions of dollars by writing his own appeal letters.

In 1984 he was deservedly nominated for the Nobel Peace Prize with these words: "Schwartz is proof that our world can be made a more peaceful and harmonious place in which to live through individual effort."

---

[11] For Michel's renovating, educational ideas and plans, see Mortimer Adler's interesting account in *Orate Fratres*, vol. 13 (22 January 1939), 123-129.

He put up many more havens and hospitals than I can mention here. When President Ronald Reagan and his wife, Nancy, visited South Korea, one of the many places they chose to see was one of Father Schwartz's orphanages. To this institution they donated a grand piano. (I saw it delivered—carried by six men.)

In Pusan, Korea, Father Schwartz gave me a guided tour. He described his many projects for the poor and dispossessed, among them the home for abandoned men who had been literally rotting in a shed. He told me (and this practice is common in the Third World) that parents who don't need the money send their children dressed in dirty rags to beg in the streets. HLI was able to show him various films and videocassettes dealing with abortion and allied subjects; he had them translated into Korean and Spanish and reproduced them by the thousands. The man's accomplishments were truly incredible. On 16 March 1992 he died at sixty-two of Lou Gehrig's disease. Asian Relief, Inc., is one of the largest and most successful individually run charitable organizations in the world, operating on a fifteen-million-dollar budget. It currently harbors 16,000 orphans; the total operation houses, feeds, educates, and finds jobs for 18,000 children and youths. Thanks to Father Schwartz's foresight in providing for its future by choosing a wise Filipina nun, Sister Michaela Kim, as his successor, this massive charitable relief project continues. He was a blessing to know.

John Kaiser was a star on my championship track and field teams in the 1940-1950s, a star wrestler who, after college, ended up as a trainer of paratroopers. He told me that after taking his first jump he knew he should be a priest; thus, after that stint with the paratroopers, he joined the Millhill Missionaries. I spent two weeks with Father Kaiser in the hinterlands of Kenya known as Kisii. I was astonished at his accomplishments: he had built many churches and more schools; he heroically protected the native rights of certain tribes, whom he served with jeep and motorcycle; and most important, perhaps, he defended and promoted theological orthodoxy and refuted a few rambunctious theologians among the Millhill Fathers and other groups. Do not ask me when he found time for all this.

In Kisii, when a person dies they bury him near the hut. When the missionary finds time later, he comes by to offer a funeral Mass, in one of which I participated. The funeral was followed with "lunch" in a typ-

Here I am with Mother Teresa (of India) and Fr. Anthony Zimmerman (of Japan).

ical family hut. My good former student and friend, fearful that I might become ill, coached me carefully as to what foods I could sample.

On one occasion he and I heard confessions for hours, sitting on chairs beside the church. Penitents lined up outside at a distance, confessed, received their penance, and then walked ten or fifteen yards to kneel down and offer their prayers. When my line finally came to the end, natives were still waiting for Father Kaiser. He admonished them to come to me, exaggerating fearsomely, "The other priest is Father Marx; he taught me everything I know. Don't be afraid to go to him."

One day we went hunting in a game preserve in his jeep. With his gun thrown across my chest and pointed out the window, he shot an impala, commenting, "Now we have meat for a week." His hunting skills helped supply food for some eighty girls attending his boarding school. What an experience to hear the natives singing, accompanied by their murmuring drums! And how consoling to see the Church's wonderful missionary work!

In Africa, breast-feeding is done openly. Father Kaiser told me that a young Irish missionary—seemingly "hung up" on sex—was shocked by the native custom according to which the women receive Communion with baby at breast, and so forth. When one of these breast-feeding mothers came to the sacristy, the young missionary thought he had a chance to admonish her to modesty. In all kinds of ways he tried to advise her to cover up; she did not know what he was talking about. Finally she seemed to understand: she removed her shabby skirt and put it around her shoulders, to the consternation of

Here with His Eminence Cardinal Francis Arinze, President of the Pontifical Council for Interreligious Dialogue, from Vatican City.

this young Irish missionary. As Father Kaiser commented, "She learned him fast."

In four work-missions to India I met **Mother Teresa** several times—whenever she was home. I encountered her twice in Japan; here she addressed Father Zimmerman's NFP conferences, gracing their huge crowds of doctors, nurses, and lay people. Mother Teresa was revered in Japan from the moment she stepped off the plane and was, of course, mobbed by the print and electronic media.

Several times she has written words of encouragement to us at HLI, and, of course, we meet her sisters in our ministry all over the world and help them wherever we can. I recall addressing her fifty-six novices on abortion in Calcutta in 1974. Nor shall I ever forget a breakfast meeting in Tokyo, attended by most parliamentarians, with whom she minced no words about abortion while also cleverly praising the good things in Japan. She told me later she had no idea what she was going to say when she walked in, to their loud ovation. They responded to her gentle scolding about abortion with a huge collection; she asked that the leftover food be given—as with a banquet earlier—to the poor. On one occasion she spoke at length to millions over national TV. Because it was baseball time, many people missed her and demanded a repeat—and they got it.

CARDINALS

*G*reat friends and early supporters of HLI were **Cardinal Jaime Sin** of Manila; **Cardinal Ricardo Vidal** of Cebu City, who gave us an office; **Archbishop (now Cardinal) Francis Arinze** of Onitsha,

Nigeria; **Cardinal Ernesto Corripio-Ahumada,** the former cardinal of Mexico City and the late **Cardinal Dominic Ekandem** of Abuja, Nigeria. The latter transported me with his chauffeur to various lecture sites in 1991.

Cardinal Simon Lourdusamy, who came from India, the former head of the Congregation for the Evangelization of Peoples in Rome, gave two grants totaling $60,000 for international pro-life work. Knowing what we were doing in his native country, he understood and was totally encouraging. **Cardinal Maurice Michael Otunga** of Nairobi, Kenya also endlessly encouraged our workers in Kenya. A financial supporter was gentle **Cardinal John Carberry** of St. Louis. I once visited him in his retirement. He told me that he and all his auxiliaries supported Pope Paul VI when he issued *Humanae Vitae,* for which the Pope was personally "very, very grateful." The Cardinal then flattered

Bishop Austin Vaughan, who has spent time in jail for the unborn, and me.

me by saying that he had followed my pro-life work "from its beginning." Ever since he was Bishop of Springfield— Cape Girardeau, **Cardinal Bernard Law** has supported and encouraged us, saying in the presence of Father Richard Welch and Gail Quinn on 18 December 1996, "Father Marx, I thank you for all you have done for the pro-life movement in this country and worldwide."

BISHOPS

Here with Bishop John Scanlan, the late great pro-life bishop of Honolulu, Hawaii.

*M*any bishops encouraged me along the

The late Cardinal Dominic Ekandem of Abuja, Nigeria.

With Cardinal Sin in Manila.

(l to r) Myself, Cardinal Bernard Law, Fr. Welch, Fr. Habiger, Cardinal James Hickey and Bishop William Lori, Cardinal Hickey's secretary.

Cardinal Maurice Michael Otunga of Nairobi, Kenya.

Meeting Cardinal Ernesto Corripio-Ahumada at Our Lady of Guadalupe Shrine in Mexico.

way; there is no space to mention all of them here, but some were
Bishop George Speltz of St. Cloud; **Bishop (now Cardinal) Bernard
Law** of Springfield—Cape Girardeau, **Bishop Glennon Flavin** of
Lincoln, who had me do a day-long seminar for all his priests in the
1970s; **Bishop John Scanlan** of Honolulu, who always offered me
words of encouragement in my frequent stops to and from the Orient;
and **Bishop John Paschang** of Grand Island, Nebraska, the oldest
member of the American hierarchy. The first bishop to be jailed for
resisting abortion was HLI's great friend and supporter **Bishop Austin
Vaughan**, who fre-
quently addressed our
seminars and symposia.
To those priests who
foolishly wish to
become bishops, I pass
along Bishop Vaughan's
observation: "Once you
become a bishop you
will never eat a bad
meal, and no one will

Martin Humer, Dr. Carolyn Gerster and me.

ever tell you the truth." As to this latter point, I feel particularly innocent: in several chapters I have not evaded the truth in mentioning
some bishops and archbishops in Latin America and Africa.

LAY LEADERS

*G*iving me undue credit for pushing them into the pro-life movement are **Jack and Barbara Willke** and **Joseph Scheidler**, whose
superb pro-life activities have presented many a headache to the
abortionists. The marvelous pro-lifer in Phoenix, **Dr. Carolyn Gerster**,
once publicly referred to me (in an excess of enthusiasm) as "the
George Washington of the pro-life movement." **Magaly Llaguno** was
active among Hispanics before I met her in 1983. She heads up our
Miami office, whose five staffers work exclusively in Spanish-speaking
countries, particularly in Latin America. An escapee from Cuba's
Castro, she—a convert from Methodism—began her pro-life work in

The saintly Frau Elisabet Backhaus (of Germany), one of the most knowedgeable people in the world on pro-life issues, and a treasured advisor.

Florida in the seventies. Since joining us, she has done so very much for Latin American countries. I do not know a single woman who has worked harder or done more; she is too unassuming and modest to appreciate my saying it.

I would be remiss if I did not mention **Frau Elisabet Backhaus** of Münster, Germany. I know of no more intelligent and well-informed woman on pro-life issues. This remarkable woman wrote insightful tracts on abortion and distributed them all over Germany, not neglecting the bishops and intellectuals. I could have had no better advisor and educator about the contraception/sterilization/abortion/euthanasia situation in German-speaking countries than this holy woman. I have saved twenty years' worth of correspondence with her, and some future researcher will find in it a gold mine of information.

In the early 1970s I spent a long afternoon and evening with **Frank Duff**, founder of the Legion of Mary in Dublin in 1921, one of the largest organizations in the Catholic Church, with members on five continents. A civil servant, he had read a book about devotion to Our Lady and concluded that "to love is to act." Today the Legion numbers several million members worldwide. Frank was a truly holy, apostolic layman who immediately sensed what being pro-life is all about. (The historian Warren Carroll, founder of Christendom College, is another.) Frank Duff almost shocked me when he warned me in the early 1970s that doing pro-life work "is going to bring you a kind of crucifixion. Be ready." He then charitably told me of his own persecution at the hands of people—religious, clergy and bishops included—who should have supported him as their ally in the beginning. That afternoon/evening's long conversation—truly an insightful blessing—was unforgettable. Frank is one of those to whom I pray. He is now a candidate for beatification, having died in 1980 at ninety-one.

In 1970 I stopped in Honolulu on my way to Australia where I

delivered thirty-two lectures in thirty
days. In Honolulu I met for the first
time **Robert Pearson** who organized the
first pro-life march in the United States,
in Honolulu, in protest of relaxing the
abortion law in 1969. Robert Pearson
used to fly around the Islands saving
girls from abortion and he started a
large pregnancy service in Honolulu.
From there branched out a whole team
of such centers across the country, many
of which Planned Parenthood sued with
a view to snuffing them out—and they

The tireless Robert Pearson.

succeeded all too often. Pearson, a convert, came from Michigan to
Hawaii to build a huge condominium in which he and his large family
would live while fighting abortion across the world. Unfortunately, the
business venture collapsed, and he came back to the mainland to build
Pearson's baby-saving operations. Bob often spoke at my seminars
throughout the country; he had a unique way of getting girls and
women into fighting abortion, and I have no hesitation to say that he
saved more babies than any man in the United States. While still active
in the pro-life movement, some years ago he moved his large family,
natural and adopted children, to the rolling foothills of the Ozark
Mountains in the quaint and tiny town of Hardy, Arkansas. Here he
established the Star of the Sea Village in which scores of Catholic families established themselves because they want to live in a totally
Catholic environment to raise their children properly in the faith. All
this work, moving, construction in fighting Planned Parenthood has
not been without poverty, pain and suffering. Bob knows he is working for the Lord; that gives him not only patience but great courage.[12]

There are many laymen who deserve mention, but let me remind
the reader of **John Cavanaugh-O'Keefe**, who worked several years for
HLI in Washington, D.C., and is the real pioneer of the rescue movement. As an employee, he would keep on working even in jail.

---

[12] *Sursum Corda*, vol. 2, n. 1 (winter 1996) 21-33 has a feature story
about him.

I have never personally engaged in rescuing, even though I have fostered it—always with some trepidation—since I am leery of the long-run effect of civil disobedience. However, I feel nothing but admiration for those who lay down their bodies in front of abortion

John Cavanaugh-O'Keefe receiving a Blessing for a Rescue Mission.

chambers to stop the slaughter within and to liberate the poor women misled by greedy abortionists. However, be that as it may, I have done my share of prayerful picketing, in which I believe deeply. It is precisely this picketing that has stopped many an abortion-bent doctor who does not relish attracting the publicity or the hassle that comes from being singled out and confronted.

During our world conference in Toronto in 1988, I ventured out to see a rescue operation. I arrived too early and began talking to the guard who was protecting the killing enterprise. Just then, the police came along to warn me about not stepping over a certain line. Carelessly, I did step over that line and was duly escorted to the police car. Strangely, I was not handcuffed; sitting in the backseat, I could have killed the two policemen in front, had I so wanted. We carried on an interesting, pleasant conversation on the way to jail. One of the officers was a Catholic, the other a Protestant. The latter turned to me and said, "Reverend, I suppose you think we will be going to hell for taking you in?" "Well," said I, "I wouldn't exclude it." Both of them chuckled. Along the way I suggested they might better serve society by arresting doctors who betray their profession by killing babies for money. Their response: "We do what we are told." "That is what the Nazis on trial at Nuremberg informed the judge—and they hanged the Nazis! Perhaps they should hang you?" They winced. So went the banter along the way until we arrived at the jail, where I overheard the Protestant tell the Catholic, "Our wives will really give us hell for arresting a priest."

Well, the authorities in jail wanted $500 from me; I said I was a poor missionary and had no such money. Eventually I called Bob Lalonde at the hotel, asking him to send the $500. Meanwhile, my friends, including foreigners, were angrily pleading my cause inside the jail's lobby, while others clamored outside. The officials were only too glad to get rid of me, sans money. Meanwhile, Bob collected $1,600 from participants

Alice von Hildebrand with John Finn, who has raised millions for the pro-life movement.

attending our symposium—and would you believe it, next year he wanted me to go to jail again, since we needed the money!

I landed in jail the second time in Portland, Oregon. Here again I had stepped across a line. It is a strange feeling to be handcuffed and to sit in back of a police car fully decked out as a Roman Catholic priest. Upon seeing you, people do wonder what crime you committed! In this case, I was hurried into a cage with the criminals, rapists, and robbers of the night before. They were surprised to see a priest join them and immediately wanted to know my crime. I told them that I had been picketing the Lovejoy Abortion Center. Alas, the dozen or

Myself with Mike Engler and Randall Terry.

so detainees in the cage—all of them pro-lifers—cursed the police eloquently, and I became an instant hero. Finally my turn came to be
processed, finger-printed, and so on. The guard yelled "Marx!" A
dirty, bedraggled hippie who hadn't washed for ages shouted back to
the guard, "*Father* Marx to you!" The embarrassed guard, a Catholic,
I found out, was from my adopted home town of Minneapolis. A tall
black was in charge of the total operation; some priest must have done
him favors, because he couldn't rush me out of jail fast enough after a
lawyer-friend, Russ Niehaus, called him. Someone once told me that
these days you can hardly claim to be a good Catholic if you haven't
been in jail. Well, I guess I qualify.

Very early I met the quiet but most effective **John Finn**, a list broker
who, it seems safe to say, has helped pro-life groups collect millions of
dollars over the years. Without his assistance I would never have been
able to publish *The Mercy Killers* in 1971. A close colleague and collaborator with John Finn and HLI is **Mike Engler**, a wise advisor and
the editor of our *Special Reports* and other publications. And in that
connection I must not overlook the perceptive **Virginia Gager**, who
edited *Love, Life, Death Issues*, the *International Review of Natural
Family Planning*, *The Death Peddlers*, *The Mercy Killers*, this book,
and other publications. Her advice and skills were incalculable in getting out our many publications.

And then there is **Bonnie Manion**, with whom I founded the
Northwest Natural Family Planning Center at St. Vincent's Hospital in
Portland, Oregon. In Chapter 5 I have related the story of our pio-

neering NFP symposium and our many subsequent weekend conferences conducted in various parts of the country.

Among the many
significant people I
met during my grad-
uate-school days at
the Catholic
University of
America in
Washington, D.C.,
was **Mary
Hayworth**, estab-
lished as the premier

Virginia and Ellis Evers, the "Precious Feet" people.

advice-giving columnist before the twins Ann Landers and "Dear
Abby" came along. Mary was an enthusiastic member of the group of
women with whom I met to discuss the apostolic life and the liturgy
every month. She had lost the faith—had given up church-going—but
eventually came back to it strong. She once told me that these monthly
meetings greatly affirmed her wavering beliefs. And I distinctly recall
her saying that the novices Ann Landers and Abby were far too shal-
low to suit her tastes. Mary Hayworth herself did write a rather substantial commentary on the problems of life, women, and marriage.
I was at lunch with her at a restaurant on 22 November 1963 when
news came that President John Kennedy had been shot in Dallas. As
we walked to the post office afterwards, I remember her remarking
that "people always kill their prophets."

There are very many more persons I wish I could adequately
acknowledge, for instance, **Virginia and Ellis Evers**, the "Precious
Feet" people.

Like Virgil Michel, I could easily fill fourteen pages with just the
names of other wonderful pro-lifers whom I have encountered through
the years. I regret that it is impossible to do so here. Be assured that I
remember each and every one of you—generically, if not specifically!—in my prayers every day. Thank you all.

CHAPTER 8

Marx in Communist Countries

ROMANIA

*T*hanks to the indefatigable Randy Engel, I was part of a twelve-person delegation of pro-lifers financed by $30,000 from her friends to attend the First World Population Conference in Bucharest, Romania, in 1974. It was to be a most profitable experience, never to be forgotten. After this infamous conference I spent working visits in Turkey, Iran, India, Thailand, the Philippines, Taiwan, Japan, South Korea, Hong Kong, and Singapore. (Because of visa problems I missed Indonesia.) I was away from home ninety-five days, my longest foreign missionary journey: the world had become my parish.

The Bucharest delegation, headed by the economist Al Kapusinski and co-chaired by yours truly, included Drs. Patrick Dunn of New Zealand and Herb Ratner; Prof. Charles E. Rice of Notre Dame; Fathers Anthony Zimmerman, SVD, of Japan, Pedro Richards, CP, of Uruguay, and Michael Welters of Haiti, and Brother Lawrence Carmody of Italy; John Harrington, Fran Frech, and George Barmann.

International Planned Parenthood Federation (IPPF) had set up a separate sideshow called "The Tribune" in a huge tent in which they sponsored many pro-abortion lectures. IPPF also circulated a daily newspaper called *The Planet* and showed pro-abortion propagandistic films, including brazen demonstrations of how abortions are done. For instance, Harvey Karman, the inventor of the Karman canula for "menstrual extraction" (early abortion), presented a film demonstrating his patented technique for killing. Karman, who had a doctorate in psychology, had been in jail several times for engaging in pseudo-medical practice.

The IPPF authorities steadfastly refused to show my four pro-life films. I finally told a certain Ms. Henderson, who was in charge of this activity, that if I could not screen my films the world would surely hear about it. She then relented. But for every one of my films, they showed six of theirs. Meanwhile we sent out international news releases, refuted the abortionists (wherever we were allowed) with lectures and rebuttals, and left a trail of literature.

Virtually every big-name abortionist attended this international conference, and all were extremely annoyed by our exhibit of abortion literature in great abundance; especially were they disturbed by our pictures and posters showing aborted babies. Of course, a whole array of notorious feminists like Betty Friedan, Margaret Mead, Mrs. Alan Guttmacher and others were there.

My good Protestant friend and staunch pro-lifer from Holland, Dr. Karl Gunning, referred to the "copulation explosion," suggesting that the world should seek to reduce the high level of sexual irresponsibility in order to solve the alleged population problems. He reminded me of Chesterton's famous remark that birth control often means "no birth and no control."

In addition to Dr. Gunning, I recall meeting Dr. Siegfried Ernst from Germany, Prof. Jerome Lejeune from France, and other prominent pro-lifers. Among the notorious abortionists were Lawrence Lader, the author of the flagrantly untruthful but extremely influential books *Abortion One* and *Abortion Two*.[1] (Incredibly, Justice Blackmun, in writing his justification for the infamous *Roe v. Wade* decision, quoted Lader eleven times but did not cite the world-famous fetologist Dr. A. W. Liley even once!) Lader wrote two other devilishly clever books, the obscene *Breeding Ourselves to Death* and *A Foolproof Method of Birth Control*. The latter praises the National Association for Surgical Contraception (sterilization), another gulper of tax money, whose operations are now fully international. Lader's Abortion Rights Mobilization group took the U.S. Catholic hierarchy to court, aiming to strip the Church of tax exemption.

Leading the six-person Vatican delegation was Archbishop (now

---

[1] Note what Dr. Bernard Nathanson had to say about Lader in his *The Hand of God*, pp. 76, 84, 86—91.

Cardinal) Eduardo Gagnon. Periodically, at meals and at other long sessions, he would brief us on what was happening in the official meeting. He told us that Paul VI, in naming him head of the delegation, carefully instructed him to follow strictly the guidelines of *Humanae Vitae*. All the other members would have to accept *Humanae Vitae* before being appointed, the Pope insisted, and they were to come from different academic specialties.

While selecting the delegates, Archbishop Gagnon asked the Jesuit Philip Land, an economist, whether he accepted *Humanae Vitae*; Land responded, "Oh, I can live with it." Needless to say, he was not accepted and his place was taken by a Brazilian economist. Other members of the papal delegation were Prof. Jerome Lejeune, Monsignor Di Rietmatten (head of Pope Paul VI's Commission on Population and Birth Control), and Monsignor (now Bishop) James McHugh. Archbishop Gagnon told us that the abortionists had requested for the official meeting an address from the Archbishop of Jakarta, the capital of Indonesia. This Indonesian archbishop had dissented to *Humanae Vitae*, and according to Gagnon, Paul VI asked him not to go; however, if he insisted on going, he must make it clear he was speaking neither for the Catholic Church nor for the Holy See. That ended that.

At the Vatican-called press conference, Archbishop Gagnon, speaking for the Pope, was asked whether the Church's teaching on contraception was evolving, responded forcefully, "In no way, not at all!" In a private conversation Professor Lejeune later remarked that if there had been even the possibility of such a change, he as a doctor would never have joined the papal delegation. Twenty-one Jesuits attended the press conference, including Father General Pedro Arrupe from Rome. (The chairman of the Vatican delegation told a number of us, off the record, that the Jesuits constituted the greatest semi-official opposition to *Humanae Vitae*.)

Whenever the little Vatican State calls a press conference, a huge crowd always assembles, and so it was this time. I recall that some reporter with a thick English accent asked the first question: "Why not abortion? Millions of babies are born yearly only to starve, suffer, and die within five years. Why not legal abortion?" Gagnon signaled Lejeune to respond and the latter administered a characteristically per-

Carrying HLI "goodies" to people all over the world.

fect put-down: "Sir, you want to kill them five years earlier?"

In a personal talk with the Jesuits' Father Arrupe, I told him that no two Americans had done more harm to the pro-life cause in the United States than Dan Callahan, with his infamous, fence-straddling book *Abortion: Law, Choice and Morality*,[2] and the Jesuit Robert Drinan, with his pro-abortion voting record as a Congressman and with his careless, virtually pro-abortion articles. Callahan, to subsidize the four years he spent researching and writing his noxious book, had received grants from the pro-abortion Ford Foundation and the anti-life Population Council of New York. (Is there a Ford in your future?) Incidentally, in October 1975 I had the opportunity to remind the New Zealand chairman of the Royal Commission on Contraception, Sterilization and Abortion in Auckland about the pro-abortion financing of Callahan's book, which this chairman was in the midst of quoting to me. On the occasion of that debate, a pro-abortion lawyer grilled me for two hours, but I survived to address pro-life doctors on euthanasia.

As for Robert Drinan, in his fifth term in the House of Representatives, after a campaign to oust him had been initiated, mostly by the laity, the Pope intervened and had him removed. In the *New York Times* of 4 June 1996, Drinan shamefully defended President Clinton's veto of congressional efforts to ban partial-birth abortion. The president of the St. Ignatius Society of Georgetown

---

[2]   Daniel Callahan, *Abortion: Law, Choice and Morality* (London: Collier-Macmillan, 1970).

University has asked the Archbishop of Washington to at least remove Drinan's faculties. As of this writing, seven months later, nothing has been done overtly. So Drinan goes on snubbing the bishops, scandalizing hard-working pro-lifers, and offending the many Catholics and other citizens who consider government-tolerated infanticide to be a moral outrage.

When Arrupe and I parted, he tapped me on the shoulder and said, "Pray for Father Drinan." What did he mean, I wondered: had Drinan lost his faith? Or was he deploring Drinan's activities while doing nothing about them? Now it transpires that Father Arrupe explicitly, repeatedly and from the very beginning opposed Drinan's deep involvement in politics. However, Drinan's immediate superiors *did* approve of his decision to run for Congress and even encouraged him to ignore orders from Rome.[3] In the end, it was the Pope, not Arrupe, who forced Drinan out of the House of Representatives. In any case, Drinan continues unchecked in his subtle pro-abortion maneuvers and scandalous writings. Why are the bishops afraid to "bash" him?

Two weeks in Bucharest was a great learning experience. We lived in the Drumul Apartment Complex, in small, primitive apartments specially constructed for the conference and later to be used by families. We wondered what liberals and feminists like Betty Friedan and the anthropologist Margaret Mead thought of "liberated" women sweeping the streets. We saw the death peddlers feverishly working and plotting with their meetings, press conferences, lectures, and a daily newspaper called *The Planet*—but they did not succeed.

In the official meeting it was the Argentinean delegation and developing nations that saved the day; the chairperson from Argentina boldly told the rich countries that it was not their business to decide how many children the families of the developing countries would be allowed to have. That position was strongly supported by many countries, but above all by the developing nations.

---

[3]   See an unbelievable account of Jesuit disobedience and the sad, dishonest maneuverings of Father Robert Drinan, by James Hitchcock, "The Strange Political Career of Father Drinan," *The Catholic World Report*, December 1996, p. 38-45.

At the Great Wall in China in 1983.

Strangely, the Vatican and Red China were on the same side. The Red Chinese Communists proclaimed that overpopulation, as Karl Marx had maintained, was a function of inhuman, imperialistic capitalism. Huang Shutse, the Chinese vice minister of health, fumed, "It is owing to overpopulation that unemployment and poverty exist today? No, absolutely not. It is due to the exploitation, aggression and plunder of the superpowers. They are the chief culprits for unemployment and poverty."[4] Alas, the Chinese have changed their minds. In five years came their brutal, inhuman one-child policy. We left Bucharest after marveling at the largest array of food I have ever witnessed at a national banquet. The Romanian President Nicolai Ceausescu sponsored this feast to impress all the delegates with Communist largess.

BULGARIA

*W*ith no lectures to give in Western Europe, I spent Christmas week of 1975 in Bulgaria. Through Martin Humer, for whom I had been lecturing in Austria, I got to know a pro-life economist who worked for the Communist government. Having been advised to stay in the "best" hotel in Sofia, I offered up bad food and worse service for a week; I celebrated an uneventful Christmas, with no evidence of any festivities to be seen. The Communists made much fuss about New Year's, their holiday—anything to distract from the Christian feast. Greeting cards bore pictures of birds and flowers. I recall going

---

[4]   United States Coalition for Life: *Special Report on the United Nations World Population Conference: Tribune,* 1974, assembled by Randy Engel.

to the apartment of my economist-friend several times and telling him on one occasion that I had conversed briefly in German with some caretaker at the door three floors below. He instantly became agitated; he wondered what I might have said and then brought out a strong drink when he found out I had been clever enough not to speak out of turn. I had, of course, been well briefed on what to say and do and what not to say and do. Never was it more consoling to offer the Holy Sacrifice of the Mass daily in a hotel.

Conditions in Bulgaria were horrible. One has to live in these circumstances to experience the real, deadly Communism and its appalling social effects. In that "best hotel in Sofia," waiters and waitresses didn't care whether they served you or not, since they got the same small paycheck every Friday in any case. And, of course, you rarely met anyone with whom you could converse, given language difficulties and the fear that you might be dealing with a spy. Today the country is in a terrible condition. Abortion on demand had been legalized in 1956 with the usual consequences. In 1996 there were two abortions for every live birth, because in Communist ideology there is no sexual morality; abortions are highest in the 15-19 age bracket.[5]

One real respite was to attend the Orthodox liturgy in the local cathedral. And in foreign countries I always love to walk through large department stores to see what goods are available, what the prices are, and so forth. Doing this in Sofia did not take much time, because there was little to observe or buy! On leaving, how relieved I was when—lost!—I was rescued by some good woman who guided me through the thickest fog of the city back to the train station. On my way to Austria some government bureaucrat had all kinds of foolish questions for me, especially dealing with money. How glad I was to get back to Vienna!

---

[5]   *Nuntiatura Apostolica* in Bulgaria: No. 280, 14 November 1996. See also *Statistical Yearbook of Bulgaria*, 1994. A good source as to how the legalization of abortion came to European countries is *Abortion in the New Europe: A Comparative Handbook*, edited by Bill Rolston and Anna Eggert, and published by Greenwood Press of Westport, CT, and London.

CHINA

*I*n 1977 I spent two weeks in Red China. My friends wondered why I wanted to go there, asking me whether I wasn't afraid. "Why should I be afraid?" I asked. "After all, my name is 'Marx.'" The one-child family policy was already in force in large cities. Get pregnant a second time and you are forcibly aborted even if they catch you in the ninth month of gestation. If a second baby should be born, the parents may lose their job(s), or may be fined, and they can say goodbye to any thoughts of promotion.

One of the saddest experiences in China was to see grandparents watching their one grandchild, the only one they would ever have. For ages it was the custom in China and in Asia that the oldest boy had to take care of the parents. That was their social security. So if you are allowed to have only one child, what are you going to have? A boy or a girl? Of course, a boy. Now, raised alone, he often becomes "a little Napoleon." If a mother is pregnant with a girl, the baby is often aborted, or, if born, she is frequently left to die. While in China I was told by reliable people that there were at least 500,000 female infanticides every year. There are very many more today. Preferring boys to girls has produced a serious disturbance of the sex ratio, which means that there are more boys than girls, creating a serious problem for the future. And now we have heard about "dying rooms" in hospitals, designated mostly for baby girls and very sick children who were lucky enough to be born, but obviously ran out of luck shortly after birth. How many abortions are there in China? No one can know, but surely more than in any other country in this land of 1,100,000,000 people.[6]

When I heard that meat is sometimes garnished with some kind of fried worms, I excluded meat from my diet. Fish seemed often served. Even though I come from a fresh fish state—Minnesota with 10,000 lakes—I don't like fish. Because I could not explain how I wanted

---

[6] Steve Mosher, *A Mother's Ordeal: One Woman's Fight against China's One-Child Policy* (New York: Harcourt Brace, 1993); *Broken Earth: The Rural Chinese* (New York: Macmillan, 1983).

boiled eggs for breakfast, I
eliminated them as well. I
ended up living for two
weeks mostly on beer and
bread. (I do not like rice.)

Since my name was
"Marx," I breezed through
customs and found awaiting
me on the other side a clunker
of a car (which, however,
never clunked out) and a
guide, carefully chosen.
Obviously he had sociological
training, judging from the questions he asked me and the answers he
gave to mine. Of course, said he, there was no religious persecution in
China. Of course there was nothing but freedom, more than in any
other country! Of course there was no unemployment, since such does
not exist in Communist countries, unemployment being the bitter fruit
of monopolistic capitalism. He told me other stories.

In China in 1978, with the only child she is allowed to have.

I saw the Great Wall, the famous Ming Museum (underground),
and in Beijing an incomparable display of gymnastics, truly the greatest I have ever seen in my life. There were few cars in the streets, either
because the people could not afford them or because cars had been
banned. But I saw my share of bicycles. As they said, in China everybody has a bicycle, except grandma—she has two!

Since my visit there, the Chinese have gone into massive sterilization
programs, and have shown a great interest in Natural Family
Planning, thanks to Drs. Lyn and John Billings of Australia. China is
undoubtedly a country of immense future problems, given its disturbed sex ratio, the aging population, and so on, and I doubt that the
soon-to-be 1,200,000,000 Chinese will stay within their borders, once
they get on their socio-economic feet. And they are fast getting there.

Concerning the underground Church, it would be irresponsible to
say what I know. The Patriotic Church, having missed Vatican II,
offers Mass in Latin. HLI is building an orphanage in northern China
in hopes of bringing threatened babies—especially unwanted girls—
out of the country for adoption. At HLI we have a program ready and

have already printed *An Examination of Conscience* in Chinese.
Through Hong Kong, we manage to get pro-life materials into China.

RUSSIA

*R*ussia was the first country in modern history to legalize abortion-
on-demand on 8 November 1920 and divorce-on-request at the
same time. The reason? Lenin wanted to eliminate Christianity
overnight, and the best way to do that is to attack and destroy the
family, the generator and tender of culture.

Traveling with me was Dr. Antun Lisec, a young Croatian surgeon
who once told me during one of our symposia in Yugoslavia, that he
would work full-time for me for $1,000 a month. "You're on," I said,
and he has been working with us ever since. He used to wonder why Tito
made him study Russian for eleven years. "Now I know as providential,"
he said; "so I could work in Russia and neighboring countries."

Dr. Lisec and I visited various hospitals and abortion centers, all of
whose directors, incredibly, gave us free access and even invited us to
lecture! In Russia, 75 percent of doctors are women, who seemed to
sense the tragedy implicit in massive abortion and the suffering
inflicted on women. I recall that in one hospital the director asked us
to address thirty-five girls who that afternoon would be aborted!
What do you tell such a group? I racked my brain; I said a prayer;
then I rattled on from the top of my head, with Antun translating. I
spoke for more than thirty minutes. He spoke longer. What a sight—
these poor women about to have their babies killed! But that was
hardly novel. We were told by hospital authorities and medical people
that there were at least seven or eight abortions for every married
woman in her lifetime. The government reports three. Today Russia
has the lowest birthrate in the world: 1.1 children per family.
Strangely, the average life span has dropped to fifty-seven years,
thanks to vodka, smoking, poor medical care, and other factors.

At our conference in Moscow two years later, attended by 600 people including some thirty doctors, our people were told by doctors that
only about 35 percent of Russian women were capable of carrying a
child *in utero* for nine months and then giving healthy birth, chiefly

In front of St. Basil's Cathedral, near the Kremlin.

because of Russia's seventy-seven-year history of aborting. One fruit of this sojourn in Russia is a branch in Moscow run by a wonderful Russian lady professing the Orthodox faith, very much opposed to contraception and abortion. Her name: Galena Seryakova. Our second symposium will take place in St. Petersburg this year (1997).

We visited four cities, supposedly taking our lives in our hands while flying Aeroflot. In European Siberia we visited the city of Siktivkar, capital of the Republic of Komi. Here I was astonished when a hospital director showed me HLI literature she was using! Through the years I have sent pro-life materials into many countries of the world, whenever I had any assurance it would be used. This policy has paid off enormously.

In St. Petersburg we lectured in the largest abortion clinic in Russia. Here I bought a mailing list of 20,000 doctors, to all of whom Dr. Lisec sent pro-life literature! Later, during another visit, he spoke to the gynecologists of the twenty-five Russian medical schools. On still another occasion, Dr. Lisec broke up a doctors' meeting sponsored by the Dutch drug company Organon in order to sell its abortifacient

With lady abortion doctors in St. Petersburg, Russia.

pills. Medical and hospital personnel were totally open to our message in these abortion centers and in these pitiful, rundown hospitals.

When it rained, the streets in Moscow became little rivers because of poor or nonexistent storm sewers. In Moscow the subways are deep in the ground in anticipation of a possible atomic exchange with the West. We treated our Russian guests at McDonald's; it takes a Russian worker a month's salary to eat there. It was the best meal I ate in Russia.

We went to see Archbishop Tadeusz Kondrusiewicz in Moscow; he is the apostolic administrator for Catholics in Russia. We learned much from him, and left him $3,000. The Orthodox Church fears what it calls "Western Catholic evangelizing." But that influence is minimal, compared with that of the sects and Protestant groups who are proselytizing all over Russia with lots of money.

Everywhere one sees these seemingly endless, long, drab, gray, unpainted, concrete apartment buildings ten to twelve stories high, where eight families would have to cook on one stove. Lavatories were few. A friend took us to one such apartment. The elevator reeked of urine, and when we came to the eighth floor, we were carefully ushered into the one apartment we were allowed to see. There we had a meal that we paid for, given the poverty of the kindly inhabitants.

Every morning on radio and TV the Russians were told that they had the highest standard of living in the world, and of course that is all they heard—no counter messages, ever. Society was totally regimented; you needed a passport to travel from city to city, and, naturally, police surveillance was everywhere in the Communist days.

Of the some ninety Catholic priests attached to Moscow at the time, only three were natives. Today two seminaries function. Russian people in general know that the Orthodox Church—perhaps in order to survive—cooperated somewhat with the Communists, and they are therefore inclined to look more favorably upon Catholics in union with the Holy See, who were brutally persecuted and often executed.

Plunging into the drab void left by the collapse of the Evil Empire, one finds neither the bombed ruins of war nor the proud defiance of a vanquished enemy, but rather a murky pool of despair left as the main legacy of a tragic social experiment conducted by godless men on helpless, unwilling subjects. As my friend Father Werenfried van Straaten, O. Praem., observed, it is going to take a hundred years to straighten out Russia economically. After seventy-four years of regimenta-

In front of a Lenin statue in Kumi, western Siberia.

tion, almost all personal initiative and sense of responsibility have evaporated. Every Friday each one customarily received his measly check for work assigned in an economy and society totally organized from the top down. Today, in the post-Communist era, in a time of attempted democracy and limping free enterprise, corruption is rampant; the Mafia has taken over; the soldiers and others are unpaid; the worker is confused and often hungers after his formerly assured small weekly check. That is why some workers think the predictable

Getting briefed by Archbishop Tadeusz Kondrusiewicz (of Moscow).

Communist system was better—and so some remain Communists and, in other countries, vote Communists back into government.

The country is a topsy-turvy nation where taxi drivers are more valued than physicians; where pro-life missionaries can walk into hospitals and talk women out of abortions with the approval of the mostly women abortionists; where women dress modestly but abort two out of every three pregnancies; where (as I noted earlier) the highly regarded pro-life video "The Silent Scream" is worse than ineffective because it teaches abortionists how to do their job better, because it was made in America, and because it impresses women by showing shiny, clean instruments of death. Before the revolution in 1917, they believed in God and the king; after the revolution they believed in Lenin and Stalin; today they believe in nothing. The result is complete confusion and an enormous social breakdown.

Even before the collapse of Communism in December 1989, International Planned Parenthood Federation (IPPF) was there; at their earliest opportunity, representatives had a national meeting with the World Health Organization, the Russian Medical Society, and significant others to plan the introduction into Russia of modern methods of birth control with a view to reducing the number of abortions! Again and again Dr. Lisec and I talked to the medical authorities in Moscow and elsewhere, trying to convince them that contraception was no solution to abortion, that much modern "contraception" was actually abortifacient, and that there was no country in the world in which widespread contraception co-existed with a flourishing family life and a good birthrate. The concepts of sexual abstinence and chastity seem totally foreign or unrealistic to Russians. Obviously, we did not convince them. Today Russia has not only the lowest birthrate (1.1 children per family) but also the highest alcoholism and divorce rates in the world.

With no sense of democracy, free enterprise, or true civil liberty, things seem (and are) upside down everywhere. Abortion is something of a national allegory: life and hope—the future—have been systematically destroyed and sucked out of Mother Russia by those who offered much in terms of material benefits but in the end provided only death, sterile emptiness, spiritual and material poverty, and an enormous anxiety about what may follow. And what may follow, with all its agonizing insecurities and uncertainties, cannot be pleasant.

UKRAINE

Giving the "Precious Feet" to a newly appointed bishop in Ukraine.

*A*fter a long delay, we finally entered a Ukrainian airplane with broken seats and an endless stream of passengers, each loaded down with God-knows-what, including little crates of chickens! So many people came on board that we wondered whether they were leaving through a door in the back. Cabin personnel and pilots seemed dressed like everyone else. After a long wait, wondering whether we would ever take off, we finally departed. When we hit the last pothole, we knew we were airborne. From a jug of water and the same cup, the flight attendant tried to

With nuns in Ukraine.

slake passengers' thirst. After a bumpy ride and many prayers we were in Kiev, arriving late at night and fleeced by immigration agents. After the usual rigmarole in getting registered at a hotel, we were in bed.

Here was the same run-down drab society, with people poorly dressed but very pleasant indeed. We met the Greek Catholic Bishop Sofron of Ivano-Frankivsk and his auxiliary bishop, who welcomed us at the airport in his broken but understandable English. The bishop had 1,000 seminarians. He was waiting for the return of his seminary, his episcopal house, several parish churches, and a few convents.

In one such convent, that first night, we had dinner in the kitchen after Mass.

Dr. Lisec treated a sick nun (there were seventeen nuns in that small convent, formerly a family dwelling, and some twenty-one novices in another building). Bishop Sofron told us of his trials in Communist courts and his brief stay in jail, where he had landed because he was an "enemy of the people," as the Commies knew

Concelebrating the Greek-Catholic Mass in Ukraine with Fr. Maksymilian Podwicka.

One goes all lengths to bring the pro-life message to Ukrainians.

from his sermons. He said that the accusations were so outlandish that he could not suppress spontaneous laughter, which kept him in jail a little longer. The bishop assured us that at least 15,000,000 Russians were starved by Stalin in the 1930s, and—hard to believe—in their hunger the Ukrainians ate human flesh. The ruthless Russian dictator had put the farmers' wheat on the international market, prompting some Marxist American university professor to extol the Communist economy. We were told about all the sad effects of the Chernobyl nuclear disaster—things you never read or hear about outside Ukraine.

One evening the bishop gathered some ten intellectuals, among them doctors and professors. I will never forget an old woman, once a professor, who told us, "Father, for seventy-three years the Communists raped us—psychologically, morally, spiritually and intellectually." But in all their sufferings there is a grandeur about these people, so cruelly persecuted for so long and now overwhelmed by the enormous magnitude of social, political and economic problems. Dr. Lisec and I spoke to a large crowd in the Civic Center. The response was very enthusiastic. Here, as in Russia, we spoke to several medical groups. Because we were foreigners—and they had seen few foreigners in the last few decades—they seemed fascinated by what we had to say, and of course, we said it as it is in a pro-life way. Bishop Sofron accompanied us everywhere, even into abortion centers!

We visited old museums, preserved churches, and a nuns' convent, driven from building to building by female abortionists in their primitive ambulance. These women asked the nuns why they weren't working in the hospitals to counsel girls out of abortion like this American and Croatian! Never in my life did I imagine that I would see what I saw in Russia and Ukraine, and hear what I heard! But now HLI has a base in Ukraine, and in 1993 we presented a successful pro-life seminar in Kiev. We are doing what we can, which is very little indeed compared with the gigantic problems and the heartbreaking need for restoration in countries where conditions are so primitive and the future so uncertain. And so it will be when we put on a seminar in St. Petersburg, Russia, in May 1997.[7]

HUNGARY

With the Health Minister of Hungary, 1980.

*I*n 1987 I stopped for three days in Budapest while driving from Poland to Yugoslavia. Vocations to the religious life and priesthood were (and still are) few, as I learned when staying at a huge, empty monastery and lecturing on pro-life themes at a major seminary of seven students.

After the Communist crash in 1989, I spent twelve days in this ancient Catholic country whose history of Christianity spans more than ten centuries. Legal abortion came in the middle 1950s and quickly ballooned, so that today one of two babies is aborted, the result being a very low, nonreplacement birthrate. As the saintly Cardinal Joseph Mindszenty wrote in 1962:

---

7   For a full account, see *My 21 Days in Russia and Ukraine* (Gaithersburg, MD, Human Life International, 1993).

Conferring with Hungarian bishops.

At birth clinics and elsewhere, we find a shocking tolerance of abortions on a scale that amounts to mass murder of unborn babes. Guilty hands slay healthy offspring; godless women, spurning motherhood, forcibly stay the Hand of God.

In line with revealed and natural law, the Church's stand is crystal clear. Either we accept the responsibility of children as a result of marital intercourse, or heroically abstain for a time, or entirely. No other moral alternative exists. Marriage thwarting procreation becomes lust. Ill-starred the union that breaks God's law.

The mere thought of quenching the spark of life is sinful; and who so aids, abets or permits abortion forfeits the Church's communion—for this sin of sins against nature, God, child, mother and nation.[8]

A Hungarian bishop told me that when authorities transferred Cardinal Mindszenty's body back to Hungary from Austria, they learned it had been preserved. He saw the body. In the cathedral of

---

[8] . . . *the World's Most Orphaned Nation* (New York: Julius Tarlo, 1962), p. 63.

Esztergom are buried all Hungarian cardinals. I had no trouble praying at the grave of the suffering, holy Cardinal Mindszenty. Thanks to

President Eisenhower, the cardinal was
able to escape into the American lega-
tion, where he lived and suffered for
years—and then he suffered more when
Pope Paul VI asked him to leave
Hungary because he was considered an
obstacle to the Vatican's *Ost-Politik*.

*With the Abbot/Bishop of the
famed Pannonhalma Abbey in
Hungary, 1992.*

The country is churning around in the
usual turmoil following the Communist
collapse. For whatever reasons, Hungary
has had a consistently high suicide rate.
Divorce and alcoholism are enormous problems. Generations have
received virtually no moral or religious education. Planned Parenthood
works with the evil government. The Association of Families with
Many Children was founded in 1987, and I addressed these heroic
people who are struggling to make their way in a society in which 30
percent exist under the poverty level. For ten minutes I also spoke in
German to the hierarchy assembled in Budapest. The beleaguered
bishops, having to deal as well with an unfriendly government, have a
multitude of problems, to say the least.

I visited with various Hungarian doctors I had met in other countries. Some of these doctors were working heroically to establish some
kind of pro-life movement in the prevailing chaos. As a former abortionist put it, "Finally and mainly, the victim is the future. A cannibal-
istic civilization that devours its own children is able to destroy even
the future of itself, the future of us all, of mankind." But that can be
said of most parts of the world these days. Some doctors, now pro-
life, moaned over the killings they had done.

I visited the large, world-famous Benedictine monastery of
Pannonhalma, with its well-known ancient library and school. Given
its important role in Hungarian history, the Communists never disturbed this famous Abbey, which produced the renowned theologian-
physicist Father Stanislaus Yaki, who deservedly won the prized
Templeton Award some years ago.

CZECHOSLOVAKIA

I made two working visits to Czechoslovakia when it was still under the Communist regime. One Sunday evening my host family in Prague took me to church to offer Mass with the pastor. At first he declined to allow me to do so. Any foreigner coming into the country had to be reported to authorities within twenty-four hours, and I was not reported. The pastor agonized over permitting me to concelebrate with him but finally summoned his courage and said, "Oh well, your name is Marx; we'll take a chance."

I engaged in a long, interesting, unforgettable conversation with the ninety-year-old Cardinal Frantisek Tomasek of Prague. He had

Being coached by the late Cardinal Frantisek Tomasek of Prague.

a magnificent record of resisting the worst of Communism. The Commies feared him. He coached me how to proceed with my cause in Communist lands, warning me that I'd be dealing with the Devil. He was a most delightful, gentle, wise person, whom the Communists could not bully.

One has to live and travel in Communist countries to realize how stifling their life is, with spies and police everywhere and people living in constant fear. Under the Communists there were twice as many abortions as today, where there are two births for every surgical abortion. The situation has slightly improved, but still the nation is dying from a very low birthrate. Pro-life activities are few. Abortions are freely performed in maternity hospitals. To picket in front of these hospitals would invite brutal treatment from the police, among whom many Communists still remain.

Once a year about 1,000 pro-lifers march in the streets of Prague. Amazingly, national television broadcasted Dr. Bernard Nathanson's film "The Silent Scream." The bishops have established some offices to help pregnant women. What I heard and saw in Czechoslovakia in three visits would fill a fair-sized book. In northern Monrovia a new church is dedicated to Blessed Mary, Mother of Unborn Children. Sex ed in schools is pornographic. I spoke in various Czech cities and twice at an international pro-life meeting in Bratislava, the capital of the more Catholic Slovakia, now separated from the Czech State as a distinct country. The Church in Slovakia is flourishing; I witnessed many seminarians and a lot of good Catholic doctors, some of whom were promoting NFP. The bishops were most friendly and cooperative. I spoke for twelve minutes to the national hierarchy in Brno, one of the largest dioceses in Europe.

YUGOSLAVIA

The real pioneer of the pro-life movement in Yugoslavia was an economist, Marijo Zivkovic. He and his wife, Darka, were two-term members of the Pontifical Council for the Family. In a visit to the United States in 1973, he discovered Father William Cogan's pioneer film "Abortion: A Woman's Decision," which featured Dr. Eugene Diamond. Earlier, posing as an abortionist early in the abortion battle, I had secured an abortion teaching film from a secret foundation in Delaware promoting permissive abortion. The film, produced in England, presented the English gynecologist Dr. Dorothy Kerslake demonstrating techniques in five suction abortions. The abortion procedure in Cogan's production came from this teaching film, as did Dr. Jack Willke's demonstration of a suction abortion that he sold and screened throughout the United States. I gave Cogan's and Willke's opuses even broader circulation, adding foreign countries to the coverage.

Zivkovic showed "Abortion: A Woman's Decision" all over his country, mostly in churches, using a translated commentary. Eventually, Father Cogan put it into the Croatian language. In the summer of 1979 Mother Teresa ran across the grisly film in Zagreb and insisted that it be shown to all young people before they encountered the problem of unplanned pregnancy. In the winter of 1978-79, Cogan and Zivkovic discovered that the film had been secretly copied 500 times in official Communist laboratories in Poland. For what purpose, one wonders.

On my way to Bucharest for the World Population Conference in 1974, I was to make a side trip to Yugoslavia. Because I would be on my way to the Orient after attending the Bucharest meeting, I began sending materials to Marijo Zivkovic instead. I actually got to "Titoland" only in 1984, bringing loads of materials and five other films, as well as various slides depicting preborn life.

I returned to Yugoslavia in 1987 for another working visit; in a meeting with Archbishop Frane Franic of Split, he agreed to allow us to organize an international conference in the undercroft of his large, new cathedral on the twentieth anniversary of *Humanae Vitae* in 1988. The conference drew some 500 people; in the audience, and already appointed, sat the future Archbishop of Split, Monsignor Ante Juric. His appointment was announced publicly a few days later. Having attended the conference, the new archbishop said that, after taking care of his priests, he must now also promote family life in every possible way; his decision, he acknowledged, was the fruit of attending our meeting.

I visited Medjugorje four times over the years, once kneeling in the sacristy with the four alleged visionaries during their alleged encounter with the Blessed Virgin. Archbishop Franic believed deeply in the phenomenon at Medjugorje and said no one should criticize it who had not heard confessions there. Most of his priests, I sensed, did not buy the story of miraculous appearances. Nor did I.

In September of 1990, HLI sponsored and financed a conference in Slavonski Brod on medical ethics and the family, attended by 2,000. Marijo Zivkovic and I immediately initiated, and began to recruit speakers for, a big pro-life Congress in Bratislava in the spring of 1991, April 26-29. Through Mr. Zivkovic I met many bishops, priests, and people at sponsored events all over the country.

After the Slavonski Brod symposium, we presented a one-day conference in Katowice, Poland, 2 May 1991, and then moved on for a two-day symposium in Vilnius, Lithuania, 4-6 May. After speaking to seminarians at Kaunas, Marijo and I addressed a Communist medical meeting of 1,000 in Grodno, Belarus. (The Polish Catholic hero of the American Revolution, Tadeusz Kosciuszko, hailed from Belarus.) We also addressed students of the primitive seminary, which was just recovering from the horrible days of Communism and awaiting the restoration of the nearby cathedral. The following year we returned to Grodno for a two-day conference.

On one occasion, during the Communist era, I gave a pro-life address in the seminary in Sarajevo. The rector was Father Vinko Puljic, now the cardinal-archbishop of that city. My lecture had to be approved ahead of time by local Communist authorities, who later were in attendance as spies. To tempt the seminarians, the Communists kept a loud nightclub open all night across the street.

I held a memorable conversation with Zagreb's Cardinal Franjo Kuharic, whose pamphlet on chastity we published. I traveled with Bishop Tomislav Javlanovic, who was jailed as a young priest at twenty-four and endured solitary confinement until he was thirty-one. Once traveling on a plane with the bishop I asked about Tito. The bishop immediately put his finger to his lips, indicating such talk was dangerous. During my several visits in Yugoslavia, I learned of the shocking number of abortions there; there has been a considerable reduction in Catholic areas recently, largely because of Zivkovic, Dr. Antun Lisec, and our massive shipments of pro-life literature and audiovisual aids. The law permitting abortion may still be turned back in Croatia.

One of the remarkable priests I met was a collaborator of Marijo Zivkovic, Monsignor Marko Mystorovic, for whom HLI bought a $12,000 printing press that operated secretly in a hidden part of his church, producing pro-life and catechetical literature. Here, too, I met Father Don Ante Bakovic, who started the One More Child Movement, out of which came my booklet *Eight Reasons Why You Should Have One More Child*. This publication, we know, is responsible for inspiring the birth of at least 125 babies in Canada and the United States—with many more to come, we hope.

EAST GERMANY

*S*everal times in the 1970s and 1980s I sneaked through the Iron Curtain into East Germany with the late Friedolin Huber, who served as my chauffeur for many trips in Germany. On one occasion, we stayed in East Berlin with a Ford Motor Company representative whose home stood about fifty feet from the Iron Curtain, that rude reminder of hideous Communism.

I learned a lot about life in this tragic Communist country just from observing the sadness in the faces of the people. Despite being prodded by the highest family allowances in the world at that time, the birthrate remained low (today it is less than one child per family), necessitating the bringing in of workers (*Gastarbeiter*), mostly the

Moslem Turks who were to make East Berlin eventually the second largest Moslem city in the world.

My long chats with the pastor of a parish in East Berlin impressed on me the great difficulties of carrying on pastoral work in an officially godless country. In the first place, merely crossing the border either way was no small ordeal; the bureaucratic hurdles were enough to test the

Trying to get into a Planned Parenthood meeting in East Berlin, 1985.

With Russian soldiers in East Germany.

Wet in Communist East Germany in 1975.

patience of Job, to say nothing of a restless Benedictine monk. I was further irritated at being refused permission to enter a large meeting of International Planned Parenthood Federation (IPPF) sponsored in part by the Pathfinder Fund.

Apparently my reputation had preceded me. Several good people gave me twice the amount of East Germany's D-Mark for my American dollars; I passed along the surplus German money to a very delighted pastor who was heroically trying to educate the children of his parish with the help of a few nuns. The nuns, by the way, had to wear civilian clothes in order to get by.

Twelve years later I participated in the first pro-life symposium in Dresden, organized largely by Dr. Siegfried Ernst. Dresden, which had been at one time one of the most beautiful and cultured cities of Germany, was virtually destroyed with fire bombs late in the war as Britain's revenge for Hitler's destruction of Coventry. Surviving Germans told me how burning people jumped into the river to snuff out the flames on their clothes. I was told, too, that some thirty-five nuns suffocated in a basement where they had gone to save themselves from the roaring Lancaster British bombers. It was fascinating to try to converse with Russian soldiers patrolling the streets. The symposium, by the way, was a huge success and well attended.

Archbishop Jerzy Stroba of Poznan, Poland.

POLAND, LITHUANIA AND BELARUS

*I*n the 1980s, when the Communists were still in the saddle, I ventured into Poland. I shall never forget seeing on my first visit, the primitive, old, barnlike airport in Warsaw, the poorly dressed people, the same huge, gray, dull, unpainted, concrete apartments one sees in Moscow and the usual shabbiness one finds in all Communist countries.

I spoke in many large cities and was terribly appalled at the number of abortions procured in this very Catholic country—thanks to the Communists. In 1956 the Communist government legalized abortion, virtually on demand, and not a few Poles resorted to it in the following years. One might cite Poland as an example of how important it is to have a law forbidding abortion. Remove the law and the killing sets in immediately—and lots of killing, even in a Catholic country. One good Polish bishop told me that for years there were an estimated 300,000—500,000 abortions annually in Poland, a nation of 38,000,000. In later years the number of abortions has been greatly reduced, even though Poles can go across any border to dispose of an unborn baby. Today the birthrate is not at replacement level. Poland, however, thanks to Pope John Paul II and his early promotion of marriage-preparation and family-life centers in parishes, has the largest

With our busy twosome, Lech and Ewa Kowalewska, HLI leaders in Poland in the early 1980s.

percentage of NFP practitioners and still fosters many vocations. Many priests trained in Poland are working in various countries, not least Russia, Belarus, and Ukraine.

Poland is the only country in Europe that has ever modified its abortion legislation toward better protection of the unborn child. The new law that was passed on 7 January 1993 permitted abortions only in rare cases such as rape, incest and danger to the mother's life, or if the "conceived child" were "irreparably damaged." The number of abortions dropped sharply. An attempt to relax the law was vetoed by President Lech Walesa in 1995. Walesa, however, lost the next election; pro-abortion President Kwasniewski took over and prepared the people for a new abortion bill, which, unfortunately, passed by a vote of 222—195 with 16 abstentions. The new law allows abortion up to the twelfth week for women "who find themselves in difficult living conditions or where they have other important personal reasons." For the first time abortion is allowed in private clinics. If a baby has a defect, killing him is allowed until he can survive outside the womb. The new law also introduces compulsory pornographic sex education beginning in the first grade and lowers the price of contraceptives (abortifacients, too) by 50 percent. In no other nation were there such massive demonstrations against this tragic type of bill, and HLI was totally involved. At this writing the Communist government is attempting to pass a law allowing the crudest pornography.

There is a second most serious problem facing the Polish people: The movement towards European Union and NATO. The media is all for it and allows the many opponents no hearing. There is total unanimity on the subject on TV, radio and in the major papers (mostly owned by godless Germans). The Church is totally excluded. While there is much talk about human rights, God's rights are forgotten.

Our work in Poland is growing by leaps and bounds. Collaborating with the alcoholics counselor Andrezj Winkler of Rybnik and his Society for Responsible Family Planning, the gynecologist Dr. Helena Gulanowska of Lublin, and others, we managed during various working visits to sponsor three national meetings and several lectures. Dr. Gulanowski's daughter, Beata, who is also a gynecologist, was very helpful. The Gulanowski home was always available to us.

In 1993, HLI set up a large center in Gdansk, headed by a remarkable editor, who speaks Russian fluently, Ewa Kowalewska. She receives much help from her husband, Lech, who is a computer expert. From this center, staffed by six persons including a theologian-priest, Father Janusz Balicki, an excellent newsletter and a lot of literature flow throughout

Archbishop Tadeusz Goclowski of Gdansk receives "Precious Feet" from me.

the country. The center's trained NFP teachers and general pro-life workers came from various Eastern European countries, including Russia, where, as I have mentioned, we now have a Moscow branch. Most helpful have been the printer Pawel Wosicki and, of course, all the bishops, who are totally cooperative and appreciative of what we do.

Our literature has been placed in every one of Poland's many seminaries, where our organization Seminarians for Life also flourishes. And the Pope is very much aware of our past and present activities in his native land.

Next we launched into Lithuania, where we have put on two

A pro-life prayer walk in expiation for the sin of abortion in Lithuania. See the small coffin at the right to be buried.

national conferences with delegates from the neighboring countries of Latvia and Estonia. In Lithuania we snuffed out a proposed horrendous sex-education program the government was about to embrace at the urging of International Planned Parenthood Federation (IPPF). On this trip, after conducting sessions in Vilnius and the seminary in Kaunas, our team moved on to Grodno in Belarus, where I addressed the seminary on two occasions and, with Marijo Zivkovic, a meeting of Communist doctors, who at that time did not know what to think of Comrade Gorbachev. The following year HLI sponsored a weekend conference in Grodno, with the full cooperation of Bishop Aleksander Kaszkiewicz. While all forms of birth control are used to produce a non-reproductive birthrate, sterilization is fairly rare.

Of late, Lithuania's Catholic bishops have expressed their concern at signs of the country's moral decline, such as alcoholism, drug abuse, sexual promiscuity, organized crime, abortion, and the declining birthrate. The most commonly used means of birth control is the IUD, routinely fitted after childbirth. Strangely sterilization is minimal. In a national statement the bishops advised the faithful to vote for politicians who respect human life and dignity from conception to natural death, freedom of religion, conscience, the promotion of moral values, and an educational system that allows courses in religion and ethics.

In 1991, on one of my last missions in Poland, I spoke to some 250

A seminary in Kaunas, Lithuania which I addressed.

About to address seminarians in Belarus.

seminarians, all of them dressed up in black cassocks or suits—no slacks, shorts, or overalls such as one might find in an American seminary these days. It was quite a sight to behold, these future priests so intent on learning all about the anti-life movement from contraception through euthanasia. I feared I would never see this vision again. But two months later I did—in Nigeria, where on the first round of talks I was granted the heartwarming experience of seeing 480 major seminarians in white cassocks, the faculty in front seats, and an archbishop introducing me!

Sneaking into Cuba, 1995.

CUBA

For years Magaly Llaguno, head of our international pro-life center in Miami—which, as I have noted, works exclusively in Latin America and other Spanish-speaking countries—has been sending pro-life literature and audiovisual aids to Cuba, her home country. She has accomplished this feat through use of the Vatican's diplomatic pouch and in other clever ways. In various countries of Latin America I have met pro-life Cubans here and there, and have worked through them insofar as possible.

During the week of 9-16 July 1995, I spent a week in Cuba helping to lay the groundwork for a national pro-life movement. I spoke twice at a week-long pro-life training seminar. Arrangements for this amazing meeting of young people were made by an HLI branch, the Asociacion Defensa de la Vida of Costa Rica under the leadership of Prof. Alejandro Leal and Drs. Hector and Conchita Morales, HLI coordinators for Cuba. Six of Cuba's eight dioceses sent delegates; Cardinal Jaime Ortega y Alamino of Havana offered moral and financial support. And indeed, out of this historic gathering Pro Vida d'Cuba, a Catholic pro-life national organization, emerged.

The once beautiful city of Havana, numbering more than 2,000,000 people, sustains an estimated 35,000 "ladies of the night," many of whom lined the dark road we took from airport to hotel. The city itself is one big semi-slum, more or less unlit at night. The country is like a gigantic prison, from which tens of thousands, including doctors, lawyers and academics, have fled in flimsy boats and rafts. Many

Cubans have drowned in the waters between Cuba and Florida, turning this area into the largest cemetery in the world. More than 400,000 Cubans, however, have successfully fled to the United States.

For generations, tourists sought sun, sand, sin, and sex in Cuba. A sex capital much like Bangkok, Havana used to be called the Brothel of the Americas. And after at first shutting down prostitution, Castro has started it up all over again in his desperate need for tourists and their money.

Thanks to the almost continuous social turmoil, pirating, exploitation, rebellions, and revolutions, the Catholic Church has never been strong in Cuba. In the past, people complained that the Church was too closely identified with the rich. Whether that charge was true or false, Castro accused her of educating mostly the children of the wealthy and doing little for the poor, whose education and medical care his system tried to foster, with limited success. In 1959, when the Reds seized power, there were some 1,000 priests and 3,000 nuns; today there are about 230 priests and 1,000 nuns. It remains to be seen how the Cubans will mob the Pope, who has demanded and received from Castro unlimited movement during his upcoming visit.

Speaking with Castro's guards in Havana.

With Cardinal Jaime Ortega of Havana.

Fidel Castro once quoted Lenin's famous thesis that the way to take over a country is to destroy its morality. Castro has done a good job of that! In such an environment it is not easy to do pro-life work, and yet we were amazed at the number of young people who came out of their poverty to learn to resist the anti-life/anti-family culture.

As early as 1940, Cuban courts allowed abortion for rape and alleged danger to the mother's life; divorce became legal at the same time. Today, getting a divorce is easy and dissolutions are rampant. In 1965, Planned Parenthood (PP), known as Sociedad Cubana de Demografica, persuaded the Reds to legalize abortion-on-demand.

In 1991 the Ministry of Public Health admitted that 78.4 surgical abortions were performed for every 100 pregnancies, by far the highest in the Americas. Many Cubans use the abortifacient Pill, Norplant, Depo Provera, the IUD, and the "Morning-After Pill." Cuba is the first developing country to authorize use of the RU-486 abortion pill. Besides recording one of the world's highest abortion rates, Cuba has surely achieved Latin America's lowest birthrate: 1.9 children per family, not enough for national population replacement (needed, 2.2).

During my week in Havana, I did not see even five babies, nor five obviously pregnant women. The National Center for Sex Education, something like the United States' infamous Sex Information and Education Council (SIECUS), promotes irresponsible sex and unlimited eroticism, facilitates premarital sex, and offers "menstrual extraction" or surgical abortion in cases of contraceptive failure. This governmental policy has devastated Cuban youth and the family. Together, the National Center for Sex Education and the Cuban

Society for the Defense of the Family control all matters of sexual morality, marriage, family life, youth work, and so forth. It has infected Cuban family life with all the venom that Marxist atheism can produce. The young people at our seminar told me that most young women do not even envision a loving boyfriend-girlfriend relationship without fornication. Sterilization, too, is widespread, but because of *machismo* doctors, it is performed mostly on women.

The last National Fertility Survey showed, among other horrible statistics, that one-third of young women aged 15-19 have surgically aborted at least one baby. Cuba was the first country in the world to transplant the brains of aborted babies in an attempt to cure Alzheimer's disease; foreigners come for these "treatments" and for abortions, putting welcome cash into Castro's coffers.

Mother Teresa started a small convent to help children and sick people. When she gave Castro a miraculous medal, he told her that, if the Reds labored as hard as her sisters, it would be a better world. In this horrendous moral climate and inhuman culture of death, HLI's heroic pro-lifers work for the good of love and life.[9]

---

[9] See the writer's pamphlet *A Pro-Life Missionary in Castro's Cuba* (Gaithersburg, MD: Human Life International, 1995).

CHAPTER 9

Further Journeyings

UNITED KINGDOM

n 1972, when Phyllis Bowman, then head of the Society for the Protection of Unborn Children (SPUC) in Great Britain, invited me to do a lecture tour in the United Kingdom, you could still get out the crowds on the abortion issue. I remember addressing some 1,700 in the city of Preston and showing the stunned audience that demonstration film in which Dorothy Kerslake—an English doctor—killed five babies by abortion. I spoke in various other cities and then celebrated Christmas in Scotland.

About the last thing the British needed was a permissive abortion law, since their birthrate was already low. But the international, imperialistic birth-controllers had to persuade England to relax its law so that the forty countries in the British Commonwealth of Nations would follow suit. Indeed, India did follow the leader in the early 1970s, and others fell into line behind her.

I was on a second working tour in England when *Roe v. Wade* was issued on 22 January 1973. As already explained, I had two thoughts: (1) as a nation we have seen our best days; (2) now we are on a slippery slope; things will get worse fast. All I've seen and experienced in ninety-one countries since then confirms my conviction.

In the 1980s Father Joseph Lyons accompanied me through four hospices for dying patients, including the first, St. Christopher's. The British have pioneered the development of these places where people go to spend their last days, to die in peace. Some of the dying say their stay at the hospice turned out to be one of the best times of their lives. A hospice's aim is to make the patient comfortable, control his pain, leave him rational and aware. Everything is done to keep life as normal as possible. Thus little shopping carts come by weekly for women

The tireless Dr. Peggy Norris of the United Kingdom and I during a radio call-in show.

to do what they did all their lives—shop. In one such hospice the patients can see school children playing outside. Teenagers come to visit. Clergy are always at their service. I asked again and again whether it was true that the staff can control all pain. "Yes," was the consistent answer: "if we get to it in time." Masters at palliative care, they use a regimen of drugs to still pain, including the illegal (in this country) heroin. Again and again hospice experts moaned that doctors are not trained in palliative care. Nor need anyone die in pain, I was assured. For a doctor every patient's death is a defeat. Medical personnel must be trained to handle the last phase of life—but never to be a part of euthanasia. Incidentally, Father Lyons started his own hospice in Leeds, which I also visited later.

GREECE

*I*n 1959, I went to Athens to give a week-long series of presentations on the family to Air Force chaplains stationed in Europe. My stay in this beautiful city stretched to fifteen days. I had many long conversations with an American gynecologist who was taking

*With Archbishop
Nikolaos Foskolos
of Athens.*

care of American women at the air base. He told me that the chief gynecological problem in Greece was the miscarriages due to the many previous abortions.

Almost twenty years later, on a second working visit, I learned that the birthrate in Greece was below replacement level and that abortion was very common in this nation of eleven million people. I remember how shocked Archbishop Nikolaos Foskolos was when he saw my films. In fact, I gave him one. Although I found no pro-life effort in existence, two bishops did express their willingness to organize some kind of pro-life program. One Roman Catholic bishop had organized a lecture tour for me on his island; unfortunately, airline problems made it impossible. A bishop told me that where an Orthodox priest and wife had the care of an island, women were afraid to go to Confession because of fear the priest would talk to his wife. My pro-life efforts with Franciscan Father Dennis Lambiris failed, and I never found time to return to the friendly Greeks. My travel agent's failure to include a visa to India prevented my attending the Second International Federation of Right to Die Society's convention.

IRELAND

*I*n 1969 the Irish Family Planning Association (IFPA) moved in to lobby for contraception and, of course, eventually and inevitably

At Our Lady of Knock Shrine in Ireland, 1992.

for abortion. Today IFPA is one of 140 tentacles of that worldwide baby/youth/family/church-destroying octopus known as the International Planned Parenthood Federation (IPPF).

During my first lecture tour in Ireland in 1972, I went to see Dublin's Archbishop Dermot Ryan to alert him to the devious schemes of IFPA—describing how they first work to introduce contraception and then move on to abortion. The archbishop would hear none of it: "Ireland is Catholic, Father," was his response. "Abortion? Unthinkable." Later in the conversation he admitted that contraception—then illegal— *might be a future danger.*

I described how I had seen IPPF connive and plot in thirty countries, always starting with contraception, then introducing explicit sex "education" and then infiltrating the government's health and education departments—and finally, ever so subtly, promoting abortion. This gracious, recently appointed archbishop, a Scripture scholar, recognized no such dangers. He refused to accept the documentation I hesitantly tried to hand him, and after a half-hour's conversation he courteously saw me to the door. I remember my thought: "Your Grace, you will see the day."

To his credit, a few years later he did see the dangers and reacted commendably. Eventually he became head of the Congregation for the

Evangelization of Peoples in Rome. If he had not collapsed and died in St. Peter's Basilica, I am sure he would have helped HLI financially. Twice in the 1970s that Congregation, then known as the Society for the Propagation of the Faith and placed under the leadership of Cardinal Simon Lourdusamy, had helped our international pro-life/pro-family missionary work with two $30,000 grants.

I recall speaking during that lecture tour to a Catholic high school in Cork conducted by nuns who at first were reluctant to allow me to show films. I assured them that the girls would be quite capable of digesting what they were about to hear and see—one suction abortion on film plus a set of slides with comments. After the program, several girls came up to tell me that they knew of classmates who had already gone to England for abortions! I recall, too, the Christian Brothers refusing me permission to speak at their high school in Cork. I was under attack from the Irish press, which had made me out to be some kind of dangerous monster, and apparently the Brothers were afraid I would contaminate their tender boys. The headmaster at the Benedictine Glenstal Abbey School grudgingly allowed me to speak the next year to his high school boys—then wondered afterward why he had hesitated.

Soon the anti-life forces in Ireland, through vicious propaganda, clever legislative moves, and court challenges, succeeded in legalizing contraception, at first for the married and eventually for singles too, with a few restrictions that soon vanished. I had become a prophet!

During one of several working tours, I was scheduled to lecture at Ireland's then-large national seminary of Maynooth, where the dissenting Father Enda McDonagh—the Father Charles Curran of Ireland—taught. A few days before the event, my appearance was abruptly canceled. My host, the engineer John O'Reilly, took the case to the rector, the future Archbishop of Dublin, Father Kevin McNamara, who reversed the decision immediately. During my presentation I showed slides of healthy babies who had been aborted and a film depicting abortion by suction. Six seminarians fainted almost simultaneously! To this day I don't know whether this incident was faked or real. In any case, it did not faze the future Archbishop of Dublin, who gratefully congratulated me and then treated me to crumpets and tea (and something a little stronger). I recall his remark: "When people see an actual abortion on film and no one faints, then we are indeed in a bad way."

Twice in subsequent years the Irish beat back, by referendum, attempts to authorize abortion. HLI went all out to educate the Irish nation against such legalized baby-killing. We poured in much pro-life literature; we even brought over Dr. Bernard Nathanson, as you may remember my noting, to warn the Irish. But the wording of the 1983 referendum left a tiny loophole; later court decisions and another referendum in 1992 made it legal to obtain abortions in England and to peddle abortion "information" in Ireland, although they prevented the legalization of abortion in Ireland itself. Sadly, the bishops could not come up with a common strategy on the three-point referendum and let each prelate decide how to oppose this subtly worded bill.

Today, the abortifacient Pill and sterilization are the chief means of birth prevention in Ireland. Last year Dr. Jane Quinlan, who for years taught Natural Family Planning (NFP) in Cork, wrote the manual *How to Get Pregnant*. She told me the number of sterile women is going up, thanks to the Pill, venereal (now "sexually transmitted"!) disease and so on. Today Ireland's birthrate is barely at replacement level. Depending on whose numbers you accept, between 1,500 and 4,000 Irish girls go to England yearly to have their preborn babies killed. The abortionists assert that abortion is safer than pregnancy. This, of course, is totally false. Ireland has the world's lowest infant and maternal death rate. In other words, it is the safest country in the world in which to have a baby, in spite of its low incidence of abortion. So much for the abortionists and their phony statistics!

The Irish defeated the legalization of divorce in a referendum by a margin of 67.6 percent on 28 July 1986, only to approve it by 5,000 votes in a second referendum in 1996. Each time HLI was involved, although often unobtrusively.

From my first days in the Green Isle, I helped those who were trying to foster NFP; they were receiving little episcopal and pastoral encouragement, although tax money was available for this undertaking. Particularly active were Mavis Keniry, Noreen Ryan, and Sister Maureen O'Sullivan. Once I addressed the National Association of the Ovulation Method in Cork. But NFP has never taken significant root. In fact, the Catholic Marriage Advisory Council (CMAC), funded by both Church and State and now known as ACCORD (trying to get rid of the "Catholic" connection?), has not consistently upheld *Humanae Vitae*. CMAC/ACCORD is nationally involved in marriage preparation courses. In the 1970s I tried to organize a national seminar with CMAC to promote NFP, abortion resistance and orthodoxy. No go.

During my seven lecture tours in Ireland, good Irish parents and priests have assured me that, just as in the United States, Catholic education has more or less collapsed, as young people in "Catholic" schools no longer learn their faith. An Irish father put it bluntly: "In primary schools they learn nothing; in secondary schools they discuss it." This is a Western world problem. Two years ago a lay group published the Irish equivalent of the question/answer *Baltimore Catechism*. It is selling briskly. Home schooling has begun—perhaps because sex ed has invaded.

Radical feminism has infected the women's religious communities over the past ten years; their vocations are declining, although most Irish nuns still are attired in recognizable garb. Twice I made presentations to the Irish Medical Missionaries in Drogheda, whose great medical and nursing work I have witnessed in Africa. My reward: crumpets and tea (this time without any stronger element).

Reflecting the feminist mania, all major beaches in mainland Europe now allow topless bathing, and the Irish are actually debating it! The argument: Toplessness would increase tourism and prove the Irish are European. (Starting a child-prostitution industry like Thailand's would increase tourism, too; is nothing more important than money?)

For forty years *Playboy* magazine was forbidden in Ireland; today the leftist government lets it poison minds and ruin lives. As in other countries, the Irish—North and South—suffer from faulty sex education, an abundance of theological confusion, and their share of pedophilia cases and priest/episcopal scandals. The clergy in Northern Ireland impressed me. For priest and laity, suffering and persecution can be great reminders of being truly Christian.

Today Ireland is fast becoming a highly secularized society. In no other country of the world that I have visited have I seen such vicious attacks on the Church by a public press and electronic media intent on exploiting every chance to downgrade Catholicism. In four national symposia, I learned from multiple participants that many Catholics are discouraged, feeling utterly helpless as bishops and priests fail to lead, the media have turned against Catholics, Catholic schools are losing their character, and now parents are faced with offensive sex education for their children.

Bribed with £6 million to join the corrupt European Union (EU), Ireland no longer stands unique as a Catholic bastion among the nations of Europe. And one can see the crumbling process by examining government documents that propose that the Irish constitution should no longer defend the Gaelic (Irish) language as the nation's official language, affirm that the six British-held Irish counties are Irish, mention Jesus, or acknowledge dependence on God. Further, the enemies call the Irish charter "overly Roman Catholic and nationalist" and urge "censoring out the words *Almighty God*" and the passage

> In the name of the Most Holy Trinity, from Whom is all authority and to Whom, as our final end, all actions both of men and states must be referred, we the people of Eire, humbly acknowledging all our obligations to our Divine Lord, Jesus Christ, Who sustained our fathers through centuries of trials . . . do hereby adopt, enact and give to ourselves this Constitution.

Thus the Irish secular-humanist liberals, starting with super-liberal President Mary Robinson, try to impose *their* ideology on official documents, imagining that what they propose is real and good and right.[1]

GERMANY

*A*fter not speaking German for thirty years, I began to work in Germany, Austria and Switzerland, starting in 1973, and felt obliged to try my hand—my tongue, that is—at the most commonly spoken language in Europe. I clearly remember engaging in dialogue

---

[1]   Clement Loscher, *The X Case* (Gaithersburg, MD: Human Life International, 1992). Paul Marx, *The Apostle of Life* (Gaithersburg, MD: Human Life International, 1991), pp. 91-101; see back issues of HLI's *Special Reports* for periodic news items on Ireland.

and talk shows with my limping German. My authentic German accent—honed in Wright County, Minnesota—did not compensate for a struggling performance. Still, these experiences, horrendous as they seemed to me, were the source of some merriment for the audiences, and I really should not feel too unhappy about them. I recall once "entertaining" a group of German priests on NFP with my limping German at Königstein.

Speaking in Germany.

Guiding me through Bavaria was a school teacher, Josef Kramer, who lined up many lecture opportunities in the 1970s, mostly in Bavaria, the most Catholic area of Germany. Working out of Kramer's home, I spent weeks giving speeches, showing slides and sometimes films. Sometimes I teamed up with Dr. Siegfried Ernst, the wonderful pro-life Lutheran leader.

Despite the existence of films showing an actual abortion ("Abortion: A Woman's Decision,") and depicting the developing child from conception through natural birth ("The First Days of Life"), the Germans were hard to awaken to the coming realities of baby-killing in the 1970s. I recall sitting in the German Parliament in 1975 and listening to long debates featuring the same lies, arguments, and insults one could hear everywhere.

There was little pro-life literature in Germany then. Individual persons, above all Dr. Ernst, were doing what they could here and there. In 1979 Walter Ramm founded *Aktion Leben* (Action Life), which grew into the largest organized pro-life group in Germany with the later help of Father Otto Maier, SAC.

I remember working in the 1970s with Rüdiger Dürr in Braunschweig and Dr. Hedwig Selentag in Augsburg; the latter had me slide-lecturing and showing films in other German cities for her group, *Lebens Recht für Alle* (ALFA), which has preoccupied itself with surgical abortion, like our National Right to Life Committee.

Father Anthony Zimmerman, SVD, and I once spent hours at the Frankfort airport with Monsignor Vinzenz Platz, highly stationed in the German Catholic episcopal bureaucracy, discussing a possible conference on NFP with the intention of starting a movement in Germany. Platz resisted the idea. Unfortunately, nothing came of our efforts.

In the mid-seventies I met the most brilliant German woman in the abortion fight in my experience, Frau Elisabet Backhaus of Münster, with whom I am still carrying on the longest correspondence of anyone I know in Europe. She still is the greatest source of information and acute observation; she wrote some of the finest pieces against the anti-lifers, pointed items that went also straight to the bishops. My saved correspondence with her will be a treasure trove for some future scholar who will be interested in researching how legal abortion came to Germany and how liberal theologians prepared the way while the Church leaders—both Catholic and Evangelical—more or less failed their people. According to reputable German Catholic sources, the bishops' foreign Catholic Aid Program ("Bischofliche Hilswerk, Misereor") centered in Aachen is sending condoms into developing nations afflicted with AIDS. Formerly they supported NFP programs.

The West German hierarchy's (not the hierarchy of the former East Germany) dissent to *Humanae Vitae* has had enormous tragic consequences for Germany, today a very dying nation with more coffins than cradles, as the blunt Germans say it. After bad national legislation and Supreme Court decisions, united Germany has abortion virtually on request.[2] In Germany abortion is illegal but not punished if the pregnant

---

[2]   French demographer Pierre Chaunu wrote in 1985: "Since 1964—the take-off point for most European countries—we have arrived at a process of reproductive collapse never seen before in history.... From a gradual death we are moving to an instantaneous death: Germany is dead; its situation is non-reversible (1.2 children per German woman, while an average of 2.1 children per woman is necessary to replace a generation). How is this implosion, this destruction, explained? The most blame apparently can be assigned to the contraceptive revolution which started in 1960" (*France Catholique*

Here I am with copies of Dr. Bernard Nathanson's Der Stille Schrei *("The Silent Scream"), a pro-life movie that has saved countless unborn lives.*

Ecclesia, no. 1988 [1985], pp. 3-4). See also Pierre Chaunu, *Die ver-hütete Zukunft* (Stuttgart: Seewald Verlag, 1979). For repeated reports on Germany see the following monthly *Special Reports* of Human Life International: "German Theologians Revolting Once Again," SR #110 (Feb. 1994) p. 6-9; "The 50th Anniversary of Auschwitz," SR #124 (Apr. 1995), p. 2; "I Shall Crush Christianity," SR #124 (Apr. 1995), p. 2-3; "Catholic and Nazi Crimes," SR #124 (Apr. 1995), p. 3; "Not Enough Rescuers," SR #124 (Apr. 1995), pp. 3-5; "The Abortion Holocaust: Today's Final Solution," SR #124 (Apr. 1995), pp. 5-7; "How Germany's Bishops Rejected *Humanae Vitae*," SR #127 (July 1995), p. 6; "A Cardinal's Brave Resistance," SR #127 (July 1995), p. 6-7; "The Mind of the Dissenter," SR #127 (July 1995), p. 7; "Loyal Bishop's Pastoral Suppressed?" SR #127 (July 1995), pp. 7-8; "Shepherds Bless a Death Potion," SR #127 (July 1995), p. 8; "Dire Predictions Proven Right," SR #127 (July 1995), pp. 8-9; "A Cardinal Admits His Error," SR #127 (July 1995), p. 9; "Bishops Involved in German Abortions," SR #130 (Oct. 1995), pp. 4-5; "Kiss Germany Goodbye," SR #130 (Oct. 1995), p. 5; "Theologians Destroy a Nation," SR #130 (Oct. 1995), pp. 5-6; "False Shepherds at Work," SR #130 (Oct. 1995), p. 6; "Diabolical Attacks on Christ," SR #130 (Oct. 1995), pp. 6-7; "Revolution in the Pews," SR #130 (Oct. 1995); p. 7. See also the following books by Paul Marx, published by Human Life International: *Confessions of a Prolife Missionary*, pp. 20-21, 34, 40-41, 52-54, 69-70, 87-91, 114-117, 122-124, 142-143, 155-156, 169-170, 182-183, 262-263; *Fighting for Life*, pp. 46-55, 128; *The Apostle of Life*, pp. 10-12, 15-28.

mother submits to government-sponsored-and-paid counseling and then presents a document as proof of such counseling. Despite papal warnings, the bishops are involved in the process, except Archbishop Johannes Dyba of Fulda, who has called the whole procedure "a license to kill," and his people counsel for life. Strangely, *Pro Familia* (Planned Parenthood) and Chancellor Helmut Kohl are anxious to keep the Church in counseling. For this the Catholic Church allegedly receives 16 million Deutschmarks annually. Today less than 10 percent of Catholic Germans attend Mass regularly. As more Germans drop out of the Catholic Church, the latter receives less and less church tax.

AUSTRIA

*D*uring the years 1974-75 my guide in Austria, the photographer and anti-pornography activist Martin Humer, arranged some sixty lectures, always presented with films and slides. In fact, while I was in Austria lecturing in 1975, the socialist government gave the Austrians abortion on demand in the first three months of pregnancy. Today some 150,000 preborn babies are murdered by surgical abortion yearly in this dying nation of eight million people.

Yours truly and Fr. Johannes Gruner with his delegation from Austria.

One evening in Austria sticks in my memory. When I had finished a long evening of slides with commentary and films on intrauterine life, the good pastor of the parish told me in German, "When you die, you will go straight to heaven, and 50,000 babies will be crawling all over you." "But will I have to diaper them?" I inquired. "No," he said, "not in heaven."

Humer's incredible activities succeeded in destroying millions of dollars worth of pornography at the border with Germany, which is Europe's largest producer of porn. Of course, he has many enemies; their attacks on him have made him the

Martin Humer, my Austrian friend, with Harry John and Dr. Herb Ratner.

best-known citizen in Austria. His pro-life/pro-family organization, *Europäischer Bürgerinitiativen* (European Citizens' Initiatives), has done much in German-speaking countries to save the unborn and to promote family life.

One afternoon in 1974 I spoke to some thirty nurses in a hospital in Braunau, where Adolf Hitler was born. With the Austrian Parliament debating abortion, I was astonished at how little these nurses knew about what would soon descend upon them. But really, that was the situation almost everywhere in Europe. When I finished my lecture, an old nun toddled up to me to say that, during Hitler's time, abortions were done in this Catholic hospital.

The marvelous French geneticist, Dr. Jerome Lejeune, my great friend and collaborator, gave me this account, which he insisted was true: One evening two babies were delivered by a Jewish doctor in this hospital in Braunau. The one baby was a vigorous, healthy boy, the other a frail girl, a victim of Down's Syndrome. The doctor followed the two through life. The girl survived to take care of her mother; the boy became Adolf Hitler.

SWITZERLAND

Many times in the 1970s and 1980s I lectured and showed my slides and films in beautiful Switzerland. Two of my guides were Ramon and Elizabet Granges, who are still active in that country.

Lecturing with the famous Dr. Siegfried Ernst in Switzerland.

I remember meeting several times a most interesting retired gynecologist, Mueller by name, who had a small office not far from the railway station in Zürich. (Every Swiss medical professor must do some practice of his specialty in order to stay in touch.) Off the train would come French girls and others asking him to kill their babies. Of course, he steadfastly refused, but he would sit them down and talk to them. I distinctly recall his telling me about his last case: A French lady just off the train from Paris, dressed in an expensive fur coat, demanded of him, "I need an abortion; I'm going on vacation; I want this thing away," pointing to her uterus.

I participated in conferences with Dr. Ernst and others at Bonaventure Myer's large catechetical center outside Zürich, where I met good Swiss doctors and others terribly concerned about checking the abortion advance. But success was not to be theirs. Abortion-on-demand in the first three months of pregnancy, and even later for other reasons, was legalized after a long, drawn-out fight in the 1980s. The battle for abortion had actually begun as early as 1916.[3] Currently medical students must learn to do abortions and other immoral operations in Swiss medical schools. As in England, this will severely reduce the number of pro-life gynecologists in Switzerland.

Today the rich Swiss employ well over 1,000,000 foreign workers

---

[3]   Bill Rolston and Anne Eggert (eds.), *Abortion in New Europe* (Westport, CT., and London: Greenwood Press, 1994), pp. 253-265. This volume is interesting in its revelation of the questionable groups fighting for the legalization of pro-born baby-killing.

in this nation of 6,400,000 that claims a dangerously low birthrate and the highest number of AIDS victims in Europe. If, as the Swiss have admitted to me, the foreign workers were to walk out of the country, the whole economy would collapse.

The Church in Switzerland, materially wealthy, is bedeviled with serious problems. Homosexuality is rife. Two years ago the recently appointed young bishop of Basel resigned after fathering a child. About five years ago, Bishop Wolfgang Haas of Chur had to step over protesting bodies to be installed in his cathedral. He has reformed the seminary, vigorously promoted orthodoxy, and attracted half of all the major seminarians in the country. Father Welch and I briefly addressed them in 1996. At this writing all other Swiss bishops have requested the Pope to remove Bishop Haas. Strangely, none of this controversy has appeared in the press.

In the 1980s I attended the most interesting Fifth International Symposium on Prenatal Psychology in Basel. Ironic: All of Europe was talking about permissive abortion while participants at this meeting were discussing the psychology of unborn babies and their reaction to external stimuli. Here I met for the first time the famous German embryologist Dr. Erich Blechschmidt, an eloquent defender of the unborn. Blechschmidt created the world-famous array of the developing

Here with some beautiful Swiss children.

human embryos in astonishing detail at the museum in the German
University of Göttingen. When a pro-abortion IPPF participant challenged Bleschschmidt's proof of the origin and development of human
life from fertilization onward, this German demolished him with typical German scholarship!

ISRAEL

I don't remember how I originally contacted Rabbi Mordechai
Blanck, who founded EFRAT (Society for the Advancement of
Childbearing), a tiny group of orthodox Jews trying to fight abortion
and raise the Jewish birthrate. Perhaps I learned of him through my
good Jewish friend and collaborator Dr. Kenneth Mitzner, a valiant
pro-life aerospace engineer working in California. Mitzner founded
the League against Neo-Hitlerism around 1970 to fight abortion. He
founded several other similar groups and was always a willing partner
in the defense of the unborn. Mitzner boldly exposed Jews who were
promoting abortion in high places. Thus, he informed me that the four
chief organizers of NARAL (National Association for the Reform of
Abortion Laws; now National Abortion Rights and Reproductive
Action League) were Jewish. More on this point later.

Rabbi Mordechai Blanck was shocked by the number of abortions
in Israel; he told me that the Knesset (parliament) had actually discussed the very real possibility of Israeli Arabs' voting the Jews out of
their own parliament in the foreseeable future because of a Jewish
birthrate that was low in comparison with that of the Arabs. For this
and other reasons Rabbi Blanck founded EFRAT, which has experienced remarkable growth under the subsequent leadership of Rabbi
Suleiman. I gave the good Rabbi Blanck much literature and bought
one piece of his for distribution in the United States.

In my visit to Israel in the 1970s, I was surprised to learn that some
medical professionals were convinced that active euthanasia was
inevitable. "In fact," one assured me, "it is going on already."

At this writing there are about 40,000 legal abortions annually in
Israel, which has a population of 5,050,850 (1994 estimate) in a land
area of 8,019 square miles. Even so, the Israelis have a higher birthrate

than any country in Western Europe. That may be due, in part, to the many Jews that have come to Israel from various countries, particularly Russia. Women soldiers in the Israeli army, by the way, are allowed payment for two abortions a year.

TURKEY AND IRAN

On leaving Bucharest, where I had attended the First World Population Conference in 1974, I embarked on a worldwide tour. Once again I put my life in danger by flying the reportedly unsafe Aeroflot, this time to Turkey and Iran—both Moslem countries. I spent three days each in Istanbul and Teheran, observing conditions with former students but finding little opportunity to do pro-life work.

Istanbul, Turkey, 1974.

Teheran, Iran, 1974.

THAILAND

y next stop was Bangkok, Thailand. Here Dr. Mana Boonkhanphol, head of St. Louis Hospital, had arranged a week's lectures. Among my targets were two huge Catholic high schools run by the Sylvestrian Brothers. My films and slides surely were eye-openers for these young men, who were excellently behaved

and were enrolled in a good religious-education program, so far as I could ascertain. One night one of the enterprising brothers showed me the town; I saw more than I should have!

It was also inspiring to speak at several high schools run by devoted nuns; the students came from wealthy homes, judging from the Cadillacs I saw outside the

In Buddhist Thailand, 1974.

school at the end of the day. These beautiful young ladies accorded me a polite, intelligent reception, even if I could not tell what they really thought.

The major seminary was filled with students. The Jesuits, with whom I stayed, made sure I would see all things Buddhist, since Thailand is the most Buddhist country in the world. Still, I am always impressed by the number of wonderfully Catholic doctors and other professional people one meets in these countries with a small Catholic population. These doctors arranged for me to speak to the staff of the medical school in Bangkok.

Here I had a unique experience. The doctors seemed very favorable to what I was saying until the question-and-answer period, when one woman told me point-blank that she didn't agree with me. I asked her to explain her objections. She said she didn't think that abortion killed a human being—this comment coming after I had carefully explained life's beginning at fertilization and constantly developing until natural death. The baby, I had emphasized, is no more human after birth than before, since humanity is an either/or proposition. (Remember Dr. Lejeune's "kangarooity"?) This was scientific fact, not religion.

After a certain amount of to-and-fro exchanges, I asked

Flirting with the elephants in Thailand.

her when she thought life began. There was a long pause, some hemming and hawing; finally she said, "Birth." "Well," said I, "usually the head comes first; now suppose the head is out—is it human? Let us say most of the body is out, but buttocks and feet are still in—is it human? When in the birth process does whatever it is become human?" Of course, this is the old argument of *reductio ad absurdum*. During the altercation, my medical audience chuckled, since they were mostly on my side. Later I found out that the doctor who had accosted me fitted IUDs and was a secret abortionist.

In 1960 an average Thai woman had 7 children; today, 1.8, although 2.3 is the replacement level in Thailand. In no other country of the world has the population structure changed so dramatically, thanks to Planned Parenthood and government policies. Today there is a shortage of workers in this economically booming country. The Ministry of Health reports 700,000 people with HIV. There are at least 500,000 foreign workers and ever more brothels. The government of this fast-aging nation has no choice; to survive, it must drastically change its family-planning policies. Although abortion is against the law, there is much illegal killing of preborn babies.

With Dr. Mana Boonkhanphol of Thailand and Mrs. Enni Banda of Zambia.

TAIWAN

*M*y next stop was Taipei. Here I met the woman who headed the Chinese Family Planning Association. She arranged any number of contacts and interviews for me. She was not a Catholic and was enthusiastic about contraception but totally opposed to abortion. I recall how shocked she was when I told her that the so-called contraceptive birth-control Pill was really an abortifacient. I have long ago forgotten her name, and she never did know mine. (Given sensitivities and political realities, my sponsors changed my name from "Marx" to "Mar.")

She knew the president of the Taiwanese National TV Broadcasting Company. She told me that she would introduce me to him, and because he was a Catholic I should really push for time on his network, reminding him that as a Catholic he surely had responsibilities before God to save the unborn from abortion and to inform people about the truth of this sordid facet of life.

As though it happened yesterday, I hear her saying, "Really push him hard; demand time. He is a good man, and if you insist forcefully, he will give you time." I prayed on the way to the TV station to say the right thing in the right way forcefully, as had been recommended by my solicitous guide.

In front of me in his swank office sat the chief mogul of the Taiwanese TV Broadcasting Company. After the usual courteous preliminaries, I really poured it on. I told him that if he did not give me TV time, the Lord would surely ask him why when he got to the pearly gates. He peered and peered at me with those intense Chinese eyes and showed me an inscrutable face that seemed to reveal more questions than answers. But I must have said the right thing—with the right force—because he finally said, "Yes, I'll give you fifteen minutes."

So for fifteen minutes I spoke to the whole nation about abortion; I was even allowed to show pictures of aborted babies at various stages of development. The broadcast was live. I never heard what the reaction was. The producer told me that I had spoken to at least 600,000 people. But my guide was ecstatic, wondering—in spite of her earlier expressions of confidence—what magic words I had used to secure prime time for my unusual program.

My guide told me that she had repeatedly applied for an official charter from International Planned Parenthood Federation (IPPF) in London. They had refused her, just as repeatedly, and it was obvious to me that her lack of progress was due to her stand against abortion. (Remember: this was 1974.) She told me that she eventually went to New York to plead her case with Dr. Alan Guttmacher, who was the president of Planned Parenthood, and the noted statistician Christopher Tietze, who worked for Planned Parenthood and the Population Council. At first they tried to avoid speaking to her, but finally she got to see them; they told her that so long as she was not going to include abortion in her program, even in the future, no recommendation for a charter could be given. Again, remember the date: 1974, when comparatively few countries had legalized abortion. But note the unswerving intent, the evil foresight, and the methodical plans of the abortion juggernaut: IPPF. When mainland China finally opened up, IPPF was ready to move in, fully chartered. It has repeatedly approved the Chinese one-child family policy. It has nothing to say about the dying rooms in Chinese hospitals or about the abuse of women, for whom elsewhere it feigns solicitude.

I recall receiving a wonderful response to an illustrated lecture I gave to students and faculty at the Catholic University of Taipei. Here I helped write a statement to be circulated by the bishops, opposing abortion and supporting NFP.

Moving south, I visited the Benedictine community founded by St. Vincent's Archabbey; I did a program and stayed for a day or two before moving on to visit and do more programs for the Maryknollers, headed at that time by my former student Jim Collignon.

On the way back to Taipei by train, I had an interesting experience at Taichung. A priest was supposed to meet me. But no priest appeared. I had always wondered what it would be like to be plunked down in a country where you cannot speak the language, cannot read the signs, and cannot even make a telephone call. Well, I found out. I tried to talk to a number of people in English and German but got only a polite and kindly look. Vague benevolence, of course, did not solve my problem. Eventually I spied two men who obviously were not Chinese; to this day, I suspect they were Catholic priest-missionaries. I told them my dilemma and they offered to make a phone call to the Maryknoll parish where I was headed. Lo and behold, they found out for me that indeed a good padre had come to pick me up but, as it happened, he had been saying his Office in the car for the last hour! Well, at least here was a Maryknoller who said his Office, even though it was while I was desperately traipsing around trying to find a solution to my anguish.

The Maryknollers everywhere have been very cooperative with HLI. I recall meeting a priest who conducted a good NFP program. Later he and several nuns attended my international symposia in Collegeville. One benefit of all these travels was finding such pro-lifers who became the eventual beachheads of our worldwide ring of pro-life branches.

Today, with abortion legalized and births declining the Taiwanese government is urging people to have more babies, given the shortage of workers. At the present time, over sixty nations have non-replacement birthrates because of contraception, abortifacients, sterilization, and surgical abortion.

HONG KONG

*I*n Hong Kong I found the Chinese freely going to Red China for abortions. In the middle 1970s Mao no longer allowed a ration card for a third child. I heard many horror stories describing life in Red China, with its one million barefoot doctors, wholesale contraception, sterilization, and abortion, and with a food supply that was ample but of the poorest quality. I addressed two student groups and on a subsequent visit spoke to various adult audiences, who were fascinated to hear my worldwide accounts. Hong Kong has a remarkable Catholic school system, and there seemed to be much interest in NFP. How clever of the Pope to name the Archbishop of Hong Kong a cardinal so that he will have one in China when control of Hong Kong reverts to that country on 30 June 1997!

THE PHILIPPINES

*I*nto no other country of the world has HLI poured more money and materials than the Philippines, the only Catholic nation in the Orient. It all began in 1974 when I was showing "Abortion: A Woman's Decision" to 700 students in an auditorium on the campus of Benedictine San Beda College in Manila. Coming up to me in the dark while I was running the projector was tiny Sister Pilar Verzosa. Talk about providential meetings! She was the daughter of a medical family, a Sister of the Good Shepherd, living at the time with her colleagues in the slums. Through her, HLI has been able to sponsor some ten local and national pro-life meetings, with the full cooperation of the bishops, and especially of Cardinal Jaime Sin of Manila. The cardinal has always made available his "House of Sin," as he calls it for press conferences, and the like. Cardinal Ricardo Vidal of Cebu City also has been notably helpful. In 1995 Father Matthew Habiger, OSB, finalized plans for a large national HLI office in Manila, which is doing conferences and educational programs throughout Asia, where two-thirds of mankind reside.

In 1996, HLI sponsored a huge symposium for delegates from most

Launching my book A Pro-Life Missionary *in the Philippines.*

Asian countries. It also maintains a large base in Cebu City, headed by the indefatigable Dr. René Bullecer, whom I met in 1976. He talks to many thousands of students, medical people, and others every year, with the total collaboration of our great friend Cardinal Vidal, who has graciously given him a base for operations.

I myself, on several national working visits, spoke on many islands to students, seminarians, medical personnel, and others. On one island a pastor told me how in the hinterlands the United States Agency for International Development paid doctors for killing pre-born babies by suction machines operated by batteries. I recall my shock when I discovered a Planned Parenthood unit on the campus of the Catholic St. Sebastian University in Cebu City, run by the Society of the Divine Word missionaries. I did what I could to stop that outrage.[4]

---

[4]   In our monthly *Special Report* we repeatedly pointed out the dissent to *Humanae Vitae* and other errors in Father Karl Peschke's *Christian Ethics*, vol. 2. Peschke belongs to the Society of the Divine Word. Over time we asked repeatedly for this text to be corrected. This moral theology text is widely used, particularly in the seminaries of the developing world. In the text, also, Bernard Häring and Peschke maintain that abortion before fourteen days after conception/fertilization is really not abortion. For instance, the book quotes

Häring that direct abortion in rare cases is justifiable: thus Peschke concludes on page 363, "Consequently direct therapeutic abortion seems to be admissible . . . as long as it constitutes the lesser evil in terms of physical damage to health and life." That not only contradicts the observations of the best gynecologists we have consulted but also Pope Paul VI's *Declaration on Procured Abortion* of 1975. Peschke also goes for the idea that birth control is necessary in the light of overpopulation. There are other errors. Brought to the attention of the authorities of Rome, Peschke was removed from one school of theology. But the errors went on.

Further, the Society of the Divine Word province in Japan sponsored a pro-contraception booklet. In the 12/72 issue of the German Catholic family magazine *Stadt Gottes*, Father Bernhard Bronstrange, SVD, justifies in a typically belabored German way the Pill for the married. Seminarians in SVD seminaries we have addressed obviously bought the Peschke/Häring line of dissent to *Humanae Vitae*. We have pointed out other errors. Because we could not get results from SVD spokesmen like Father Thomas Krosnicki and others, we asked our readers to boycott the Society of the Divine Word financially. We ask the readers to check *Special Reports* nos. 89, 95, 99 and 105 for details.

Eventually the usual thing happened: Father Superior General Henry Barlage complained to Cardinal Jose Martinez, head of the *Congregatio pro Institutis Vitae Consecratae et Societatibus Vitae Apostolicae*, who complained to my superior about HLI's "allegations defamatory of the good name of that Society." We then wrote to Cardinal Martinez a total description and analysis of what we had actually published, with exhibits and proofs of errors. Apparently we won our case, because we never heard from him again. Any reader who wants to see our defense and our exposé, please send $5 to HLI. This will be very enlightening as to what has happened to Catholic theology over the last thirty years.

I should add that we work closely with a number of SVD missionaries in various parts of the world, among them Father Anthony Zimmerman, SVD. In fact, we published his *Catholic Teachings on Pro-Life Issues* to counter the bad Western moral theology seeping into the seminaries in the developing world. By and large, the Society of the Divine Word does great missionary work for the Church.

At the largest Catholic university in the world, the University of San Tomas in Manila, I addressed the students on "The Nature and Need of NFP," gave a memorial lecture to the medical school on "Modern Threats to Human Life," and received a commemorative plaque. The University's faculty has been most cooperative. In 1974 the fearless, clever Sister Pilar arranged to have me speak to the large staff of the Filipino Family Planning Association. They did not like what I said.

It was always hard to leave the thoroughly Catholic Filipinos, who have inherited the mission that the Irish used to have, namely, to bring Catholicism to the whole world. Travel where you may, you meet gentle Filipinos; they are faithful church-goers. That is all the more reason, says Father Matthew Habiger, that we must do the maximum for this interesting, exploited nation of sixty-five million people. The Philippines, with its marvelous hierarchy, is now our gateway to the rest of Asia, including China.

JAPAN

*J*n October 1974 I spent a month in Japan under the guidance of my energetic pro-life classmate, the moral theologian Father Anthony Zimmerman, SVD, who has done so much for this nation in his forty-nine years of teaching, writing and missionary work. Father Zimmerman once took me to see the Minister of Health, who spoke perfect English. I asked this official why the Japanese had never approved the Pill or IUD. I got a swift answer: "All medical studies in foreign countries show that Pill and IUD are a very bad medication and device, so far as health is concerned." After further conversation he made the astonishingly perceptive statement that to scatter the Pill through society is to invite a lot of intercourse among the unmarried, "and surely that isn't a good thing." Well in the post-*Humanae Vitae* era we have indeed learned that it is not a good thing, for many reasons!

Meanwhile, the *Mainichi Daily News* of 5 December 1996 headlined, "Government Keeping 'The Pill' Out of the Reach of Women." Researchers in this report insist that there are at least three times the official figure of 360,000 abortions per year in this nation of 125 million people, now fast dying out with only 1.4 children per family.

Here 77.7 percent of men use the condom—more proof that condom use does not reduce the incidence of abortion.

In Japan there is no euphemizing of abortion; the mind-set is fatalistic: "Yes, abortion kills a baby; this is to be regretted; it is wrong; it is not good; it is not right; one cannot help it, and so it has to be." Here over 80 percent of women have had at least one abortion and often more. One native Japanese nun, an obstetrical nurse, told me that she knew a woman who had had sixteen abortions.

With Father Zimmerman I traveled throughout Japan, visiting Nagasaki, Hiroshima, and other cities. To this day I am astounded at the number of people attending his symposia on Natural Family Planning, for which he "imported" Mother Teresa several times as speaker. She had to be given bodyguards to protect her from the huge crowds that would await her descent from the airplane and then mill around her alarmingly. At lectures, Father Zimmerman would tell the press and photographers they had five minutes to take pictures, after which he would ban them.

I have mentioned the occasion on which Mother Teresa addressed parliamentarians at a breakfast. Most members of the Diet were there. They gave her not only a standing ovation but also a huge collection for telling them, frankly but subtly, the truth about abortion. It was a clever speech that flattered Japanese efficiency even as it laid out the ugly truth about abortion. Mother Teresa has a way of encouraging people. Thus she wrote to us on 19 March 1992:

> Dear Fr. Paul Marx and all at Human Life International,
>
> This brings you my prayer for all you have been doing through your newsletters for God, for life and for family.
>
> God love you for the love you have shared and the care you have given to the un-born through your writings by creating awareness among your readers of the preciousness of human life - especially that of the pre-born who are so help-less, so weak, so small, and so much in need of all the love, care and nurture we can give.
>
> In protecting the pre-born so beautifully, by using the gift

God has given you—the gift of writing—you have indeed made your own lives precious to God. May you continue to protect, promote and build up life and uphold its sanctity.

God bless you.

In 1948 the Japanese relaxed abortion restrictions in what was called the "Eugenics Protection Act." That law turned out to be a terrible tragedy, since the Japanese family now averages only 1.4 children, as I have said. Importing guest-workers, as Europe and the United States do, is difficult because of language problems. Besides, the Japanese do not appreciate foreigners unless they are tourists who leave their money as they depart. Nor has the desperate government had any success in inducing Japanese women to have children in pop- ulation-replacement numbers, now that they are working outside the home and well-enough off to travel all over the world! Lately, how- ever, Japan has reluctantly begun to welcome immigrants. Today it is the fastest-aging nation in the world. And if it cannot remedy its disas- trous decline in the birthrate, it is doomed to extinction.

At one time Japan reported some three million abortions annually. The number has declined to perhaps half that for various reasons: there is less sexual activity, including fornication; dating is uncommon, youths travel in groups; and doctors are less money-hungry. Also, remember the astonishing fact that this so-called pagan nation prac- tices proportionately more NFP than the United States does.

Father Zimmerman is convinced that the reason the Catholic Church, numbering 400,000, has made so little progress in Japan is that contraception and abortion are prevalent in this nation whose 125 million people live in a land area the size of California. The Japanese hierarchy has said little about these evils; I hope Father Zimmerman's latest book, *Catholic Teachings on Pro-Life Issues,* will go a long way in educating seminarians, religious, and priests about the evils of the anti-life movement. Unfortunately, that movement only becomes stronger in Japan and in the developing countries as Western dissenting theology continues creeping into the seminaries.

On my way home in 1974, I gave seven lectures in three days and did my 199th radio-TV program in three years. After 165 days on tour, I returned to St. John's on November 14, convinced that living

out of a suitcase on long
lecture tours is the hardest work of all. Life in a
monastery can be sheer
luxury! But there was
much more to come.

INDIA

At least four times I   *In front of the Taj Mahal, India, 1974.*
have been in India, the
first time in 1974, and I
have lectured in several large Indian cities like Calcutta, New Delhi,
Bombay, Bangalore, and Pondicherry. HLI has branches in
Pondicherry, Madras, and Bombay, to each of which we have sent
much literature and many audiovisual aids.

Imitating England, the Indian Parliament relaxed the abortion law
in the early 1970s, and the result, of course, has been nothing but a
tragedy. Previously, Margaret Sanger had spent some time trying to
convince Mahatma Gandhi to embrace Western contraception and
abortion. Dead set against both of these practices, Gandhi is quoted as
saying that the difference between a wife who uses contraception and
a prostitute who uses it is that the one gets paid and the other does
not. In his opinion, as we have seen, the only means of birth control
worthy of human beings is self-control.[5]

Pro-life meetings in India are in the planning stage. The last time I
visited this vast country of 900 million people with only 15 million
Catholics, I was told by pro-lifers that there is at least one abortion for
every live birth; this means there are 15-16,000,000 abortions yearly,
not counting the non-surgical killings induced by abortifacients.

---

[5] For more of what Gandhi told Margaret Sanger, his incredible wisdom about human sexuality and love (some of which Pope Paul VI
quoted and referred to during his visit to India), see Louis Fischer
(ed.), *The Essential Gandhi: His Life, Works, and Ideas* (New York:
Vintage Books, 1962).

With the Bishop of Pondicherry and Fr. Antonisamy in Pondicherry, India.

I had some memorable experiences in this second most populous country in the world. In 1974 I talked to Mother Teresa's novices in Calcutta. Another time I walked through a large, barnlike shed that had a wall running through the middle. On one side were a hundred male lepers, and on the other a hundred females. What a sight! Holes in the face, ears rotting away, fingers and toes gone, and so on. But I can honestly say that in my fifty years of priesthood I never saw a happier lot of men and women. They lay on simple, clean cots and were beautifully taken care of by devoted people, some of them Mother Teresa's nuns. This project was financed in part by the Kennedy Foundation.

There is much more I could say about India—the country—and its people. I shall never forget how, when I was there the last time, HLI's great friend Archbishop (now Cardinal) Simon Pimenta of Bombay gently but unyieldingly forbade me to stop at Sri Lanka because of the revolution being waged there. I was truly touched by his concern.

SCANDINAVIA

*I*n the late 1930s the Scandinavian countries became the first in Western Europe to allow abortion by way of exceptions. Christianity has decidedly not flourished in these countries. Since Lutheranism is the officially established religion, the clergy are functionaries of the State. Because of low birthrates, the Scandinavians attract their share of immigrants, including Moslems. Nationally, some 3 percent engage in religious practice; these countries are hardly ready to support a pro-life/pro-family movement. The

With the pro-life Dr. Fred Freggavagen of Sweden.

idea of contraception (now mostly abortifacients, of course) is virtually frozen into the Scandinavian mind, and abortion is almost a way of life. Welfarism has just about run its course, and serious economic adjustments are being made. Of the thirty-five nations of Western and Eastern Europe, only Sweden, Albania, and Malta have maintained replacement birthrates, but barely.

DENMARK

*I*n Denmark, as in all countries, there are always at least a few observers who see the totally destructive character of abortion, even if not of contraception. Among them are Dr. Bruce Kyle and Dr. Michael Harry, who have worked almost day and night to bring home

to the Danes the reality of *in utero* baby-killing. I met Dr. Harry only
through correspondence; pro-life Danes could not praise him too
highly. Active too, and also promoting NFP, was Dr. Ross Nicklassen.
My nephew, Father Paul Marx, OMI, who on my last visit there was
still Vicar General of the diocese of Copenhagen, was helpful as well.
That visit coincided with the Pope's pilgrimage in Denmark, where,
given the small Catholic population, he drew small crowds. As I recall,
only 1,500 attended his public Mass.

SWEDEN

*I*n Sweden I worked with a great pro-life Catholic, Theres Degen,
the kindest and most diplomatic person one could ever meet, who
explained to me the Scandinavian mind and knew how to foster pro-
life ideas in this Lutheran country. As a young girl, Mrs. Degen had
come from Switzerland to work in Sweden. Eventually she married a
very fine Catholic, a physical therapist with whom she reared a large
family, including one Catholic priest. Her work consisted largely of
counseling women away from abortion and teaching NFP to young
couples. Exceedingly successful, she always claimed that she found
much help and encouragement in our literature, which convinced her
she was not alone in the battle for life. Incidentally, religion has so
declined in this beautiful country that the union of Church and State,
forged in 1544, is to be dissolved this year, leaving a lot of loose ends.

In 1956, Sweden became the first country in the world to mandate
sex education. Planned Parenthood-inspired sex education there, as
elsewhere, has been a total disaster, although—typically!—it is often
pointed out throughout the world as having been a huge success.
Living together without benefit of marriage, having babies out of wedlock, and engaging in casual fornication—these misfortunes are com-
monplace in Sweden, as in other Scandinavian countries, where con-
traceptive/abortifacient methods are freely taught in the schools.

On my last visit to Sweden I discovered that 15,000 Latin
Americans, mostly Chileans, were living there, having escaped from
the dictator Augusto Pinochet; later I sent Spanish literature to them.

Given Polish, Spanish, and Latin American immigration, the number of Catholics has increased notably. There have been a fair number of conversions among intellectuals who—thanks to the Jesuits—recognized the Swedish sex mess for what it is and perceived the only solution to be authentic Christianity. The welfare state was already in serious trouble at that time. (We publish several widely read pamphlets on the realities of the declining welfare state.) I must not fail to mention that Sweden produced a great NFP researcher, Professor Eric Odeblad of the University of Umea. Through his pioneer studies of the female cervix, he has greatly enhanced the effectiveness of the Ovulation Method. He has shown how the progestin only (mini-Pill), abortifacient implants like Norplant and injections such as Depo-Provera destroy proper cervical functions.

NORWAY

I have been in Norway, a nation of almost five million people, only once. It is the only Scandinavian country to have an organized pro-life movement, and its activism is entirely Lutheran inspired. Its leaders impressed me. Like the American National Right to Life Committee, pro-life Norwegians oppose only surgical abortion, but they fight it as no other Scandinavian country does. Once 10,000 people marched against abortion in Oslo, the capital. In 1975, Bishop Per Lonning led a small opposition group in Parliament against abortion, but to no avail. He resigned from parliament in the same year.

NIGERIA

*I*n 1991, I made a twenty-two-day lecture tour in this largest black country in the world, which has 100 million inhabitants. My first talk was before 480 major seminarians. I have already mentioned—but it is worth repeating!—my delight at seeing all those brilliant white cassocks, sharply contrasting with ebony heads and hands, and the seminary faculty lined up ahead of me in the front row. I spoke in several seminaries, delivered by jeep by the two young men who

At one of the eight major seminaries in Nigeria (five of them have 500+ seminarians).

squired me through an empty Nigeria. On one occasion, when asked to speak to the whole assembled hierarchy, I was told I would have fifteen minutes. When I had finished, they wanted me to continue. Those who know me know that was not very hard for me to do. I went on for another fifteen minutes.

At the back of the room sat the late Cardinal Dominic Ekandem of Abuja, Nigeria's capital. This saintly man wept at my description of the abortion slaughter going on in the Western world. He spent about two days with me, hauling me around with his chauffeur, speaking here and there, totally convinced of the importance of what I was doing. I also lectured in the large city of Onitsha, where I met the most-supportive Archbishop (now Cardinal) Francis Arinze, currently head of the Pontifical Council of Inter-religious Dialogue in Rome.

Nigeria has access to enormous resources, including oil, mostly in the hands of the Moslems. The land is so rich that I was told again and again that, properly cultivated, it could feed the whole of Africa—perhaps an exaggeration, but certainly not a big one. In its immensity, Africa is the second-largest continent, more or less empty, with only some 760 million people; in spite of its many natural resources, it is greatly underdeveloped. Instead of developing the African countries, the dying Western nations use citizens' tax money to provide them with harmful birth-control materials and sex ed.

I had fine chats with bishops and doctors at meetings of various kinds. I visited the Holy Family Sisters of the Needy in Owerri, whom we support financially. These sisters operate a home for unwed pregnant girls, rehabilitate prostitutes, and take care of placing their babies for adoption. This new order is attracting many vocations. According to the latest reports, there are eight major seminaries in Nigeria, five of which are educating some 500 seminarians! There are very many minor seminaries engaged in a unique training program for future priests, some of whom have already moved to the United States. Thus, the diocese of St. Charles in Louisiana has welcomed fifteen Nigerian sisters and priests, and more are coming.

Nigeria also runs an international seminary

Cardinal Francis Arinze of Nigeria, now President of the Pontifical Council for Interreligious Dialogue, speaking at HLI's World Conference in Cincinnati, 1996.

Conversing with our branch leader in Nigeria, Lawrence Adekoya.

to train priests for foreign countries, initially for foreign *African* countries. Convents for female religious are also flourishing. In Lagos our national base, called the Human Life Protection League, employs some ten workers under the guidance of Lawrence Adekoya. Here we published 100,000 copies of *Love and Let Live*, an array of colored pictures of preborn babies before and after abortion. We cannot keep up with their requests for films, videocassettes, audiocassettes, and literature—and, of course, money for their programs. Western liberal theology is seeping in; we are countering it here, as elsewhere, with Father Zimmerman's *Catholic Teachings on Pro-Life Issues,* which is espe-

Getting interviewed in Zimbabwe.

With our branch head, Enni Banda of Zambia, at the Victoria Falls (one of the great natural wonders of the world).

Presenting the "Precious Feet" to President Kaunda of Zambia.

cially useful in seminaries in the developing nations, faced as they are with what the Vatican calls "the contraceptive imperialists."

KENYA

*I*n the 1970s we established contact with various leaders, especially Dr. Andrew Kiura, Sister Stanislaus Barry, and Father John Kaiser, MH, the former student whom I have mentioned before. We sponsored several meetings in Nairobi, and I lectured to various seminarians and other Catholic groups, who, as usual, were shocked by the abortion films into the determination that legalized baby-killing would never come to their country. Cardinal Maurice Otunga was always supportive and cooperative. So were other bishops as our work spread into their seminaries and schools. In 1993, Father Matthew Habiger led a conference in Nairobi with an international faculty, including Father Anthony Zimmerman of Japan; they followed it up with addresses at various seminaries and schools. Every week we seem to be sending pro-life/pro-family materials to Kenya, where it is used wisely and well.

ZIMBABWE

I spent a week in Zimbabwe in the 1980s. Upon arriving there, I contacted several pro-lifers, like Bernie and Paddy O'Shea. I lectured mostly in Harare, where we also conducted one seminar. Here, as in Zambia, I was shocked to hear doctors tell me about the number of AIDS victims, especially in the army. I recall participating in a long interview on national TV with an excellent black moderator. He allowed me to speak at length after I had been asked the "good questions" that I had furnished him ahead of time, at his request.

ZAMBIA

*W*ith Mrs. Enni Banda, HLI founded the Pro-life Society of
Zambia in the early 1980s. In 1985 we invested $30,000 to
sponsor a national pro-life conference in Lusaka for 400 people, most of
them from that country. Here, as in other countries, including Tanzania,
we have sustained a constant flow of literature and audiovisual aids to
active pro-lifers, above all to seminaries and schools. Always helpful in
Tanzania and elsewhere is the German Benedictine Sister/Doctor Birgitta
Schell, highly influential in medical and Church circles.

SUB-SAHARA AFRICA

*I*n Johannesburg, in the fall of 1996, we brought together heads of
seminaries, doctors, lawyers, and other potential pro-life leaders
from the sub-Sahara region of Africa for a planning meeting to guide
our future work in Africa, where the Catholic Church may discover
her future. We feel that our African mission has only just begun. In
this second-largest continent the spread of AIDS is frightening; the
opportunities for pro-life work are mind-boggling. The native African,
perhaps as the result of an animistic background, is inherently pro-life
and pro-family. On this foundation one can build great things, especially with the help of the fine missionaries whom we meet all the
time. One wonderful South African doctor, Dr. Claude Newbury, is
our highly competent coordinator. And now, as I have mentioned,
given the passage of the worst abortion law outside of China and
Russia, Dr. Newbury of South Africa cannot practice medicine in that
country but will devote himself with his wife, Glenys, to full-time
work for us throughout sub-Saharan Africa.

SOUTH KOREA

*S*outh Korea is the only country in the world where the spread of
Catholicism began with laymen. One Korean pioneer went to

China, learned all about Catholicism, and brought it back to his country. For generations the little Catholic group hid away from the rest of society, engaging mostly in the craft of pottery-making. The predominant religious group in South Korea is the Presbyterians. Today there are about 4,000,000 Catholics in a population of 45,000,000. The Church increases yearly by about 100,000.

Last year the enormously influential Cardinal Stephen Sou Hwan Kim, Archbishop of Seoul, ordained thirty priests. Even so, given the many converts, there is only one priest for every 5,000 Catholics. The Korean Catholic Church is very generous with missionaries; eighty-six of them work outside the country. When the Pope visited Korea, 600,000 attended his Mass, the

In Kwang-Ju, South Korea.

second-largest participation—proportionately, the largest—of all his missionary tours.

In the early 1980s I visited South Korea twice. My guides were Sister Mary Hughes, who was promoting NFP throughout the country, and Dr. Kwang-Ho Meng, another promoter of NFP and a professor of community medicine at the Catholic Medical College in Seoul.

I went to South Korea especially to visit the Irish missionary Bishop Thomas Stewart of Chun-Cheon, with whom I had been in correspondence. The bishop told me he had little trouble with contraception and sterilization among his Catholics, because he had promoted Natural Family Planning for years in what was called the Happy Family Movement, offering special courses for priests, nuns, and, of course, couples. At the time they were also teaching NFP to the Buddhists. I can still see Bishop Stewart as he spoke on that subject to members of a large parish whose small pastor looked like a teenager! Bishop Stewart's fostering of family life and NFP spread more or less throughout the country.

At a meeting honoring my international pro-life work, Bishop Thomas Stewart said, "No priest in the world has done more for NFP than Father Paul Marx." I then turned the tables on him, giving him a gold symbol of ten-week-old fetal feet and saying, "No bishop has done more for NFP in his diocese than Bishop Thomas Stewart, who has proven that NFP can be taught to a whole diocese."

For years the government promoted the limitation of families to two children; today, lacking workers for its booming industrial complex rivaling Japan's, the government, as also in Singapore and Taiwan, is urging parents to have more children. Unfortunately, abortion is legal. Good, active nuns assure us there are over 1,000,000 abortions per year in South Korea. HLI has sent the Koreans pro-life materials, but the language is ever a barrier. We are currently preparing for a pro-life/pro-family center in Seoul; Cardinal Kim—who, incidentally, speaks English, Japanese, and German fluently—has welcomed our presence there.

SINGAPORE

I visited Singapore, an interesting, unique island-nation of 244 square miles, twice, the first time in 1974. Some 18 percent Malaysian, the Moslems are a fast-growing sect in Singapore. There are a number of Catholic schools here; I spoke in several as well as in the seminary. The Church is flourishing under Archbishop Gregory Yong Sooi Ngean. Celebrate Life is the name of our affiliate pro-life group and its excellent newsletter; we have worked with these Singaporeans closely for years, under the guidance of the very apostolic Dr. John Lim. The government collaborates closely with their education-in- love and sexuality courses.[6]

---

[6] Most data for this and other countries comes from HLI's monthly *Special Report* and *HLI Reports*, diaries and correspondence.

Children are beautiful everywhere; here I am with a group in Singapore.

I remember having a long conversation with Archbishop Ngean in 1974. I never before had heard a bishop lay out so clearly and accurately the evil of contraception and its progression, of course, to

With the ubiquitous Sisters of Charity in Singapore, 1990.

abortion and all manner of sexual abuse. I was privileged to speak to his seminarians, to preach in a number of parishes, and also to lecture to various groups.

The government at one time promoted the slogan "Stop at Two,"

Among some of the many nuns and seminarians praying for HLI around the world (this photo taken in Malaysia).

which the archbishop fought fiercely. Today it is promoting larger families because of low birthrates and a shortage of workers.

Bishop James Chan of Malaysia and me.

MALAYSIA

*I*n the middle 1980s I did a week of lectures in various Malaysian cities. Again, one can only admire the presence of a missionary Church in a Moslem country. The bishops have many problems in dealing with the Moslem government. Where once the Irish Christian Brothers ran fifty-five schools, today they run fewer than ten. HLI is in the process of setting up a center in the diocese of Miri. Bishop Anthony Lee Hok Hin sent six of his people to our international symposium in Cincinnati in 1996, and he himself attended an earlier one.

CANADA

𝒯hanks to "Catholic" Prime Minister Pierre Trudeau, the Canadians were handed virtual abortion-on-demand in 1969, with little opposition from the bishops. At the same time, divorce was legalized. In the previous year, 1968, after issuance of the monumental encyclical *Humanae Vitae*, the Canadian bishops had released a statement subtly dissenting to this encyclical. Today they are reaping the whirlwind.

Thanks to the late Joseph Borowski, the Canadian Supreme Court was faced with determining the constitutionality of this new abortion law, after a highly publicized campaign involving world-famous scientists giving testimony that life begins with conception (fertilization). Ignoring all scientific evidence, the Canadian Supreme Court justices tragically declared the infamous 1969 law constitutional and the pro-life situation continued to deteriorate.

The abortionist Henry Morgentaler, meanwhile,

As a priest, I never know when my services may be needed. Here I am conditionally absolving the unconscious victim of a traffic accident in Montreal.

established abortion mills in various cities of Canada, always winning his court battles. In 1988 the Canadian Parliament considered passing a bill forbidding abortion but allowing such wide exceptions that the pro-life movement rightly considered the law worthless in defending the unborn. The bishops supported it, believing that they had more to gain with some law rather than with none. At any rate, the bill was defeated, and today Canada is the only country in the world that has no law whatsoever against abortion.

The average completed-family size in Canada is 1.8 children, with

Theresa Bell and I celebrating Senator Stanley Haidasz's 50th anniversary of being in politics.

the lowest birthrate in North America being recorded in Catholic, French-speaking Quebec, where some 7,000,000 Catholics have 1.4 children per family. Apparently Quebec citizens forget that language and culture walk on two legs.

In 1996, Canada took another step backward when Parliament passed a law giving homosexuality equal status with heterosexuality: there was to be no discrimination whatsoever exercised against homosexuals. Although parliamentarians did not recognize same-sex "marriages," all homosexuals working for the government were to be given equal benefits. Large Canadian business corporations could—and more and more do—grant the same benefits to paired homosexuals as to married couples.

Just before the abysmal 1969 abortion decision, I was lecturing in Canada. In fact, I have spoken in every major Canadian city at least once. Besides addressing various Canadian groups, the Human Life Center of St. John's University, Minnesota, and its continuation, Human Life International, have conducted Canadian seminars on Natural Family Planning, abortion, and euthanasia.

In 1985, HLI chose Montreal as the site of its annual international symposium. In 1988 we selected Toronto, in 1992 Ottawa, and in 1995 Montreal again. This time we were loudly and violently picketed by 2,000 feminists, abortionists, exhibitionists, anarchists, drug-pushers, and the like.

In 1984, HLI founded HLI Canada, its largest regional office. In 1988, HLI Canada moved to Ottawa, and today it has twelve paid workers plus volunteers. Here, besides English pro-life materials, we publish a substantial amount of French literature for Quebec and for shipment to French-speaking Africa. Under the leadership of Theresa Bell, our Canadian branch is truly flourishing, and in 1999 we shall be doing an international symposium in Toronto for the second time.

All things considered, it is my judgment that the anti-life situation in Canada is considerably worse than in the United States, for whatever reasons.

FIJI ISLANDS

I went to the Fiji Islands twice to see the NFP program run by the Irish missionary Father Dermot Hurley. It was really *The Fiji Islands.*
impressive, with some nuns dangerously plying the islands by boat to teach NFP! I recall speaking to a small group of seminarians, who were avid listeners, as were the few other groups that I addressed. How dangerous it was, I now realize—flying in a small plane over vast areas of the Pacific Ocean with my heavy load of films and other materials. I could never do that again. But once more I saw the beautiful work for God done by the missionaries, whom I have always found wholly orthodox and full of zeal. It is sad that so few Catholics are aware of what the Church's far-flung army accomplishes. For instance, many Catholics do not even know that the Church is the greatest provider of health care in the world, by far.

FRANCE

*I*n France, so often the rebellious "eldest daughter of the Catholic Church," HLI has been a total failure. Although in touch with pro-lifers there early on, we never quite succeeded in getting a seminar or symposium organized. We made a serious attempt in 1993 but failed. Dr. Jerome Lejeune warned us, "In France you will meet a mine field." How right he was! Through the years I had lectured here and there, and participated in various panels and meetings.

This year we shall sponsor a meeting of leaders at the Benedictine Monastere Ste. Madeleine Le Barroux, whose abbot went to jail for trying to rescue the unborn at an abortion chamber. We hope this conference will result in some kind of national seminar or symposium that unites the various French pro-life groups.

In 1920 the French government forbade contraception by law; it considered birth control propaganda as an incitement to abortion; the law outlawed all information on contraception and all practice of it. In 1923 the government categorized abortion with restrictions as an offense to be tried in a magistrate's court. In 1979, the French relaxed their abortion law in certain circumstances on a trial basis, again with restrictions. Several years after passage of this tentative law, which applied to only the first ten weeks of pregnancy, baby-killing was fully sanctioned.[7] The results have been the same as everywhere else, with the performance of more than 100,000 abortions yearly and establishment of a birthrate of 1.8 children per completed family (2.2 are needed for replacement). But the birthrate is not low just because of abortion, since the French have been ace condom-contraceptors ever since and during the post-World War I period. When Hitler's armies overran France in six weeks, Marshall Petain reminded the French nation that, if parents had done their duty for the nation, he could have called on one million young Frenchmen to defend the fatherland.

Today the low birthrate is very troublesome to the authorities of this country, whose 4,500,000 Moslems continue to follow the biblical

---

[7]   See the fascinating, subtlely biased account in Bill Rolston and Anna Eggert (ed.), *Abortion in New Europe, op. cit.*, pp. 101-112.

injunction to "increase and multiply." Muslim immigration continues. Here are the French Ministry of the Interior's observations on immigration:

Fr. René Bel of France.

> Foreigners arriving [to settle] in France must understand that from henceforth their ancestors are the Gauls and that they have a new homeland. . . . But Muslim extremists have begun arriving in France as colonizers, with goods and weapons in their baggage. . . . Today, there is a real Islamic threat in France which is part of a great worldwide wave of Muslim fundamentalism.[8]

France has a number of pro-life groups, but no organized movement. On 6 October 1996, 23 groups (5,000 pro-lifers) marched for the sixth time in Paris. The French have done some rescuing at abortion mills, and France has produced one of the world authorities on post-abortion syndrome, that is, the anguish caused by having killed one's preborn child. This healer is Dr. Marie Peeters, a co-worker with Dr. Lejeune, now the wife of Dr. Philip Ney.

One of the leaders of the French pro-life effort is Father René Bel, who has retired as a seminary theology professor, but remains active in

---

[8] As quoted by *The Economist*, 16 November 1996, p. 63.

Italy. Wise about the machinations of IPPF, Bel often addressed our international pro-life meetings and spent a year working in our Miami office. I must mention the bulletins of François Pascal, *Trans Vie* and *Famille Chretienne*, both strongly pro-life. Angela d'Malherbe is president of *l'Assoc. Provie*, and Claire Fontana leads *La Treve de Dieu*, a group of rescuers. The effective baby-saving national operation called *SOS Futures Méres* was the inspiration of Madame Genevieve Poullot. Professor Lejeune was associated with this group.

For years we have sent many pro-life materials to *Centre Intl. Pour la Vie* in Lourdes, now under the guidance of François Pascal. I lectured here and showed films in the 1980s, when the dynamic Sister Regine Michaud, OSF, was in charge. My friends and colleagues, Drs. Michele and François Guy, have been world leaders in promoting NFP while also fostering the right to life in France. Michele Guy asked me several times why a man, with a sterilized wife, so often gets another woman pregnant?

THE NETHERLANDS

I don't recall how often I have been in this country. I first visited the Dutch in 1959 with my tour group and was there, as I have mentioned, in 1974 when the World Federation of Doctors Who Respect Human Life was formed; this group never accomplished much beyond sponsoring a few European meetings, the chief reason for its futility being a lack of funds. On one occasion I stayed several days in the southern Netherlands at Rolduc, where at that time was the only orthodox seminary; I lectured there to some ninety major seminarians; those who remained until ordination would find themselves acceptable in only two of seven dioceses! I had wonderful conversations with Cardinal Adrianus Simonis of Utrecht, who once flattered me by saying, "You are the archangel of life."

The theological situation in the Netherlands is to this day pathetic, thanks to unruly theologians like the Dominican Edward Schillebeeckx. The Dutch were the first to tamper with the Mass after Vatican II, a deplorable exercise from which we still have not recovered. To this day, very few Dutch people go to church on Sunday in

Taking pictures of anti-HLI protestors in the Netherlands.

Here in front of the Dutch Society for Voluntary Euthanasia booth. It is so sinister to see those who support the Culture of Death flaunting evil so widely and openly.

this country where the Pope was miserably treated and where wild and trendy priests have offered Mass with women as co-celebrants. (I witnessed one such adventure on a videocassette.)

The Netherlands, remember, was once more than 40 percent

Bishop Bommers of the Netherlands, Siegfried Ernst of Germany and me.

Catholic and at one time produced more vocations to the priesthood and religious life than did Ireland. All of which reminds me of the Benedictine chaplain of a convent who told me how much the old nuns, now retired after a lifetime of mission work, suffer from seeing younger members in their modern clothes, boots, and a new coiffure every week. I am reminded also of the *elderly* Minnesota nun who explained her routine visits to a hair-dresser: "As a professional woman, I must look my best."

No other country has embraced euthanasia as the Dutch have. According to surveys, some 19,000 people are killed by euthanasia yearly. At least one-fifth of these many euthanasia killings are involuntary.[9] In the Netherlands, it is a civic duty to subject pregnancy to rig-

---

[9]   R. Fenigsen, "Euthanasia in the Netherlands," *Issues in Law and Medicine*, vol. 6 (1990), p. 231. See also how it all began in Susan Glyn's "Human Value—or the Scrap-Heap?" and Richard Fenigsen, M.D., "The Report of the Dutch Governmental Committee on Euthanasia," in *Information on Euthanasia* published by Human Life International, 1982. A good summary is Rita L. Marker's *Euthanasia: Killing or Caring*, (Toronto, Ontario and Lewiston, New York: Life Cycle Books, 1991.) Rachel Nowark, "The Dutch Way of Death," *New Scientist*, vol. 134, no. 1826 (20 June 1992.) Paul Marx's *And Now Euthanasia* (Gaithersburg, MD: Human Life International, 1985).

orous economic calculation. Amniocentesis is required. Infants with Down's Syndrome are routinely starved to death in Dutch hospitals.

In 1990 we presented a very successful national symposium in Holland at a retreat house near Eindhoven. Never to be forgotten were the homosexuals, lesbians, socialists and anarchists picketing the conference with all manner of screams, shouts and obscenities with music to match. Two lesbians took off their clothes and "made love." Here, too, as in every other Western country, there are heroic pro-lifers like Dr. and Mrs. G. J. M. van den Aardweg; the late Gerhart and Katrina van den Berg, in whose home I often stayed; the magnificent pro-lifer Father Johannes Koopman; Dr. Emmanuel van den Bemd; Dr. Karl Gunning, president of the World Council of Doctors Who Respect Human Life; and the powerful euthanasia opponent Dr. Richard Fenigsen. Even so, there is a budding revival of religion and common sense in the present day Netherlands.

One thing needs to be clarified: it is often reported and said that, because of sex ed and contraception in Dutch schools, the Netherlands has the lowest number of teen pregnancies in the Western world. Even *Sursum Corda* fell for this falsehood. In the Netherlands, when a teen misses a period or two, a doctor "brings on the menses," i.e., does a mini-suction also called "menstrual extraction." In short, he destroys the pregnancy. This is never considered an abortion and so not reported. Further, the huge international Dutch drug firm, Organon— drumming up future business—distributes the abortifacient Pill widely among the young, sometimes with the cooperation of sex ed teachers. In short, there is much aborting in the Netherlands, not a few Germans and others coming across the border to have their babies killed.

TRINIDAD AND TOBAGO

*T*his interesting little country off the coast of Venezuela has a very good and influential archbishop, Anthony Pantin, who invited HLI to do a weekend seminar there. It was well attended, and the following year the archbishop sponsored his own national pro-life meeting.

While there I addressed the regional Seminary of St. John Vianney. Unfortunately, I was kept too busy to visit the Benedictine Abbey of

Mount St. Benedict in Tunapuna. Five Caribbean bishops concele-
brated the final Mass of our seminar, which was followed by an
impressive procession through the capital city of Port-of-Spain. To my
surprise I learned of the presence of several million Catholics in the
Caribbean (apart from Cuba), and we are in the process of establishing a branch there under the leadership of a fine, intelligent priest-
writer, Father Leonard Alfonso of Barbados.

BELGIUM

*L*egal baby-killing came to Belgium on 3 April 1990. The Belgium
king must sign all bills. He refused to sign this one. In true
Machiavellian fashion, the pro-abortion parliament pronounced the
king unfit, and dethroned him for one day while ministers signed the
bill. Thus, they derailed democracy in a truly totalitarian way.

According to the abortion law, pre-born babies may be killed at any
time in the first three months of pregnancy, and thereafter for social
indications or if the mother bears a handicapped unborn child. For
these two reasons abortions can be committed up to birth. There are an
estimated 30,000 abortions in this nation of ten million, double the
estimated number before the law was passed. Like other Europeans,
some Belgians go to foreign countries for their baby-killings to stay out
of medical records. The abortifacient Pill is widely used, the abortifacient intra-uterine device less so, and sterilization is increasing rapidly.

The pro-life movement began with the late law professor Charles
Convent in 1971. Almost from the beginning I was in touch with
Professor Convent, and the Belgian Pro-life Movement is now a
branch of HLI. Gilbert Sprengers, a disciple of Convent, works with a
staff of three, and is very effective in the schools, where he teaches virtually every day. According to his reports, things are fast getting
worse, also in the schools. Effectively using our aborted baby pictures,
Sprengers has been cited in court several times for pornography!

As elsewhere, Planned Parenthood is very active in the schools with
its biological sex education program, starting with children at five
years of age.

The Catholic Church has "neutral" and "charitable" organizations,

At a cemetery in Belgium, the final resting place of the soldiers who fought at the Battle of the Bulge.

some of which give out the condom. The Pope's encyclical V*eritatis Splendor* is mostly ignored, and *Evangelium Vitae* is not taken very seriously in Catholic schools and churches.

The average family has 1.5 children, far below replacement. More than one-fifth the population in Belgium is Moslem; Catholic schools often have a majority of little Muslims. The Masons openly boasted on TV that they were responsible for passing the abortion law in 1990. Along with much sexual abuse and drugs, Belgium has its share of VD, about which the government does not give out exact figures. Rare is the pro-lifer at the world-famous "Catholic" University of Louvain, where at its hospital they do abortions and engage in the immoral *in-vitro* fertilization. "Why don't the bishops speak out?" I asked. The answer was what one hears so often: "They are afraid of the media." "More afraid of the media than of God?" I commented.

When I was in Belgium the last time, the *Catholic Catechism* was not yet available; but Catholics estimated that it would be given the same brush-off as *Veritatis Splendor*. The secular press said that this document dealt only with contraception.

A stalwart prolifer is Dr. Philippe Schepens, with whom I have worked often and who is the secretary for the World Federation of Doctors Who Respect Human Life. His wife does much for NFP. While I have lectured several times in Belgium, I recall distinctly talking to an assemblage of priests on 25 October 1985. The Flemish-Walloon ethnic problem has never been resolved; it creates its own difficulties in this small nation, where the faith is weak and the problems many. Last year several children were killed in a notorious pedophilia case, badly handled by the government. It finally brought 300,000 angry citizens into the streets of Brussels protesting the pervasive corruption in government.

This by no means includes all the countries I have visited. Hopefully I left some pro-life traces in Iceland, Tanzania, Italy, Spain, Luxemburg, and others where I lectured.

CHAPTER 10

Accusations

"In every generation there must be some fool who will speak the truth as he sees it." —Pasternak, from an interview with the *New York Times*, 2 February 1959

*H*uman Life International adopts a total approach to the life issues by working against contraception, sterilization, abortion, euthanasia and explicit sex education, while promoting chastity, natural family planning, homeschooling, theological orthodoxy and serious preparation for marriage. This strategy is bound to rouse opposition and engender accusations, even blatantly false ones.

Even so, in over thirty-five years of pro-life/pro-family efforts, we have been the subject of comparatively few rational complaints. Of course, one need not take seriously the unsigned letters from fanatics or the occasional signed letters from crackpots. But even these have been few. More seriously, people have sometimes falsely accused HLI of bishop-bashing and of being divisive, anti-woman, anti-Semitic, anti-Muslim, racially prejudiced, and self-righteous.

BISHOP-BASHING

*N*o single bishop, so far as we know, has ever explicitly accused HLI of bishop-bashing, although (as I will note below) our vigorous pro-life orthodoxy has incurred disfavor in some episcopal circles. I can recall one critical letter from a retired bishop. I have forgotten his minor complaint. No more than two letters from laymen have made that accusation. The charge of bishop-bashing is a fairly recent development. Let it first be said that presenting the truth, accurately reporting major, proven religious irregularities, upholding orthodoxy, and refuting dissident theologians and writers should be characterized not as bishop-bashing but rather as legitimate reporting. In our publications we have always scrupulously, and I hope prudently, attempted to report abuses and failings correctly. This policy seems to result in responsible and legitimate journalism. There is nothing in the teaching of the Catholic Church that says its adherents must be blind and mindless, following any leader at any price.

Thus, unraveling the late Cardinal Joseph Bernardin's seamless garment may be considered bishop-bashing by some; and reporting that this liberal Chicago cardinal stopped a good priest from sponsoring a widely attended Holy Mass and Holy Hour intended as penance for the sin of contraception may be deemed scandalous by others.[1] I know of no experienced pro-life leader who is not convinced that Cardinal Bernardin derailed the American pro-life movement at Fordham University in 1983 with his unwise "Consistent Ethic of Life" lecture. Bernardin's "consistent ethic" became popularly known as the "seamless garment," in whose folds abortion was considered just another social problem.[2]

In 1987 Pope John Paul II asked theologians to cease discussing contraception, since it had been settled with *Humanae Vitae* and

---

[1]   See HLI's *Special Report* no. 125 (May 1995).

[2]   James Hitchcock, "The Bishops Seek Peace on Abortion," *Human Life Review,* vol. 10, no. 1 (winter 1984), 27-35. In the middle 1980s Mike Engler and I produced a document, "What Bishops Could Do about Abortion" (HLI Reprint 29), translated into five languages. A few weeks before the 1996 national election the bishops urged the Catholic electorate to pick and choose from among the issues listed in the October 1996 U.S. bishops' pastoral, "A Religious Call to Political Responsibility," among which abortion was one of equal rank with eighteen other highlighted issues. Is this why 53 percent of Catholics voted for abortion President Clinton? The British hierarchy did much the same, enraging seasoned pro-lifers (London: *Sunday Telegram,* 27 October 1996). The bishops' reward seems to have been to have Vice President Al Gore bashing Catholics after the election: See *The Wanderer,* 30 January 1997.

through the consistent teaching of the Catholic Church over the centuries. How then, would reporting that Saginaw's Bishop "Call Me Ken" Untener asked for reconsideration of the validity of *Humanae Vitae*, at a semi-annual bishops' conference be bishop-bashing? Would reporting how several bishops actively participated in the horrendous Call to Action meetings be bishop-bashing?[3] In discussing the theological errors of several speakers at Cardinal Roger Mahony's annual catechetical congress and making known the strange goings-on at Catholic universities like Georgetown, Notre Dame, and the Catholic University of America (the last institution being the bishops' own pontifical university)—would that be bishop-bashing? Some consider such accounts out of order, but to others they are legitimate journalism. To say and do nothing while the faithful are misled by obvious infractions and toleration of false teachings is highly irresponsible. As St. Augustine wrote, "It is better that the truth be known rather than scandal be covered up." Apparently several American cardinals are activated by the same spirit. Read on!

Speaking with the police in Portland, Oregon outside the Lovejoy Abortion Clinic.

The accusation "bishop-bashing" can now be directed at some princes of the Catholic Church. In August 1996, Cardinal Bernardin, often called titular head of the American Church, announced his peculiar "Catholic Common Ground" project, also known as "Called to be Catholic." Boston's Cardinal Bernard Law dutifully pointed out "inconsistencies and ideological bias," qualities that Cardinal Bernardin's project elsewhere decries in others. "The Church already has 'common ground,'" Cardinal Law explained. "It is found in

---

[3]   See HLI's *Special Report* no. 145 for a description of what went on at the Call to Action meeting in Detroit, November 1996.

Extremist?

Sacred Scripture and Tradition, and it is mediated to us through the authoritative and binding teaching of the Magisterium."

He went on to say: "Dissent from revealed truth or the authoritative teaching of the Church cannot be 'dialogued' away. Truth and dissent from truth are not equal partners in ecclesial dialogue. . . . Dialogue as a way to mediate between truth and dissent is mutual deception."

Cardinals Anthony Bevilacqua of Philadelphia and James Hickey of Washington engaged in similar "bashing," as did New York's Cardinal John O'Connor, who also rather thoroughly bashed the retired Archbishop John R. Quinn for his criticism of Pope and Curia in his widely publicized lecture at Campion Hall, the Jesuit Hall of Studies in Oxford, on 29 June 1996.[4] In that lecture the former archbishop of San Francisco did what HLI has never done or would do: he questioned the exercise of papal authority within the Church and the role of collegiality; he further queried why topics such

---

[4]   *Catholic New York*, 25 July 1996. For a most insightful discussion of American cardinals and bishops "bashing" each other and the irreconcilable differences among bishops in the American hierarchy, see Michael Gilchrist, "U.S. Catholicism: how far will the dissenters go?" *AD 2000*, vol. 9 (October 1996), 3-4. The divisions within the U.S. hierarchy were underlined in 1995 with the "restructuring proposal" approved by the forty more radical bishops, including Archbishop Rembert Weakland of Milwaukee and Bishop Thomas Gumbleton; this proposal criticized aspects of the Holy See's policies and, in effect, sought a U.S. Church more independent of Rome.

as contraception, the ordination of
women, general absolution, the
celibacy of priests and "liturgical
inculturation" had been closed to
discussion. Thus Cardinal Hickey
wrote that Cardinal Bernardin's
project "tends to reduce authoritative Church teaching to a partisan
voice in debates on neuralgic [sic]
issues." The cardinal rightly goes
on to observe that the "Catholic
Common Ground" statement "seems to
give too much weight to the opinions of
Catholics who do not really agree with
the Magisterium." As an example he
cites its reference to the "gap between
Church teachings and the convictions of
the faithful."

HLI's ten newsletters, our many
books, booklets, pamphlets and articles—all of our publications in all languages—have repeatedly made the same
points as the cardinals who disagree with
Cardinal Bernardin, though perhaps in

With a bishop from Argentina.

*With Bishop Vivas Bosco of
Nicaragua.*

*Fr. Habiger and I with Cardinal Trujillo at the First International Conference for Life
and Family in Santiago, Chile, August 1994.*

Here with his Eminence, Alfonso Cardinal Lopez Trujillo, President of the Pontifical Council for the Family.

stronger language. That is why I wrote to Cardinal Hickey on 21 August 1996: "Alas! I never thought I would see the day when cardinals (you and Cardinal Law) would 'bishop-bash' cardinals! (We secretly feel vindicated since we have pointed out these and other abuses for decades!)" Strangely, a few weeks before he died, Cardinal Bernardin observed that these criticisms "to some extent,. . .confirm the need for this initiative."

On 22 January 1997 Vice President Al Gore, speaking to a meeting of the National Abortion and Reproductive Rights Action League (NARAL), characterized the pro-life stance as "an extreme" position, held only by a minority of American citizens. Contrary to all evidence, Gore proclaimed that the best way to reduce the number of abortions is the promotion of contraception (today mostly abortifacient). He scoffed at the pro-life minority and then said, "The truth is that the minority within the minority also believes that family planning, in the form of birth control . . . is morally wrong." Three times he favorably cited Cardinal Bernardin for his efforts to "construct a dialogue aimed at understanding." Is this the fruit of Cardinal Bernardin's Catholic Common Ground effort? It is surely very interesting that Cardinal Bernardin should have become the Catholic leader most favorably regarded by the abortion lobby and by pro-abortion Gore.

SEX EDUCATION

*H*LI has published critiques of six of the most explicit sex-education tion programs in the United States. Sex education in this land,

and elsewhere, is an unnatural disaster. Judging from our mail, phone calls, and many conversations with Catholics across the country, the U.S. bishops did the Church a disservice at their semi-annual national meeting in 1990, when they approved by a close vote a secretly produced, barely discussed set of guidelines for Catholic-school "sex education." It bears the pretentious title *Human Sexuality: A Catholic Perspective for Education and Lifelong Learning*. Why was this sex-ed document composed in such secrecy, by an unnamed committee, and with virtually no parental input? The strange document ignores the latency period of child development, flagrantly disregards parental rights, wavers on the need for moral/spiritual formation, and presents a fatally confused and muddled concept of human sexuality with "New Age" overtones, and so on.

Names of the committee members leaked out, of course. Some of them—authors and publishers of sex-ed literature—could hardly have been disinterested members. For instance, Father John Forliti's public-school curriculum, *Human Sexuality: Values and Choices*, was approved by the abortion-committing, anti-Catholic Planned Parenthood! A public dissenter to *Humanae Vitae*, Forliti serves as a theological consultant for the anti-Magisterium *New Creation* series discussed below, which includes a recommended reading list of books and authors representing the dregs of the sexual revolution: Sol Gordon, Wardell Pomeroy, William A. Black, Planned Parenthood's abortion-pushing Alan Guttmacher, and the teen novelist Judy Blume—all hostile to Catholic morality. Father Forliti was also the director of youth programs for the Minneapolis-based Research Institute, a front for Planned Parenthood. An entire section in Forliti's *Issues in Sexuality*, particularly the film portions, opposes Catholic teaching. At least three other members of the twenty-person secret committee are known dissenters to *Humanae Vitae*.

At the bishops' 1990 meeting, Bishop Edward M. Egan of Bridgeport, Connecticut, pleaded for an opportunity to study the "guidelines", complaining that he had been given no time to read it. The theologically astute and courageous Bishop Austin Vaughan remarked that this was the first time he had ever received an embargoed document. He too claimed that the bishops had had no time to read it. At this meeting, Bishop Vaughan asked for the confidential list of committee members. It was denied him, perhaps because he had charged that there were dissenters on it. HLI had asked for the list long before the meeting and was also refused.

Did the bishops approve a document they had not read? Why the rush to push through an inherently controversial document, potentially fraught with the most serious consequences and kept out of sight for two and one-half years, with, again, almost no input from parents whose basic right and duty—not the bishops'—it is to educate and form their children in chastity?

Astonishingly, Auxiliary Bishop William Newman of Baltimore, chairman of the sex ed committee, revealed in a news conference that he was not familiar with the pivotal document quoted by virtually every Pope since 1929, Pope Pius XI's *Divini Illius Magistri*—a monumental document on Catholic education that includes an insightful section on sex education.

If the reader is tempted to think this discussion of the NCCB/USCC (National Council of Catholic Bishops; U.S. Catholic Conference) 1990 document is exaggerated, let him consult an analysis prepared by Catholics United for the Faith.[5]

HLI has continued its efforts to alert the bishops, as pastors charged with the care of millions of souls, to the need for them personally–not through delegation-to-staff–to examine carefully all sex ed programs used in Catholic schools, to consult with parents and to ensure that Catholic truth is not evaded.

Thus in 1991 I asked an Archbishop whose *imprimatur* appeared on the *New Creation* Series to consider an HLI critique of *New Creation* that, I believed, showed it to undermine Catholic teaching. I repeat here a few of the concerns I expressed because the *New Creation* Series is still in use:

> Recently Fargo's Bishop James Sullivan wrote in the
> newsletter of Catholics United for the Faith his own

---

[5]   See the insightful analysis of the bishops' *Human Sexuality: A Catholic Perspective for Education and Lifelong Learning* by Catholics United for the Faith, 827 North 4th Street, Steubenville, Ohio 43952; telephone: 614/289-2481.

thorough critique of the *New Creation* Series wherein, he said, there was no Catholic doctrine, and wherein he pointed out that the Series had been brought to the attention of the Pope, who considered the Series unfortunate.[6]

...The *New Creation* Series contains a total dissent to *Humanae Vitae* and has in its bibliography secular, humanist, godless authors like Sol Gordon and Wardell Pomeroy who believe that morally any behavior from fornication to bestiality is okay...

...In the *New Creation* Series ... there is a total dissent to *Humanae Vitae* in the teacher manuals. Quoted is an ex-Maryknoll priest and now a psychology professor, who eloquently rejects Paul VI's prophetic encyclical...

My correspondence on this series also states that:

We are evaluating all the major sex education programs to see if there is a worthy one, that is, one promoting chastity in the context of learning one's whole faith. We realize also that without the spiritual means of confession and Eucharist, prayer and penance, the obedience to the Ten Commandments and the practice of the spiritual/corporal works of mercy and the cardinal virtues, chastity is indeed impossible. As Pius XII stated, the reason the young get into trouble sexually is 'not ignorance, but weakness of will and poverty of spiritual life.' As the Scriptures say, chastity is a gift from the Lord, and no mere organ recital or the best of biological, human knowledge about sex and its function is going to produce chaste living.

---

[6] Five letters from Rome to various individuals concerning the *New Creation* Series are in HLI's possession. They were all written by Cardinal Edouard Gagnon, then president of the Pontifical Council for the Family. In one letter Cardinal Gagnon says that he showed the *New Creation* Series to the Pope, who was decidedly displeased.

Parents have written and called us constantly over the years, from all parts of the country, to tell us about sex ed in their so-called Catholic schools—to say nothing of the explicit biological education in so many public schools. Some parents have proven to us that there are, by and large, *less* offensive sex ed and *more* parental consultation and control in their public schools than in the local Catholic institutions. We are convinced that nothing destroys the faith and morals of youth more today than pornographic, explicit, detailed, often "value-free" sex ed—unless it is pornographic TV.

In 1993 we raised concerns about the TeenSTAR program with the staff of a Cardinal Archbishop in whose diocese the program was being used. We did this after hearing repeated complaints from parents across the country about the TeenSTAR program, after a staff member attended a seminar intended to train teachers of the program, and after the promoters of TeenSTAR claimed the approval of the Cardinal Archbishop.

Later, a group monitoring sex education in the United States published excerpts from TeenSTAR as an advertisement alerting parents in the Archdiocese of Washington to its dangers. The editors of the *Washington Times* found the excerpts so objectionable and pornographic that they actually censored parts of the advertisement.[7]

HLI's efforts to "raise the consciousness" of the American hierarchy generally about sex-ed programs used in Catholic schools and, more broadly, the need for strong episcopal leadership for life, were the subject of concern on the part of some members of that hierarchy. These concerns were brought to the Pontifical Council for the Family and its president, Cardinal Lopez Trujillo, an outstanding defender of life.

Cardinal Trujillo has done a tremendous job in arousing the whole of Latin America to the abortion issue. I cannot say enough about his great pro-life work there and elsewhere. As Archbishop of Medellin in Colombia, Cardinal Trujillo resisted the worst of liberation theology. I once had occasion to examine the seminary library with a colleague in Medellin. Only orthodox theology books are there. The cardinal has also bravely and totally condemned value-free, biological sex educa-

---

7   *The Washington Times*, 14 November 1995.

tion in Latin America. Cardinal Trujillo was also the chief architect of the Vatican's definitive and magnificent document, *The Truth and Meaning of Human Sexuality: Guidelines for Education within the Family*.

Several times I asked Roman authorities whether the then-forthcoming encyclical, *Evangelium Vitae* (Gospel of Life), would include a condemnation of contraception. I was always assured it would . Then I got a request from the Pontifical Council for the Family for evidence that the practice of contraception did indeed lead to abortion. Assembling the evidence took more than a week. Again, I spent days gathering the names and addresses of the world's pro-life leaders as requested by the Pontifical Council for the Family on behalf of the approaching Third International Meeting of pro-life leaders in Rome, 3-5 October 1995. Assembling this list took another week. The first such meeting brought about 300 to Rome; the second, about 500; the third brought almost 1,200—70 percent of whom were or had been HLI contacts.

Notwithstanding HLI's efforts to assist the Pontifical Council, following the October 1995 meeting the Council raised with us the concerns brought to the Council regarding HLI's policies. Suffice it to say here that I hope and believe that the Council now has an accurate picture of HLI's efforts and of HLI's compelling desire to continue its work with the approval of, and in open communication with, the Council.

In explaining HLI's concerns to Cardinal Trujillo as President of the Council, I noted, among other points, how HLI's efforts had been welcomed by many bishops throughout the world:

> At our meeting 5 October 1995 you mentioned how dialog solved the contraceptive statements eliminated for a Spanish translation of Willke's "Question/Answer" book on abortion. You may not be aware that that dialog began with Mrs. Magaly Llaguno, who heads our office in Miami. I hope your next trip to the U.S. will take you to our Miami office where six people work throughout Hispanic countries, and above all Latin American countries. Virtually every Latin American bishop who comes through Miami

visits Mrs. Llaguno because of her magnificent pro-life work in their countries. A Brazilian cardinal once offered Mass in her home. HLI's Hispanic pro-life work began in 1972, when I visited every major country in Latin America with a view to starting a pro-life movement, convinced that the death peddlers would come sooner rather than later to the only Catholic continent in the world. Indeed they have! And they meet HLI everywhere.

Seventeen Latin American countries had representatives at our congress in Chile in 1994. We have organized congresses in Nairobi, Kenya twice. HLI organized a conference in 1982 and two in 1995 in South Africa; we've done two in Nigeria; one in Zambia, one in Zimbabwe, one in Lithuania and two in Yugoslavia. Representatives from ten countries attended our symposium in Mexico City in 1985, seven in Port of Spain, Trinidad, 1989; five in Santo Domingo in 1993; we have done several conferences in Brazil in the 1980s and in Colombia (Bogota) twice; we sponsored three large meetings in the Philippines for Asians; in Moscow in 1993; Ukraine in 1994. Our president, Fr. Matthew Habiger, just returned from almost three weeks in the Philippines and South Korea. In Manila he conducted a training course for 300 Asian leaders with our staff, Filipino doctors and professors. Result: a large Asian center in the Philippines into which we have poured over the years more money and literature than any country since it is the only Catholic country in Asia, which comprises two-thirds of mankind. Seoul's Stephen Cdl. Sou Hwan Kim invited HLI to do a conference there next year.

Let me frankly say that except for HLI, there would be very little pro-life activity in Latin America and Africa. We have done three international symposia and four national conferences in Latin America as well as numerous lecture tours in the various countries. Right now we are organizing a weekend conference in Panama City with the collaboration of Archbishop José Dimos Cedeño. You attended the St.

Louis, Chile, Ukraine and California HLI conferences so
you know what we do. We have done the same conferences
in various countries of the world over the last thirty years
with full collaboration of the bishops. We have seven
regional offices in various countries, 75 branches in 57
nations and employ over 80 paid workers helped by many
volunteers....

My letter to Cardinal Trujillo also noted widespread lay desire for
strong pro-life leadership from their bishops:

I hope Msgr. Elliott reported to you the repeated complaints
by pro-life leaders . . . at your 2-4 Oct '95 conference in
Rome, about their main problem in their pro-life work
being with priests and bishops. . . . On complaints about
bishops, see "A Holy Alliance" about the meeting in Rome;
this appeared in one of the most respected Canadian week-
lies, *The Alberta Report* for 23 Oct. 1995:

With the exception of the Italian working group,
every final report contained biting criticism of the
inertia and apathy of the national Catholic hierarchies in the developed countries. The English criticized their bishops' failures to excommunicate or
even criticize pro-abortion Catholic politicians and
medical workers. The French condemned the folly of
permitting secularist dissent in Catholic-funded institutions. The Americans chided the failure to organize and energize the individual parishes in support
of life. And in passing, one working group was
regaled by the story of the Calgary diocese's obstruc-
tion of an upcoming Human Life International conference.

"The bishops must institute a mechanism to educate
and discipline the priests of their dioceses in the
Church's teaching on life," barked the chairman of
the German working group—only to be interrupted

by 10 minutes of forceful, continuous applause from about 1,000 delegates. "Wait! Be quiet! We have other things to say to our bishops!" he finally shouted, while a dozen clerics looked on, some surprised, some glum. . . .

The Catholic laity's criticism of their ordained leaders received some support from evangelical activists. "The Catholic church has got to clean house," says evangelical pro-lifer Doug Scott, author of the book *Bad Choices: A Look Inside Planned Parenthood.* "It's hard for us to work with a church that won't kick out politicians like Teddy Kennedy or Mario Cuomo—the guys who say they're 'personally opposed' but continue to support the killing of unborn infants."

Not surprisingly, the international criticism of the Catholic national hierarchies has found echoes in Alberta. "Priests speak out on funding Catholic schools, and bishops defend social programs, but I've never heard of a single Catholic MLA [Member of Legislative Assembly] being contacted by his church over the issue of defunding abortion," says Joanne Hatton, spokesman for the Committee to End Tax-Funded Abortions (CETFA). "We've gotten tons of support from the Catholic Women's League and the Knights of Columbus, but nothing from the hierarchy. It's embarrassing. We've got evangelical and completely faithless people, fighting tooth and nail to defund abortion in this province, and then they ask me why Catholic politicians and lawyers are cheerfully permitted to disobey the church's teaching. The grass-roots Catholics are wonderful, but we could sure use some of the leadership."

Despite 65% to 70% popular support for the provincial defunding of abortion, the local Catholic hierarchy may identify more with the secular political elite than they do with their Church. When a CETFA representative first contacted the Calgary diocese eight months ago, a member of the bishop's pro-life committee told him that they could not support the defunding of abortion "because that would restrict a woman's choices." In August, when the Tory caucus was actually debating the issue, a local CUL [Catholics United for Life] member called the diocesan Family Life director to ask what the bishop's office was going to do to help. "Nothing," she was told. "The purpose of the pro-life committee is to receive reports and study issues."

Demonstrating an equally comfortable attitude, the Catholic Health Association of Canada (CHAC) criticized the Klein government on October 2, for considering the defunding of abortion rather than attacking its "root causes" such as unemployment. CHAC accepts the church's teaching that life begins at conception, its head explains, but it has not taken a position on whether abortion should be publicly funded.

Catholic pro-life activist Joe Scheidler of Chicago, speaking in Rome, says that the lack of Catholic pro-life leadership is almost universal. "In the encyclical, the Holy Father focuses on Christ's death," he recounts. "And we're called to go and do likewise. We're supposed to take up our cross in defense of life, but most of our bishops just aren't that committed. We sure could use the leadership. We look to our shepherds for leadership, and when they don't... (from: *Alberta Report* for 23 October 1995).

Vancouver's Abp. Adam Exner, representing the Canadian bishops at the Pro-Life Leadership Conference in Rome, asserted in the 23 October 1995 *Western Catholic Reporter* that "in every nation pro-lifers want to see stronger leadership from clergy and bishops on life issues. They are really begging for that leadership."

The whole sex-ed controversy should have ended with the Vatican's promulgation of *The Truth and Meaning of Human Sexuality: Guidelines for Education within the Family*, but the document has been subtly boycotted by a few bishops and downplayed through a release from the National Catholic News Service. Has not the failure of bishops to discipline dissenting theologians and other teachers under their jurisdictions caused most of the prevalent theological confusion and strange teaching that goes on at virtually all levels of Catholic education?[8] This is the most common complaint I have heard repeatedly in the last twenty-five years from the best of thinking Catholics who love their Church. In *Veritatis Splendor* the Pope goes so far as to say that bishops should withdraw the name "Catholic" from programs and institutions that do not deserve that name. In instructing Titus St. Paul writes that "there are many irresponsible teachers. . .and deceivers. They must be silenced. They are upsetting whole families by teaching things they have no right to teach—and all for sordid gains."[9]

ANTI-SEMITISM

*I*n 1987 HLI made a careful study of involvement in the worldwide abortion movement. The undisputed conclusion of this study was that a disproportionately large number of Jews who are disloyal to Jewish teachings have led and are leading the campaign for legalized abortion. We then consulted with Orthodox Jews who con-

---

[8] Cf. James Naughton, "Mass Protest" (describing the Jesuit parish of the Holy Trinity), *Washington Post*, Sunday: 25 August 1996. (See also his book *Catholics in Crisis.)*

[9] Titus, 1:7-11; 2:1-8.

Here with Rabbi Yehuda Levin at a press conference in Montreal defending HLI against accusations of anti-Semitism.

firmed these findings.[10] If a large and prominent group of Mormons or Indians (both of whom, thankfully, are pro-life) had surfaced, we would have published this, too. We have deplored the horrendous Holocaust, in which some six million Jews died at Hitler's hands, and have compared it to the greater worldwide "holocaust" of unborn babies slaughtered daily. At no time have we ever condemned the Jewish people—our targets have been only Jewish abortionists, and not because they were Jewish. The Jewish people, after all, have a

---

[10] *Confessions of a Prolife Missionary* (Gaithersburg, MD: Human Life International, 1995), pp. 268-274; see also Brian Clowes, "Confronting the Canadian Anti-life Network," (Vanier, Ontario, Canada: Human Life International—Canada, 1995.)

great pro-life heritage, and as Pius XI observed, "Spiritually we are all Semites."

However, according to official Jewish sources, only about 10 percent of the Jewish people are ortho-dox/conservative and true to their Jewish pro-life tra-dition. We were deeply dis-appointed to find that not more Jewish people were pro-life, given their magnifi-cent tradition and the horri-ble example of the Holocaust. In mentioning this anomaly in *Confessions of a Prolife Missionary,* we did no more or less than what former editor Norman Podhoretz has done in the Jewish journal *Commentary.*

Dr. Judith Reisman (above) and Rabbi Levin (below), a noted Jewish writer, at HLI's world conference in Montreal.

HLI's 1978 study also mentioned that, in the sev-enty countries I had visited up until that time, I found, and collaborated with, a small Jewish pro-life group, EFRAT (Society for the Advancement of Childbearing in Israel.) Today EFRAT has grown into Israel's largest ortho-dox pro-life association, now under the able leadership of Dr. Eli Shusheim. The 1978 study also pointed out and deplored the fact that there were countless Catholics and Protestants in high places who helped to legalize and finance mass abortion in Western countries, from Supreme Court Justice "Catholic" William Brennan to "Catholic" Senator Ted Kennedy. So we did not just single out Jews—we criticized abortion supporters as a group.

From the earliest days of the abortion fight I had been in contact with a Jewish aerospace engineer, Dr. Kenneth Mitzner of California, who, in 1970 or thereabouts, founded the League against Neo-Hitlerism to fight abortion. He also founded and led other pro-life groups. After the Supreme Court's Black Monday decisions in 1973, Mitzner wrote, "It is tragic but demonstrably true that most of the leaders of the pro-abortion movement are of Jewish extraction." [11] In a letter to me of 17 July 1987, he declared:

> Jews must decide whether we condemn Hitler and his followers because mass murder is intrinsically evil or whether our quarrel is just with their choice of us as victims. If our concern is only with the killing of Jews, we have no claim on the sympathies of the rest of humanity. Some Jews ask the world to weep with us for the Jewish victims of Nazism, at the same time they promote the murder of innocent babies by abortion. Such Jews are the most contemptible of hypocrites.

And so, one could say, are avowed Christians who approve or affirm the "right" to kill the unborn, like hypocritical politicians who solemnly proclaim, "I am personally against abortion, but. . ."

In the 1970s I collaborated with Rabbi Mordecai Blanck, founder of EFRAT, to which I referred earlier. This little group of orthodox Jews in Israel was trying to raise the Jewish family birthrate because it was sinking to dangerously low levels. I visited him and his colleagues in Israel to enhance cooperation between our organizations. The reader will perhaps recall my prior remarks about exchanging literature with Rabbi Blanck.

---

[11] *Confessions of a Prolife Missionary* (Gaithersburg, MD: Human Life International), p. 269.

Why, if I am anti-Semitic, have I worked with so many Jews over the years? I have featured such Jewish leaders as Dr. Bernard Nathanson, Dr. Hymie Gordon, Dr. Judith Reisman, Rabbi Yehuda Levin, Dr. Rudolph Vollman, Rabbi Daniel Lapin and others on the various HLI conference faculties I have assembled across the world.

Notwithstanding HLI's record in this respect, columnist Monsignor George G. Higgins, in a weird release by National Catholic News Service in February 1995, accused me of being over the years "a divisive force within the pro-life movement." Worst of all, he wrote, "Alongside this, there has been what I would call a flirtation with anti-Semitism." We at HLI and others sent a rebuttal to each diocesan newspaper that had published Higgins's column (not all did). Not one printed our rebuttal, although we know they each received a bundle of protesting letters. A number of Jews also immediately came to our defense. Among them were Rabbi Yehuda Levin of the Jewish Anti-Abortion League and the prominent Jewish leader Rabbi Daniel Lapin, founder of the organization "Towards Tradition."

Asked by the journalist Arthur Brew whether "Father Marx was anti-Semitic," Dr. Bernard Nathanson responded, "Father Marx doesn't have a racist bone in his body!" Asked about Monsignor Higgins's statement regarding the high rate of abortion in Israel, Nathanson replied: "It is absolutely true. Everyone knows that Israel's rate of abortion is very high, definitely one of the highest anywhere." Asked about my statement in 1987 that there are a large number of abortionists and pro-abortion medical professors who are Jewish, Dr. Nathanson replied, "That's correct. For some reason Jewish doctors seem to be attracted to abortion work."[12]

Besides Nathanson, forty-three Jewish leaders, rabbis, and thinkers, such as Dr. Norman Kurland, Midge Decter, Dr. Judith Reisman, Rabbi Lapin, and others, came to HLI's defense in an HLI news conference held in Montreal.[13]

---

[12] Arthur Brew's refutation of Higgins and defense of HLI in a submission to the *New York Catholic*, 29 February 1995.

[13] *Montreal Gazette*, 28 February 1995.

HLI has collaborated with pro-life Jews for years. In 1995 Rabbi Levin and Father Matthew Habiger, president of HLI, signed a "Christian and Jewish Pro-Life Alliance Joint Declaration on the Sanctity of Life" designed to save both Jewish and gentile babies from abortion, with a special effort directed towards educating Israeli Jews on the importance of being pro-life. With that agreement in mind, we are planning a pro-life seminar in Israel. Also, we are funding (in part) Rabbi Levin's Jewish Union Developing Education and Assistance (JUDEA) and working closely with him. Note that he sits on our board of advisors. Is our attempt to save Jewish babies anti-Semitic? HLI is *pro*-Semitic!

The charge of anti-Semitism, as received and amplified by Monsignor Higgins, originated with Planned Parenthood in New York. Prof. Stephen Scheinberg of Concordia University in Montreal, speaking for B'nai Brith, repeated it.[14] On good Jewish authority we were told that Scheinberg and his cronies need to make periodic accusations of anti-Semitism on the part of prominent persons or groups in order to raise funds. Our Canadian staff and Father Matthew Habiger met with Scheinberg at length to answer his questions and concerns, to refute his charges, and to present evidence suggesting the unfairness of his accusations. Nonetheless, Scheinberg's outlandish untruths were further broadcast by Planned Parenthood of New York, which sent them out on worldwide Internet. In a flurry of mud-slinging, it added that HLI was neo-Nazi, racist, anti-Muslim, liberal-hating, anti-woman, and you-name-it objectionable. I am grateful that my reprehensible sweet tooth managed to escape Planned Parenthood's attention.

A dissenter to *Humanae Vitae*, Monsignor Higgins may have been too busy defending dissident theologians to investigate what HLI really stands for. Higgins's charge that HLI is "divisive" says much regarding the shallowness of his own views about pro-life issues, summed up by his repeated defense of Cardinal Bernardin's seamless garment fallacy, which has allowed so many Catholic politicians and

---

[14] *Frontline Research*, vol. 1, no. 1 (June 1994). See also half-page advertisement in support of HLI in the *Montreal Gazette* for 28 February 1995 signed by a number of Jewish leaders and activists.

others to ignore the massive baby-killing going on in their own back-yards. As if a reply to Cardinal Bernardin's seamless garment theory, Pope John Paul II wrote in *Christifideles Laici*, art. 38:

> Above all, the common outcry, which is justly made on behalf of human rights—for example, the right to health, to home, to work, to family, to culture—is false and illusory if the right to life, the most basic and fundamental right and the condition for all other personal rights, is not defended with maximum determination.

In all our work and writings published worldwide through the years, HLI has been scrupulously loyal to Magisterium and Pope. No one has ever proven the contrary, nor can it be proven. How, then, could HLI be ideologically "a divisive force in the pro-life movement," as Higgins asserted? Was Higgins divisive when he staunchly defended the dissident Notre Dame theologian Father McBrien's *Catholicism*, a book whose errors twice inspired the American hierarchy to call for correction? Or when he defended Father Charles Curran, who led the precipitous dissent to *Humanae Vitae* and was later declared not fit to teach Catholic theology?

We received comparatively little mail over the Higgins column, but it is interesting that in 1987 some pro-abortion Jewish leaders complained to the American Catholic Bishops' Conference, raising the mythical charge of anti-Semitism. I wished that the staff persons who received such complaints had gone straight to HLI for a factual response to the charges. Alas, that did not happen initially. The complaints concerned HLI's *Special Report* no. 34 (reprinted in *Confessions of a Prolife Missionary*, pp. 68-74).

Sadly, it was only after the Conference staff had written to an eminent archbishop who served on HLI's Advisory Board, that we learned about the charges. Our substantive—and I believe conclusive—rebuttal emphasized the following, which I repeat here only to underline the point that HLI's opposition to certain Jewish groups that advocate abortion is due solely to their pro-death advocacy (an opposition shared by pro-life Jewish leaders):

It is indisputable that the mainstream of Jewish teaching
has condemned abortion for centuries. . . . The Union of
American Hebrew Congregations (UAHC) and four of the
other five Jewish organizations I mentioned all belong to
the Religious Coalition for Abortion Rights (RCAR), which
was formed *specifically* to advocate abortion in the name of
religion. Do not those who abandon the teachings of their
religion to advocate the murder of innocent babies deserve
the public criticism . . .?

The UAHC and the American Jewish Congress (AJC)
advocate the legalized murder of millions of babies, including millions of Jewish babies—an "unspeakable crime"
against the Jewish people. Have you asked these groups or
any other pro-abortion groups with which you are "in regular contact" to stop advocating the mass murder of Jewish
babies? Will you now? If not, why not?

According to Israeli sources, more than 1.2 million babies
have been killed in Israel since 1948. Hundreds of thousands or even millions more Jewish babies have been
aborted in Europe and the USA. The UAHC, AJC, etc.,
publicly approve of these killings. HLI opposes them. Who
is acting in the interest of the Jewish people?

If [one] truly find[s] it difficult to think of today's abortion
carnage as a holocaust, please read the enclosed book, *The
Abortion Holocaust—Today's Final Solution*, by William
Brennan, professor of social service at St. Louis University.
Note the atrocity-by-atrocity, euphemism-by-euphemism
parallels between what the Nazis did and what the abor-
tionists are doing. In particular, I draw . . . attention to
Ch. 3, on abortion in Nazi Germany.

ANTI-MUSLIM

*A*nother ridiculous charge made against HLI by Planned
Parenthood and B'nai Brith is that we are anti-Muslim. To
point out the growth of Muslims throughout the world is hardly being
"anti-Muslim." The evidence of such growth can be read in many
publications—even newspapers—and not least in the *Encyclopedia of
Religions*. Before our 1995 World Conference on Love, Life and the
Family in Montreal, three HLI staff members met for five hours over a

Here meeting with a group of Muslims.

meal with Muslim leaders in that city at their headquarters. The aim
of the meeting: seeking common ground and reconciliation.

At our 1996 World Conference in Cincinnati, the Vatican's Cardinal
Francis Arinze, who is Nigerian, gave a keynote address on Christian-
Muslim relations. At the infamous Cairo World Population
Conference in 1995, HLI representatives worked with Muslim leaders
against the horrendous anti-life, anti-family aims and machinations of
the UN and its aggressive anti-life arm, the United Nations Fund for
Population Activities (UNFPA). Is this anti-Muslim?

When the Pope sent his representative to the dedication of the huge mosque in Rome, not very far from St. Peter's, to say that he hoped the freedom granted to the Muslims in the Eternal City would be matched by equal freedom for Christians in Muslim countries—was he anti-Muslim? Incidentally, the chief Muslim authority in Cairo publicly thanked the Pope on prime time TV for alerting Muslims to the enormous crimes proposed by the enemies of life and the family at the notorious UN anti-population conference in his city.

Dr. Hassan Hathout, the well-known Muslim authority and professor of obstetrics and gynecology of the University of California at Los Angeles (he was formerly at the University of Kuwait), would be amused at the outlandish charge that HLI is anti-Muslim. Twice each time at HLI World Conferences (New Orleans, 1989 and Santa Clara, 1991), my friend Professor Hathout lectured on "Islamic Morality and Abortion," "Islamic Morality and the Sexual Revolution," "Islamic Sources of Biomedical Ethics," and "A Puzzle Called Islam." His overall theme (reflecting my intention in inviting him) was achievement of an understanding and reconciliation between Christians and Muslims. The accusation that HLI is anti-Islam is unproven, inflammatory and intentionally confusing, and amounts to cynical manipulation to hobble HLI operations internationally. And, of course, it is propagated by racist Planned Parenthood, which twice labeled HLI "public enemy no. 1." We meet them everywhere.

RACISM

*T*he accusation that HLI, and particularly yours truly, is racist is so outlandish that there is danger of overkill in responding. After fifty years of priesthood, I have addressed groups on many topics, including racism, in forty-nine American states. I have lectured in ninety-one countries, including five African countries; I have written six books and hundreds of articles. For us to be accused of racism is an enormity that only the vicious International Planned Parenthood Federation could perpetrate for its evil, satanic ends and purposes.

Some facts that are already familiar to you but that deserve being repeated in this context: The abbey to which I belong and the university at which I taught for years (St. John's Abbey/University in Collegeville, Minnesota) was one of the first to admit black members and students. A popular black novice and my dear friend, the late Father Prosper Meyer, OSB, was in my novitiate class of eleven (1941-42). He became a great missionary in the Bahamas. My abbey pioneered the missions in the Bahaman islands, where 99 percent of the inhabitants are black. Over forty years in a friendly environment with black students and monks bred not even a grain of racism in me.

For very good reasons we at HLI are concerned about protecting minorities in this country. They are victimized most of all by the abortionists and Planned Parenthood: 24,202,000 white women and 12,203,760 minority women have undergone surgical abortions since the first states legalized this prenatal child-killing in the late 1960s. Because there are currently about 46,000,000 minority people living in the United States, the latter abortion figure indicates that more than one-fifth of our country's minority population has been wiped out by surgical abortion.[15]

Currently the average annual number of surgical abortions obtained by white women is 1,031,500 (66.2% of the total), and the average annual number of surgical abortions obtained by minority women is 526,500 (33.8% of the total).

During the time period 1980-1996, 25.5% of white women's pregnancies ended in surgical abortion, while 40.1% of minority women's pregnancies have been aborted. This means that a pregnant minority woman is 57% more likely to abort than a pregnant white woman.

---

[15] U.S. Department of Commerce, Bureau of the Census. Reference Data Book and Guide to Sources, *Statistical Abstract of the United States, Washington, D.C.* United States Government Printing Office, 1995. Table 12, "Resident Population—Selected Characteristics, 1790-1994, and projections 1995 to 2050." Cf. Also *Washington Times*, 10 January 1997.

The average 1980-1996 abortion *rate* among white women of childbearing age is 22.4 abortions per 1,000; the average abortion rate among minority women is 55.8 abortions per 1,000—two and a half times higher!

Obviously, abortionists target minority women. The eleven U.S. cities with more than 70% minority populations had 52.74

The Rev. Mr. Johnny Hunter, founder of LEARN.

abortionists per million persons, and the eleven U.S. cities with less than 10 percent minority populations had only 15.75 abortionists per million persons. This tremendous disparity represents nothing less than a systematic pattern—which can fairly be called genocidal—directed against minorities by abortionists and other abortion advocates.

To summarize: there are 235 percent more abortionists in minority neighborhoods than in white ones!

Similarly, Planned Parenthood has planted into minority high schools most of the so-called "school-based health clinics," known for their contraception/abortion referrals.[16]

In August 1994, HLI paid for the first black American pro-life conference in Orlando, Florida, giving black leaders $12,000 to organize their congress as they wished. We partly financed a second black conference. The Rev. Mr. Johnny Hunter, the evangelist who founded LEARN (Life Education and Resource Network) and who organized the two black pro-life conferences, has served on the faculty of two

---

[16] See Brian Clowes, *The Facts of Life* (Front Royal, VA: Human Life International, 1997).

Here with some beautiful children in Zimbabwe.

HLI World Conferences and four seminars in South Africa sponsored by HLI. Members of HLI staff have repeatedly picketed abortion centers in Washington, D.C., where genocide against black unborn babies is going on.

HLI sponsored and financed nine seminars in Africa. In November, 1996 we sponsored a large meeting of African leaders in Johannesburg, South Africa, with a view to organizing a pro-life/pro-family movement in Sub-Saharan Africa. We have sent an enormous amount of literature, equipment and audio-visual aids to Africa since the late 1970s.

In 1991 I spent almost four weeks lecturing in various Nigerian seminaries. During that time I addressed the national hierarchy of Nigeria, among whom I saw only one white (Irish) bishop. I was a collaborator in setting up the Nigerian Human Life Protection League with Lawrence Adekoya as its head. We have generously financed him and his staff, with the total cooperation of the bishops.

HLI also financed the participation of five black African bishops and archbishops to our World Conferences in the United States, which some of them addressed. In fact, Archbishop John Onaiyekan of Abuja, Nigeria, opened our Montreal Conference in 1995 with Mass and a sermon. HLI likewise sponsored and largely financed two seminars in Kenya, one in Zimbabwe, in Zambia and others elsewhere. HLI sends enormous amounts of literature and audio-visual aids to

African countries every week. We published in Nigeria 100,000 copies of our popular pictorial pamphlet "Love and Let Live" which shows aborted and preborn healthy babies. In 1988 HLI spent $30,000 financing an international seminar in Zambia. We have put into Africa 10,000 models of three-month-old black fetuses to educate people on the realities of abortion. HLI would do much more for Africa, with more financing.

Archbishop John Onaiyekan of Abuja, Nigeria at our world conference in Montreal, 1995.

Dr. Claude Newbury, the head of our office in South Africa, whom we financed and with whom we have worked for years, has credited HLI with defeating the South African abortionists twice, as we have seen in Chapter 9. Most unfortunately, we recently lost the fight.

Adolf Hitler wrote in *Mein Kampf* that if you tell a lie often enough, people will believe it. IPPF must have learned this lesson from Hitler, because the lies accusing HLI of being anti-Semitic, racist, anti-Muslim, and misogynist appeared again and again on the Internet, in the publications of Planned Parenthood, and were quoted against us by a whole bevy of people, including some Catholics, who should know better! We were astonished to learn that some professors at Notre Dame believed and repeated all these lies about us, disgracing themselves in South Bend newspapers as representatives of a so-called Catholic institution supposedly interested in the truth.[17]

---

[17] *Special Report* No. 139

With a group of seminarians in Nigeria.

If you are not accomplishing anything, the liars and maligners of this world will not attack you, as our Lord reminded all of us. Therein lies our consolation.

And so we have come to the end of this painful chapter. HLI's mission is to promote the culture of love and life and the enhancement of family life. Let it be said that our activities, our literature and our many publications are open to anyone who cares to examine them.

Visiting with a number of Nigerian women and their babies.

CHAPTER 11

Interviewed on Radio and Television

$\mathcal{I}$n the last thirty-five years I have been interviewed by representatives of the press, radio, and TV several thousand times. I recall one of the first such experiences in the early 1970s.

It was on a TV program in Chicago: a debate of three pro-lifers vs. three pro-abortionists. The great pro-lifer and law professor Dennis Horan was on my team, with another stalwart whose name I have forgotten. Shy, afraid, and inappropriately polite, I made a contribution that was short and feeble, and Mr. Horan told me so. He exhorted me to be bold and to politely cut in, because the enemy always tries to use up all the time. He taught me a lesson I never forgot. Too bad, I thought: Why are not all priests trained to confront the enemy, as Horan so eloquently did?

In the early days of the battle, the propaganda had it that abortion was a narrowly "Catholic" issue. This invention kept many Protestants from becoming active in the pro-life fight. That is why, too, as I explained earlier, my superiors allowed me to wear a business suit in fighting the abortionists; a priest speaking publicly against abortion in the media would only be proclaiming "the Catholic line," as the abortionists were asserting. That is why my book *The Death Peddlers: War on the Unborn* was released in December 1971 as authored by "Paul Marx, OSB, Ph.D." Still, we weren't deceiving anyone, because any reader who gathered that I belonged to the Order of St. Benedict could figure out that I was a Catholic.

In 1972-1973 I was interviewed, mostly about *The Death Peddlers*, one hundred thirty times on radio and TV talk shows.[1] There were

---

[1] *New York Times*, 8 July 1995.

In the last thirty-five years I have been interviewed by representatives of the press, radio and TV several thousand times.

also many interviews with the press. The widely distributed *The Mercy Killers* in 1971 also was the subject of many media and press interviews. The reader may be surprised that mercy killing had already become a subject of popular discourse in the early 1970s. I recall doing two-hour discussions on abortion/euthanasia and family topics twice on an international radio hookup out of San Francisco. I spoke to millions. I used to joke with my confreres at St. John's Abbey/University that I talked to more people in one year than the whole faculty did. That was undoubtedly true.

In the 1970s I conned leaders at Planned Parenthood meeting in California into giving me a chance to explain natural family planning. They graciously allowed me fifteen minutes. The reaction was good until abortionist Dr. Sadja Goldsmith asked me what I thought of "outercourse." My response was inadequate; I tried to get by by saying that I'd thought this was a scientific meeting, not a religious one. A week later we tangled on a large San Francisco talk show before an audience of about forty people. This time I appeared as a priest. I think the moderator enjoyed the fierce exchange even more than I did. Trying to be friendly at the beginning, I made the mistake of calling the abortionist by her first name, "Sadja." Perhaps justified, she retorted full steam: "Call me Dr. Goldsmith!"

I remember being interviewed in 1972 on a large radio station in suburban Los Angeles in a program entitled "Kitchen Chat with Sam." Delightful, outgoing, and amiably Italian, Sam personally interviewed his guests the week before going on the air, and I gave him *The Death Peddlers* then. A week later, just before we went on, he happened to read, "Paul Marx, OSB., Ph.D.," and wondered what the

"OSB." meant, vol-
unteering the infor-
mation that it must
be "another degree
in obstetrics."
(From then on, I
jokingly told people
who asked about
"OSB." that it was
an abbreviation for
"Bachelor of
Obstetrical Science."
We had many a
good laugh about
it.) But just as Sam
asked me again
what OSB. meant,
the engineer sig-
naled to him to
begin the program,
and I didn't have to
answer! All went
well. Obviously,
Sam had not read
the book and knew
very little about
abortion. He
allowed me to say
virtually anything I
wished. I was not
so lucky on other
occasions.

In Chapter 3 I
discussed my hour-
long TV interview in
San Jose, Costa

Unforgettable was the one-hour program on the second largest TV station in Tokyo in 1974. I had been instructed not to dress as a priest.

Rica, in 1972 and the proposed three-hour TV program canceled because

With the press at a banquet in Nairobi, Kenya.

Being interviewed in Argentina.

of a strike in Montevideo, Uruguay. Twice in the 1970s I was "victimized" on the Gay Byrne show in Dublin, a Johnny Carson-like program that most Irish adults watch. One of these programs had to do with natural family planning, the merits of which I did my best to explain. When I finished a doctor (Catholic?) denied most of what I said.

Unforgettable was an interesting one-hour program on the second largest TV station in Tokyo in 1974. It was unique insofar as the questions and answers were subsequently published in both Japanese and English, in a booklet used to teach the English language. I had been instructed not to wear a Roman collar and to appear as the sociologist "Dr. Marx"; and that is the way I was introduced.

The interview went well until the moderator threw me a curve: "Dr. Marx, I happen to know that you are also a Catholic priest. Would you mind a sensitive question?" "Of course not," I said bravely. "Well then, tell your audience why the Catholic Church is against birth control." My response: "That's news to me. Actually the Catholic Church is very much *for* birth control. She teaches that there should be no intercourse before marriage and no living together before marriage: that would eliminate a lot of births. The Church teaches

I'm obviously not a woman, but I was interviewed for this program anyway!

that once validly married, always married, until death do you part: no divorce—and that would eliminate a lot of births. Furthermore, the Catholic Church insists on fidelity within marriage—and that would eliminate still more births."

I went on:

> The Catholic Church believes that couples who get married should be seriously taught about the difficulties of married life and parenting, marriage being a demanding vocation, as the number of divorces would seem to prove. In other words, a couple shouldn't get married unless they are emotionally mature, spiritually deep, economically ready, and prepared for parenting. If no one married unless so prepared, marriage would take place later, and any number of births would not occur. This would be a good means of birth control. And it would foster good family life, without the burden of single-parent families.

Then, knowing that many wealthy Japanese have mistresses, I emphasized, "The Church also teaches that, once married, there are to be no playmates on the side. The Church believes in strict monogamy, with no sexual playing-around; no sex tourism, of which Japanese men are so fond. Again, this involves fertility control, doesn't it?"

The moderator, a bit taken aback, then said, "But I mean birth con-

At the March for Life in Toronto, Canada, 1988.

trol within marriage. The Church believes in this. . . in this. . . Rhythm . . . this abstinence from sex for birth control." "Well, yes," said I; "abstinence sometimes, yes, if the couple engages in the most healthy form of fertility control, which is natural family planning—of which a great Japanese gynecological surgeon was the pioneer." That scored a point and led into a discussion of NFP, a subject that, curiously, seems to attract and interest many people, even if too few of them practice it.

In the early 1980s, I once arranged an interview with Dr. John

With moderator Jim Eason of KGO in San Francisco on a one-hour talk show.

Billings and Mrs. Mercedes Wilson over a large Twin City TV channel. I followed the next week with an interview on abortion. The station manager told me that the Billings-Wilson interview had brought them the largest reaction to any program ever. The Liturgical Press sold many of Billings' books as a result.

On the radio in Ottawa, Canada.

One thing about being interviewed about abortion across the world is that after a while there remain very few new or unique questions. You know what the interviewer is going to ask before he finishes the first sentence. In the United States, Europe, and even somewhat in Catholic Latin America, the attitude of most interviewers is almost always hostile. A few moderators have confided to me privately that they greatly oppose abortion but have to play the devil's advocate, given their job. But one could almost feel the anger of radical feminists and other pro-abortion adversaries—most of whom, I sensed, either had abortions or were involved in some way.

A number of times I debated or was interviewed along with members of Planned Parenthood. Too often I said too much, or spoke too angrily. Sometimes you met your adversaries in advance. I remember

On the TV program "In Focus" in Milwaukee.

in some studio on the West Coast faced with an attractive young lady, easy on the eyes and speaking for PP. I asked her before the program began whether she ever had an abortion. The question stunned her, and I was not surprised when she suddenly blurted out, "Yes," and then, when she realized she had said too much, begged me not to refer to this admission during our live encounter on TV. Psychologically healthy women are never happy about having killed their babies; there *is* a real post-abortion syndrome. I have counseled women who have agonized over abortions, one of them for as long as forty-nine years. What has always struck me is the latent, deep-seated anger simmering in feminist, pro-abortion interviewers. (Often it is not latent!)

An amusing thing happened during an interview in Denver. I had explained to the moderator, in answer to his question, that there was no real overpopulation problem. Just then, one of three children carefully guarded in a neighboring room by a solicitous mother escaped and shouted a word or two clearly picked up by the microphones. My interrogator then dryly asked me whether I still thought there was no overpopulation.

In Africa the situation is different. Most black people are inherently pro-life, because they love children and family. The media reflects this attitude. Also, as in every country but especially in Africa, a foreigner is always considered to be an expert. I have recounted my experience on Zimbabwe's national TV network in the city of Harare, where the

On the July 1990 cover of the German magazine pur-magazin.

nice young interviewer actually asked me what questions he should ask me! Never have I faced more intelligent queries or been given more time for my response!

I was always delighted to be interviewed in the Philippines. The gentle and kindly Filipinos are always forthright and honest, with no trickery to catch you. In the city of Baguio in northern Luzon, the only cool city in the Philippines because it is in the mountains, there was

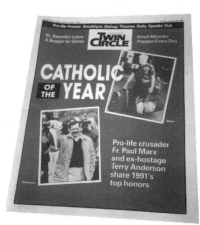

Proclaimed "Catholic of the Year" in 1991 by Catholic Twin Circle.

the usual kindly chat with the moderator. What was unusual were the two birds in separate cages outside the hotel, seemingly large parrots. If you told one of the parrots, "Go to hell!" the bird would ceremoniously raise his head slowly, look around a bit and then respond, "You go to hell too." The children from the town came to tell the bird "Go to hell" so often that the poor parrot grew hoarse, actually almost losing his voice, so the

On TV in El Paso, Texas, May 1994.

proprietor told me. At that point the children were told to find their fun elsewhere.

A TV appearance in Australia in the 1970s was highly unusual. Without warning, a middle-aged woman with a large shawl over her head and her back to the cameras told the moderator that she was a Catholic, that an angry priest had warned her not to abort, but that he relented when she informed him she was pregnant by another priest. It was a totally programmed "plant." And I, too inexperienced, surprised, and stunned to collect my wits, reacted very badly. Dr. Kevin Hume, the great pro-lifer who had arranged the interview, was too polite to dwell on my miserable performance.

On another work tour, I was interviewed on euthanasia seven times in Australia. All but one moderator thought that the Catholic Church teaches that a doctor must continue to treat a sick patient to the very grave. The ignorance that media and newsmen betray about the Church's teachings on life issues is immense, especially when it comes to the teaching about ordinary and extraordinary means.

Then there was the two-hour interview on a large, national radio network in Ottawa, Canada. The experienced, intelligent interviewer asked me whether I did not think it unfair that where abortion is illegal the rich can always avail themselves of abortion in other countries, while the poor are forced to bear their children. My response was, "The rich can always commit sins and crimes the poor cannot afford. Thus, the affluent can rent $1,000-per-night prostitutes in New York City while the poor cannot. Unfair? Are you suggesting that we make

Being interviewed at our conference in Seattle, Washington, June 1995.

$1,000 prostitutes available to all who want them but cannot afford them?" He willingly conceded, "You won that one."

He then asked me to name the greatest promoter of abortion in the world. "Unquestionably Planned Parenthood," I responded, adding "Planned Parenthood is the most wicked organi-

On the radio in Cuba, 1995.

zation on earth, killing our unborn, destroying youth, family, churches, and society with its horrendous sex ed, lies, and blood money." "Do you wish to repeat that?" he asked incredulously. So I did. In fact, I almost said PP could stand for "Planned Promiscuity."

A week later two couriers came to my office in Washington, D.C., bearing a note from Canadian Planned Parenthood telling me that they would sue me if I did not retract my statement publicly. "Go

With Cardinal Sanchez on the "Life Matters" TV show in Detroit, Michigan.

In front of the cameras at our conference in Montreal, 1995.

Never a dull moment when you're in the pro-life movement.

ahead," I responded bravely. "All we have is debts—and you can have all of them." In Canada, at that time, once you threatened a lawsuit you had to follow through within a month or else forget about it. Several days before the expiration date, I received notification that the threat had been withdrawn, but I was warned about possible future action. By the way, I learned later that the highly competent interviewer who had elicited my appraisal of Planned Parenthood lost his job over the incident.

When it comes to press interviews, you do well to distrust the reporter. Here there is no margin to be simple as a dove. Even if the reporter accurately submits what you have presented, it may come out so different that you will hardly recognize it. Sometimes the pro-abortion city editor recasts the report. To avoid pernicious editing, the great French geneticist Dr. Jerome Lejeune would go on only *live* radio and TV.

It is good advice to be as sly as a fox and—again!— never simple as a dove. Record the interview, if you can, as protection. Actually, most radio stations will give you an audio-tape of the interview, if you ask. Raise all your antennae to detect ambushes and trap questions. Don't let them state/frame the issue, if you can prevent it. Most of the media and press are satanically pro-abortion; I suspect many of their personnel have in some way been personally involved with preborn baby-killing. Every abortion involves a number of people with thirty-four million *surgical* since 1973 and several million before that (since 1967 when Colorado became the first state to legalize abortion): think of the number of families involved, to say nothing of families involved with abortifacients. A national poll a few years ago showed that 96 percent of TV producers in the United States accepted abortion-on-request as just another medical procedure. On the other hand, the Protestant radio and TV networks have been cooperative and friendly.

How many people have I spoken to on the electronic media and in the press? I calculate well over fifty million.

But make no mistake about the power of money and the media! In a sense, we no longer live in a democracy. Did we want abortion on request? No—but we got it. Did we want pornographic TV? No—but it is here. Do we want explicit sex ed in our schools, public and private? No—but it is there. Do we want euthanasia? No—but two circuit courts have already given it to us. And if our Supreme Court is logical, after giving us *Roe v. Wade* and thus allowing doctors to kill preborn babies, why should they not allow medics to kill older babies? One could go on.

We are "educated" and manipulated by national and international media of all kinds; they often and effectively neutralize any moral or spiritual forces and opposition, already all too weak, given the weakness of the mainline churches, riddled with pedophilia, affluence, weakness of leadership and scandal. And as the great Protestant thinker Reinhold Niebuhr said, "The worst corruption is the corruption of religion." It is a sad commentary on our times that bishops should act to exclude Mother Angelica's EWTN TV network from some archdioceses and dioceses.

CHAPTER 12

The Future

A German cardinal once told me, "*Die Abtreibung macht Alles kaput*: Legal abortion destroys everything." An archbishop in South America wrote me that "to legalize abortion is to create a moral earthquake." Abortion's moral earthquakes have been propelling their shock waves for some thirty years over wider and wider areas, so that more than 66 percent of mankind now live in countries where the historic protection of the unborn has been abandoned in whole or in part.

The chief duty of governments is to guard the life of all its citizens, born and unborn. Thomas Jefferson said it better, "The care of human life is the first and only legitimate object of good government." The right to life is *the* basic right; all other rights flow from it. Failing in this duty to protect life, nations cross a point of no return, witnessed by the fact that no single Western country has effectively reversed or even permanently tightened a permissive abortion law. And like individual persons, countries do indeed influence one another; hence the international abortion plague and the expanding culture of death. We have seen that abortion, along with sterilization, has become the chief means of birth control in the Western world, and is fast approaching that status in the developing nations, thanks to the contraceptive/abortifacient imperialism of the selfish, affluent West. These prosperous nations, as they succumb to the anti-life virus of sterilization and abortion, resolutely continue to instill it into the Third World.

Some thoughtful people—even many pro-lifers—do not seem to realize that abortion is the endpoint of sexual abuse. Before there is abortion, there are fornication, adultery, and other irresponsible sexual activities. To oppose only abortion is to indulge in short-sighted preoccupation with only the results of sex-run-loose. The virtue of chastity is essential in controlling the sexual drive; without chastity, the unleashed drive wreaks endless havoc on family and society, as our modern times eloquently demonstrate. Think of all the sexually transmitted diseases, the growing rate of infertility, and the more than thirty million Americans (one out of six men, women, and children in the United States) infected with incurable herpes. Consider that almost one of three babies is born out of wedlock, as eight million single-parent families run up a national bill of $42 billion a year (remember: out-of-wedlock pregnancy is a near-certain predictor of poverty). Note that 48 percent of first marriages end in divorce, that four of

Another day at the office.

Preaching from the pulpit.

ten children will sleep tonight without a father in the house, and that emotionally crippled children are being devastated by their psychological problems.

Think, too, about these statistics from the Centers for Disease Control and Prevention: 38 percent of all ninth graders, 46 percent of all tenth graders, 55 percent of all juniors, and 68 percent of all

"A clean desk is a sign of a sick mind."

Always on the go... five days after an operation. I'm in front of our previous World Headquarters in Gaithersburg, Maryland.

In our old stock room one late night.

I attended the baptism of former abortionist Dr. Bernard Nathanson, 9 December 1996, at St. Patrick's Cathedral in New York City. Here I watch as Dr. Nathanson receives his first Holy Communion from Cardinal John O'Connor.

seniors have reported having sexual intercourse at least once.[1]

According to the latest data of the National Center for Health Statistics, illegitimate births among Caucasian girls and women are soaring: From 1982 to 1992, births out of wedlock rose 54 percent to 1.2 million a year! The trend of teenage, unwed childbearing is up: from 16.7 per 1,000 teens (aged 15 to 19) in 1965 to 46.4 per 1,000 in 1994, amounting to some 350,000 new unmarried teen mothers each year.

---

[1] *Catholics for a Free Choice Exposed: Dirty Ideas, Dirty Money* (Gaithersburg, MD: Human Life International, 1995).

And when a society has to resort to chemical castration (as in California and several countries) to discourage rape and sexual child abuse, it is sliding toward the bottom of the slippery slope.

Meanwhile, international sex tourism is big business. Western houses of prostitution are stocked with young girls and women from Thailand, the Philippines, and other poor countries. In 1996 the World Congress against the Commercial Sexual Exploitation of Children took place in Stockholm. In time for this large congress, Save the Children Fund (SCF) published a report, *Kids for Hire*, highlighting the global extent of children's sexual exploitation. For more than two years the British Coalition on Child Prostitution and Tourism had campaigned against child sex tourism. Exploiters, it seems, think they have less chance of acquiring AIDS and VD from children.[2]

With my good friend Randall Terry at The March for Life, 1992.

Fr. Welch and I speaking with Cardinal Trujillo.

---

[2] *London Tablet*, 31 August 1996, and sources listed in the September 1996 *Readers' Digest*.

In the airport with all my luggage.

Spending time with the One Who gives me strength.

Work and prayer is the life of a Benedictine.

Drug addiction consumes an enormous number of victims today, but surely not more than sex addiction does. Of course, the two are by no means unrelated. One facet of sex addiction is cohabitation, just living together, which is deadly to the institution of marriage. According to census surveys, in 1970 there were 520,000 cohabiting couples in the United States. In 1994, the figure had soared sevenfold to 3.7 million! We used to call it "shacking up." Now it is merely one of many choices euphemistically known as "alternative lifestyles."

Couples who "shack up" have a 50 percent higher rate of divorce than couples that don't have "trial marriages." More than 40 percent of couples living together ("shack mates") break off their relationships short of marriage. As a result, the number of never-married Americans has increased drastically since 1970, doubling from 21 million to 44 million during a time when the population was growing by one-fifth. Hence, too, the percent-

Praying in front of an abortion clinic, Fargo, North Dakota.

age of never-married men and women in their thirties has tripled, while there has been a 41 percent decline in the marriage rate. Cohabitation has also been a chief factor in the soaring rate of children born out of wedlock. In 1994, according to Maggie Gallagher's book *The Abolition of Marriage*, 40 percent of never-married women in their thirties had had at least one child.

The natural choice is LIFE!

The atheist Albert Camus once remarked: "A single sentence will suffice to describe modern man; he fornicated and read the papers." Does modern man still read the papers today, or does he watch pornographic TV? We are no longer "slouching to Gomorrah" (Judge Robert Bork's phrase)—we are there!

Chastity, in *and* out of marriage, is extremely important for everyone's body and soul. In the old-time and still valid understanding, chastity is the rational use (or non-use) of the human sexual faculty according to one's station in life (marriage, the single state, consecrated celibacy). As applied to the married, chastity entails the proper, loving use of this faculty to beget, educate, and responsibly form a generous number of children—who, I firmly believe, will in turn make saints of their parents. This marital vocation defines the nature, function, and meaning of the marital embrace.

For years I have waited in vain for our National Conference of Catholic Bishops to issue a national pastoral on chastity *before and within* marriage. In a pamphlet on marriage and family life issued by the NCCB in 1995, contraception, natural family planning, and

With my longtime faithful secretary, Brenda Bonk.

Humanae Vitae were not even mentioned! In fifty years of priesthood I cannot recall hearing a single specific lecture on marital chastity at any secular conference. In the last three years I have taken up that topic myself in formal lectures for married couples, always receiving a highly appreciative response. Long before his election, Pope John Paul II wrote on this subject in *Love and Responsibility.* He has several times expressed his dismay that the Catholic Church's reasonable teachings on human, Christian sexuality are so little understood and therefore so foolishly and ignorantly rejected.

As Malcolm Muggeridge said in 1978 (long before he became a Roman Catholic), *Humanae Vitae* hits "the point that really matters; to interfere with [human procreation], to seek to relate it merely to pleasure, is to get back into pre-Christian times and ultimately to destroy the civilization that Christianity has brought about."

In another context Muggeridge explained that when people lose their sense of God, sex becomes their main preoccupation. And who would deny that our affluent modern times are saturated with sex, and that sex has become recreation? It is worth quoting once more the comments of the wonderful Jesuit theologian Father John A. Hardon:

Some work, others sleep.

I do not believe the pro-life movement will succeed unless those who are strongly pro-life are also defending the teachings of the Church from the first century—that contraception is a grave sin.

For many years, I've taught a course on the history of contraception. Over more than 5,000 years of recorded history, all contraceptive societies become abortive societies. Contraception leads inevitably to abortion. And abortion always leads to the destruction of that society.

Intensely listening.

Having myself studied the history of contraception, I can confirm Father Hardon's statement; I, too, have seen the transition from contraception to abortion in many countries over the last thirty years. But note the confusing statements released by various groups. It is indeed disconcerting when the legal counsel to the National Right to Life Committee urges in

Rome at the Third Pro-Life Leadership Conference of 3-5 October 1995 that the final document of said meeting should not condemn non-abortifacient contraception! As early as the 1920s, the great Jesuit economist/philosopher Heinrich Pesch referred to the contraceptive scourge as the "White Death" creeping through the Western world. In no country of the world—and I've been in ninety-one—has legalized abortion preceded the widespread use of contraception. But in every country of the world—bar none—widespread contraception has *always* led to abortion. I

"He doesn't like me!"

defy anyone to cite a single exception to this rule. As you will recall, I have frequently challenged those who sanction contraception to show me one nation in the world that has widespread contraception, but also enjoys a good, replacement-level birthrate and a flourishing family life. There is none. There never will be.

I have told you this story before, but allow me to repeat it, perhaps with an added nuance or two. I had a chance to talk with Pope John Paul II on 17 November 1979. After thanking him for condemning contraception in virtually every country (thirty times during a ten-day tour of Africa, for instance), I expressed my deep conviction that once you have contraception, abortion inevitably follows. If parents contracept, their teenagers are much more likely to fornicate. Irresponsible sexual activity, facilitated by contraception and abortion, produces more and more venereal disease and eventual sterility, increases illegitimacy even as adoption services dry up, prostitutes the medical and legal professions, and occasions ever more divorce. And, of course, if you can kill unborn babies, you can kill the old and unproductive—the "useless eaters," as Hitler called them. The abomination of euthanasia is already very much with us! The Pope was in total agreement.

Indeed, as the Pontiff wrote in his 100-page letter to the world's

With my little friends in Zambia.

One of my little friends.

Children are the future of the Church and family—I love them!

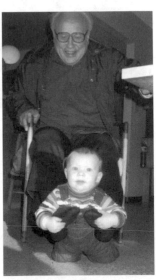

Captured by a little one!

families, "No human society can run the risk of permissiveness in fundamental issues regarding the nature of marriage and family." Tamper with sex, and you tamper with all of society.

The incomparable G. K. Chesterton put it eloquently: "All healthy men and women know that there is a certain fury in sex which we cannot afford to inflame, that a certain mystery and awe must surround it, if we are to remain sane." He also said, "A society that claims to be civilized and yet allows the sex instinct free-play is inoculating itself with a virus of corruption which sooner or later will destroy it. It is only a question of time." The destructive process is going on.

One cannot get too much of Chesterton, the wise convert:

You've got something there.

For sex cannot be admitted to a mere equality among elementary emotions or experiences like eating and sleeping. The moment sex ceases to be a servant it becomes a tyrant. There is something dangerous and disproportionate in its place in human nature, for whatever reason; and it does really need a special purification and dedication. The modern talk about sex being free like any other sense, about the body being beautiful like any tree or flower, is either a description of the Garden of Eden or a piece of thoroughly bad psychology, of which the world grew weary two thousand years ago.[3]

---

[3] "St. Francis of Assisi" in *Collected Works of G. K. Chesterton*, (San Francisco: Ignatius Press, 1986) vol. 2, p. 39.

The question presents itself: How can we teach chastity; how can we spiritually instill it into the young in home and school when this difficult virtue is not widely practiced and exemplified by parents and teachers—and, alas, too often not even by the clergy? The vast majority of fertile Catholic parents and teachers are contracepting or unknowingly using abortifacients; some have been sterilized. Some have deliberately and knowingly chosen chemical (by Pill), mechanical (by IUD), or surgical abortion, even though this choice leads to automatic excommunication from the Catholic Church if one knows the penalty. (No sacrament can be received, of course, unless this excommunication has been lifted!)

My attempt at playing Santa wasn't 100% successful!

Most parents, bishops, priests, and religious seem to think that sex ed promotes chastity. However, all studies *everywhere* in the world show that modern classroom sex education has been a complete failure; even its promoters

"Watch it — it's my fingers you're biting."

often admit that.[4]

The Pope has rightly called sex education the "aphrodisiac of the culture of the West." In the West, sexuality in sex-education courses and in the general media is often reduced to the category of bodily functions and lessons in anatomy and physiology—"organ recitals"— and the "education" itself often amounts to little more than "how-to" lessons. The proper implementation of the latest document on sex education from the Pontifical Council for the Family, *The Truth and Meaning of Human Sexuality: Guidelines for Education within the Family*, should have eliminated most of the offensive, explicit sex ed from Catholic schools. However, it seems that most American bishops are totally ignoring the document.

Those who rejected *Humanae Vitae* must ask themselves the question: Are today's youth and parents happier because of the increase in irresponsible sexual activity? The words of the French writer Jean

---

4   Barbara Dafoe Whitehead, "The Failure of Sex Education," *Atlantic Monthly*, October 1994, pp. 55-80; Arthur J. Delaney, "The Grotesque World of Today's Sex Education," *New Oxford Review*, vol. 63, no. 4 (May 1996), 11-19; "Public School Sex Education: A Report," published by the American Family Association; Bill Reck, "Sexual Education in Catholic Schools," a report published by the Riehle Foundation of Milford, Ohio; also, the various issues of *Information*, a German publication by Freundeskreis Maria Goretti, e.V., Munich, Germany; insightful articles on sex education's dangers and failures appear periodically in the German *Medizin und Ideologie* published by Europaische Ärzteaktion in den Deutschsprachigen Landern, e.V., Postfach 1123, Ulm, Germany; "Case Histories of Graphic Sex Ed in Catholic Elementary Schools," published by Paul Marx, OSB, Human Life International, n.d.g.; "What will happen to Sex-Ed?," *Challenge*, 1996, p. 8; "New Vatican Document Vindicates Concerns about Classroom Sex Education," *AD 2000*, vol. 19, no. 2 (March 1996). Steve Wood, "Sex Education: Protecting Your Children from Something Worse Than Herod's Troops," *St. Joseph's Covenant Keepers*, vol. 2, issue 6 (November 1996). The very latest and best documented description of sex ed's failure is in Brian Clowes' *The Facts of Life* (Front Royal, VA: Human Life International: 1997), 261-265. See also *HLI Reports*, vol. 15, no. 2 (February 1997), the whole issue.

Guitton, advisor to Pope
Paul VI, come to mind:
"Man's sexual need is but
slight as compared with his
sexual desire, which knows
no bounds and makes itself
known repeatedly at the
slightest stimulation. We live
in an aphrodisiac society
which multiplies our sexual
desires."

An early HLI supporter from Africa.

No amount of bed-hop-
ping assuages the monster of
sex-run-loose. In a culture
soaked with sex, especially
through movies and television, sexual activity is
expected to solve all
kinds of problems it was
never meant to solve.
The massive disillusion-
ment as to marriage and
family life is reflected by
increasing divorce rates
in this age of contracep-
tion, abortifacients, sterilization, and surgical
abortion. Need and
desire are two different
things: need is reason-
able, but desire can be
gargantuan. Love, not
sex, is what humans
need and crave—and
cannot do without.
There is more truth than
poetry in what a wise

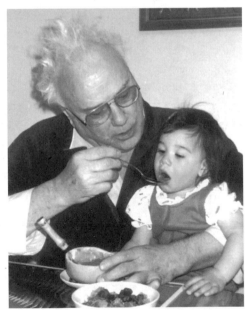

Definitely a bad hair day for me...but my young charge doesn't seem to notice!

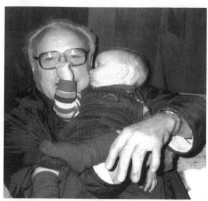

Hi Groucho Marx!

man wrote: "To live without love is a tragedy; to live without sex is inconvenient."

As the Quaker William Penn observed, "Men must be governed by God or they will be ruled by tyrants." And sex unleashed is one of the worst tyrants, in view of the consequences.

Perhaps Edmund Burke said it even better: "Society cannot exist unless a controlling power upon will and appetite be placed somewhere, and the less of it there is within, the more there must be without. It is ordained in the eternal constitution of things that men of intemperate minds cannot be free. Their passions forge their fetters." In his encyclical *The Development of Peoples* (42), Pope Paul VI wisely wrote against "a humanism closed in on itself, and not open to the values of the spirit and to God Who is their source."

In an age when we cannot build prisons fast enough, when the drug culture has consumed so many of our youth, when the mass media peddles so much pornography, when the churches are so weak, when governments are so corrupt, when the private foundations sponsor so much evil with their grants, when we suffer from a growing immoral judicial imperialism—in such an age and in such a world one can only conclude that churches and society, indeed mankind, are in total crisis. As Arnold Toynbee observed, "Every age has its own crisis and challenge which must be met—otherwise society collapses."

One thinks of deist Benjamin Franklin's dictum "A remedy for luxury has never been found." Add to this the theological confusion, the godless feminism that has contributed to the downfall of our Catholic school and hospital systems, the general absence of strong clerical and episcopal leadership—and you tend to agree with what the great Protestant thinker Reinhold Niebuhr said: "The worst corruption is a corrupt religion." Cardinal John Newman prophesied one hundred years ago, "I thank God I live in a day when the enemy is outside the

Church, and I know what he is doing, but I foresee a day when the enemy will be both outside and inside the Church, and I pray for the poor faithful who will be caught in the crossfire." Indeed, so it is in this culture of death in which most people fail to distinguish freedom from license and make up their own moral rules, especially with regard to sexual morality.

The immoral impositions of our courts, particu-

Babies—our most precious resource.

larly the U.S. Supreme Court, are frightening. Consider how in the Court's 1992 decision in *Planned Parenthood v. Casey*, Justices O'Connor, Kennedy, and Souter declared, "At the heart of liberty is the right to define one's own concept of existence, of meaning, of the universe, and of the mystery of human life." This twaddle is a formula for moral anarchy. In short, the fundamental Judeo-Christian principles on which our Constitution and nation were founded have been thrown out by the people and their courts.

It is this unprincipled mentality that caused these justices to write, "In some critical respects, the abortion decision is of the same character as the decision to use contraception. . . for two decades of economic and social developments, [people] have organized intimate relationships and made choices that define their views of themselves and their places in society, in reliance on the availability of abortion in the event that contraception should fail." As the philosopher Dr. Janet Smith has observed, this wholly permissive principle describes our times accurately. Abortion has become just another means of birth control! Anyone can see that the U.S. Supreme Court essentially proclaimed, "We need abortion so that we can continue our immoral, pleasure-seeking, contraceptive lifestyles."

"Who in the heck are you?"

You don't have to travel in many countries before you are convinced that one of the chief sources of abortion is contraception, which today, of course, is largely indistinguishable from most abortifacients.

Most Americans, most Catholics, and (one can safely say) most bishops, priests, and religious are not aware of the abortifacient character of most types of "contraception." An American cardinal once said, during a lecture in a foreign country, that there were forty million abortions in the world each year. He was quoting, of course, the guesstimate of the United Nations, which at various times has referred to an annual incidence of between fifty and sixty million *surgical* abortions. I wrote to the cardinal to inform him that very many more abortions were induced than the forty million he had cited. I then politely suggested that perhaps bishops and priests could be informed about the various chemical abortions induced by so-called contraceptives, and parishioners could be educated as well. I sent documentation and cited scientists who could confirm what I presented. I received a polite thank-you note and routine encouragement to "keep up the good work."

The founding president of Pharmacists for Life International, Dr. Bogomir Kuhar, attempts to track the true number of abortions—

Twelve more reasons to have one more child...

not merely the surgical abortions—in the United States. He estimates that in 1996 there were between nine and twelve million. One can safely say there are comparable numbers in other countries.

Never have we lived amid so much death; we exist in a veritable culture of death, at a time when the whole West is collapsing because of sexual abuse and the resultant low birthrates and family disintegration—but most people do not seem to know it! Meanwhile, Satan and his minions are trying to open the next door to oblivion, the legalization of euthanasia all over the world. Nor are the churches very helpful in fighting euthanasia at this stage. And I mean *all* churches. Note the confusing statements given out by the various church groups. Even Catholic dioceses have given differing statements on euthanasia.

Let us look more closely at the world's reproductive rates. Were it not for the babies of the immigrants—Filipinos, Vietnamese, Hispanics, and others—the United States would be a moribund country. The average American family includes 2.1 children (statistically, 2.2 are needed for replacement). Canada is worse off. In Europe the average woman has barely 1.5 children. Italy has the lowest birthrate in the Western world with 1.2 children per family; the Spanish have 1.3; France, England, the Scandinavian countries, Austria, Belgium, and Luxemburg are all seriously below the replacement level. Thirty-two of thirty-five European nations are now below replacement. In fact, more than sixty nations in the world are not replacing their populations.[5] The French demographer Pierre Chaunu, a Protestant, writes point-blank in his *Die Verhütete Zukunft* that Germany has no future, and he explicitly names contraception as the cause. Even the Irish are barely holding their own, having surrendered to the Filipinos their role of bringing Christianity to the world. The only country in Europe with

a comparatively healthy birthrate is little Malta, where the 300,000 Catholics have an average of 2.4 children per completed family. Sweden and Denmark approach the figure of 2.1.

From every demographic predictive view, Europe will soon be dominated by Islam. Almost five million Muslims live in France, and there are many Muslims in all the other European countries. There are 1,500 mosques in Germany alone. By the year 2000, there will be more Muslims than Catholics in the world for the first time in history, because the followers of Mohammed take seriously the edict

My little friend in Kenya.   "increase and multiply."

Things are far worse behind the crumpled Iron Curtain. After seventy-five years of unchecked abortion, the 148 million people of Russia proper are achieving the lowest birthrate in the world, 1.1 children per family. None of Russia's former satellite countries has a replacement birthrate, because of sterilization, contraception, and abortion. In the Far East, the average Japanese married woman has 1.43 children, and the government is desperate for more. Condom use and abortion are rampant in Japan, of course.

Throughout the Western world, the number of marriages is declining as couples increasingly "shack up" without the benefits of marriage. Boys, even girls, rent their own flats ("shacks"?), to which they invite a succession of sexual partners. It all reminds me—perhaps

---

[5]   United Nations Development Program. *World Resources 1994-5: Guide to the Global Environment.* New York: Oxford University Press, 1994, Table 16.2.

unkindly!—of Larry King's saying that he never commits adultery but just divorces his wives; I believe the count has reached eight by now.

Not least in our unbelieving world is the religious and priestly vocations crisis. (See attached tables.) Every study of vocations I have ever seen shows that most priests, whatever the country, come neither from the very wealthy nor from the very poor but from middle-class, totally Catholic couples who oftentimes are struggling a bit for economic stability. Today the large family is the exception, and in every Western country many good mothers tell me that when they get pregnant a second or third time they are ridiculed and called irre-

It's never too early to become a part of the Culture of Life!

sponsible. To those good women I say that pagans have always laughed at true Christians, adding, "Remember, you will laugh last and you will laugh forever! Have three or four more!"

Some readers may think that this whole account has been too pessimistic, too gloomy. Admittedly, one can find a Christian resurgence here and there, and the Church certainly flourishes in the Philippines and in parts of Africa. Other positive indicators are the home-schooling movement, the Marian movement (I have never before seen so many people saying the rosary as today), the charismatic movement, the many good Catholic magazines, the perpetual-adoration movement, some great bishops (for instance, John Keating of Arlington, Virginia; John Myers of Peoria, Illinois; Fabian Bruskewitz of Lincoln, Nebraska, and others) who are proving to everybody that the diocese that defends orthodoxy and fosters good family life produces good Catholic living and many vocations. For more of these positive notes, read the current and back issues of *Sursum Corda*.

I am often asked what the greatest obstacles are to doing pro-life

Some babysitter I am! After reading and ignoring the baby at my feet, I felt guilty and blessed him.

work. In posing this question, some people accuse me of bishop-bashing! But I can assure the reader that, after working for the longest time in the greatest number of countries and meeting innumerable true-blue pro-lifers, I have found that all these pro-lifers say the greatest obstacle is bishops, priests, religious, and—not least—theologians. Of course, there are exceptions in every category.

At the third Pro-Life Leadership Conference in Rome, 3-5 October 1995, someone asked this familiar question about the greatest obstacles encountered in various countries. Repeatedly, without exception, the answer was "bishops and priests." A good Canadian pro-life archbishop was present and finally could not contain his wrath: "I am sick and tired of all this bishop-bashing!" he exclaimed. But the delegates continued testifying that bishops and priests provided their greatest opposition. As for myself, I would say that this statement is true in North America, in a few Latin American countries, in some European countries, and especially true in South Africa. In the rest of the world—that is to say, in most of the world—the bishops and priests have been magnificent, and nowhere more so than in Africa, where the Catholic Church (as I have predicted) may well find her future.

The great Protestant medical missionary Dr. Albert Schweitzer once observed that "the Christian is a short-range pessimist and a long-range optimist." I am not a pessimist even at short range, although there is plenty in the modern world to be pessimistic about. God is still in His heaven; the world and all in it belong to Him; nothing happens by chance; everything is God's will except the evil we choose. The truly important thing is that we do all we can to know our world and our faith, and then unstintingly and tirelessly work under God's guidance to win the battle for life, to restore the family, and to promote religious orthodoxy.

I have little patience with the discouraged! They look for results; I do not. I leave the results to God. The Canon of the Mass urges us "to wait in *joyful hope* for the coming of our Savior, Jesus Christ." Even my confreres at times ask me whether I get discouraged. I reply with a resounding "No!" They say: "But you are losing—don't you see?" "Yes, I see it every day—but God will not ask me whether I succeeded, only whether I truly tried." And, depending on who asks me these foolish questions, I demand, "When are *you* going to try!"

The situation of Christianity and mankind is such as to remind us of the perceptive words of C. S. Lewis: "When the whole world is running towards a cliff, he who is running in the opposite direction appears to have lost his mind."

If this frank account of one pro-lifer's thirty-five years of efforts in ninety-one countries prompts more travelers to run "in the opposite direction," then the pains of writing this book will have been richly rewarded.

Building for the Future...

GRAND OPENING DAY, 15 AUGUST 1996, FRONT ROYAL, VIRGINIA—A PHOTO ESSAY

A new home for HLI—at 4 Family Life!

The new building architect, Bill Robson, explains the layout of the new World Headquarters. He is assisted by Fr. Matthew Habiger and me.

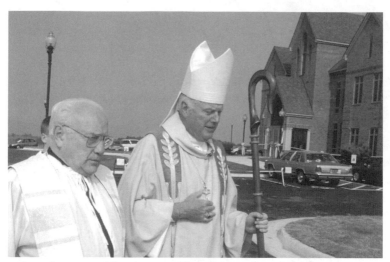

Bishop John Keating of the Arlington diocese presided over our opening Mass and dedication ceremonies. Our processional took us across the parking lot to tents set up outside.

The opening Mass was a wonderful celebration of thanksgiving for all the Lord has done for HLI, and of intercession—that we may be even more faithful to His work among the poor, the weak, and the often forgotten.

The Knights of Columbus led the procession.

Fr. Matthew Habiger and I were joined by two young friends for the official ribbon-cutting ceremony. This day was a long time coming and was only possible because of the faithfulness of thousands of HLI supporters from around the globe.

We estimate there were some 2,000 guests visiting HLI on opening day. Many thousands more have visited since then and we hope they'll keep coming! This building is dedicated to all those who fight so tirelessly for life—wherever they may be.

It really was a day of fun and joy for all!

APPENDIX A

"Contraception and the Rejection of God"

A t the origin of every human person there is a creative act of God. No man comes into existence by chance; he is always the object of God's creative love. From this fundamental truth of faith and reason it follows that the procreative capacity, inscribed in human sexuality, is—in its deepest truth—a cooperation with God's creative power. And it also follows that man and woman are not the arbiters, are not the masters of this same capacity, called as they are, in it and through it, to be participants in God's creative decision. When, therefore, through contraception, married couples remove from the exercise of their conjugal sexuality its potential procreative capacity, they claim a power which belongs solely to God: the power to decide in a final analysis the coming into existence of a human person. They assume the qualification not of being cooperators in God's creative power, but the ultimate depositories of the source of human life. In this perspective, contraception is to be judged objectively so profoundly unlawful as never to be, for any reason, justified. To think or to say the contrary is equal to maintaining that in human life situations may arise in which it is lawful not to recognize God as God.

— Pope John Paul II
to a Study Seminar on "Responsible Parenthood," September 17, 1982. Published in *L'Osservatore Romano*, 10 October 1983.

APPENDIX B

Papal Address to Participants in Natural Family Planning Course

A course on Natural Family Planning was held at the Catholic University of the Sacred Heart in Rome in December, 1990, and the participants were received in audience by Pope John Paul II, who spoke to them in the following words. This address is typical of the support the Holy Father has given NFP throughout his pontificate.

1. In giving you a heartfelt greeting, I wish to express my deep joy over this important initiative, sponsored by the Centre for Studies and Research on Natural Regulation of Fertility of the Catholic University of the Sacred Heart. The course you are participating in seeks to train teachers who can teach families natural methods permitting truly responsible procreation, in accord with the moral doctrine which the Magisterium has constantly taught. A description of this initiative's aims is enough to show its relevance to the Church's mission to the family. In the Apostolic Exhortation *Familiaris Consortio*, I reminded the bishops and faithful alike about the urgent need for 'a broader, more decisive and systematic effort to make the natural methods for regulating fertility known, respected and applied' (n. 35).

2. Church teaching about such a delicate and urgent issue in the life of spouses and society is often misunderstood and

opposed because it is presented in an inadequate and unilateral fashion. It stops at the negative judgment concerning contraception, which is always an intrinsically dishonest act; yet it rarely makes any effort to understand this norm in the light of "the total vision of the human person and vocation, which is not only natural and earthly, but also supernatural and eternal" (*Humanae Vitae*, n. 14). Only within the context of values such as these can spouses find the inspiration which allows them to overcome, with the help of God's grace, the difficulties which they inevitably face when, under unfavorable social conditions and in an environment marked by readily available hedonism, they seek to follow a path which conforms to the Lord's will. It is only by deepening the Christian concept of this "responsibility for love and for life" that one can grasp the 'difference, both anthropological and moral, between contraception and recourse to the rhythm of the cycle' (*Familiaris Consortio*, n. 32).

3. Responsibility for love and for life! That expression reminds us of the greatness of the vocation of spouses, called to be free and conscious collaborators of the God Who is love, Who creates through love and calls to love. The term "responsibility" is, therefore, ethically decisive, because in it is combined the dignity of the "gift" which is received and, on the other hand, the value of the "freedom" to which it is entrusted so that it might bear fruit. The greater the gift, the greater the responsibility of the subject who freely accepts it. And what gift is greater on the natural plane than the vocation of a man and woman to express faithful and indissoluble love which is open to the transmission of life?

In conjugal love and in transmitting life, the human being cannot forget his or her dignity as a person; it raises the natural order to a certain level, one which is no longer merely biological. That is why the Church teaches that responsibility for love is inseparable from responsibility for

procreation. The biological phenomenon of human reproduction wherein the human person finds his or her begin-
nings also has as its end the emergence of a new person,
unique and unrepeatable, made in the image and likeness of
God. The dignity of the procreative act in which the inter-
personal love of the spouses finds its culmination in the new
person, in a son or daughter, emerges from that fact. That is
why the Church teaches that openness to life in conjugal
relations protects the very authenticity of the love relationship, saving it from the risk of descending to the level of
mere utilitarian enjoyment.

4. Through this sense of responsibility for love and for life,
God the Creator invites the spouses not to be passive opera-
tors, but rather "cooperators or almost interpreters" of His
plan (*Gaudium et Spes*, n. 50). In fact, they are called, out
of respect for the objective moral order established by God,
to an obligatory discernment of the indications of God's
will concerning their family. Thus, in relationship to physical, economic, psychological and social conditions, responsible parenthood will be able to be expressed "either by the
deliberate and generous decision to raise a large family, or
by the decision, made for serious moral reasons and with
due respect for the moral law, to avoid for the time being,
or even for an indeterminate period, another birth"
(*Humanae Vitae*, n. 10).

Today science offers the opportunity for precisely determining fertile and infertile periods in a woman's body. Couples
can make good use of this knowledge to achieve several
ends: not only to space or to limit the number of births, but
also for choosing the most opportune moment under every
point of view for procreation, or also to identify the periods
of great fertility in cases where conceiving has been difficult.

5. In applying this scientific knowledge to regulating fertility, technology in no way substitutes for the involvement of
the persons and neither does it intervene by manipulating

the nature of the relationship, as in the case with contraception in which the unitive meaning of the conjugal act is deliberately separated from its procreative meaning. To the contrary, in practicing natural methods science must always be joined with self-control, since, in using them, virtue—that perfection belonging specifically to the person—is necessarily a factor.

Thus we can say that periodic continence, practiced to regulate procreation in a natural way, requires a profound understanding of the person and of love. In truth, that requires mutual listening and dialogue by spouses, attention and sensitivity for the other spouse and constant self-control: all of these are qualities which express real love for the person of the spouse for what he or she is, and not for what one may wish the other to be. The practice of natural methods requires personal growth by the spouses in a joint effort to strengthen their love.

This intrinsic connection between science and moral virtue constitutes the specific and morally qualifying element for recourse to natural methods. It is a part of the complete integral training of teachers and of couples, and, in it, it should be clear that what is of concern here is more than just simple "instruction" divorced from the moral values proper to teaching people to see that it is not possible to practice natural methods as a 'licit' variation of the decision to be closed to life, which would be substantially the same as that which inspires the decision to use contraceptives: only if there is a basic openness to fatherhood and motherhood, understood as collaboration with the Creator, does the use of natural means become an integrating part of the responsibility for love and life.

6. The Sacred Scripture unveils for us the radiant face of God Who "is love" (1 Jn 4:8) and Who is a "lover of Life" (Wis 11:26). Even amid difficulties and misunderstandings, never forget that the work to which you are devoted, dear

brothers and sisters, is a service to love and to life in support of spouses who intend to live by God's plan. Through this service, which merits the committed support of all pastors, you are giving a valid form of assistance to the Church's mission.

APPENDIX C

The following is from Our Sunday Visitor, *20 November 1988.*

Pope Urges Local Churches to Promote Birth-Control Teaching

Pope John Paul II, addressing an international gathering of bishops, said local churches should establish educational Institutes to vigorously promote the Church's teaching on birth control.

The Pope said the 20-year-old encyclical *Humanae Vitae* ("Of Human Life") was prophetic and that criticisms of its ban on artificial contraception missed the main point about conjugal love—that it is a gift from God.

He said the Church now needs to better explain its teaching, to help overcome the "crisis that has hit the morality of marriage."

The Pope spoke Nov. 7 to about 60 bishops representing episcopal conferences worldwide. They were meeting at the Vatican for two days to discuss pastoral approaches on marriage and the family.

The meeting was sponsored by the Pontifical Council for the Family, which, along with the John Paul II Institute for Studies on Marriage and the Family, was promoting a three-day theological conference on *Humanae Vitae* the same week. Both organizations have been aggressive defenders of papal teaching on human sexuality.

The Church's birth-control teaching has been unpopular with many Catholics.

The Pope said the pontifical council and the Institute were examples of what local bishops —at the national, regional or diocesan level— could and should be doing to deal with pastoral problems in marriage.

APPENDIX D

The following is the complete text of an editorial that appeared in California Medicine, *the official journal of the California Medical Association (Sept., 1970; Vol. 113, No. 3).*

The traditional Western ethic has always placed great emphasis on the intrinsic worth and equal value of every human life regardless of its stage or condition. This ethic has had the blessing of the Judeo-Christian heritage and has been the basis for most of our laws and much of our social policy. The reverence for each and every human life has also been a keystone of Western medicine and is the ethic which has caused physicians to try to preserve, protect, repair, prolong, and enhance every human life which comes under their surveillance. This traditional ethic is still clearly dominant, but there is much to suggest that it is being eroded at its core and may eventually even be abandoned. This of course will produce profound changes in Western medicine and in Western society.

There are certain new facts and social realities which are becoming recognized, are widely discussed in Western society and seem certain to undermine and transform this traditional ethic. They have come into being and into focus as the social by-products of unprecedented technologic progress and achievement. Of particular importance are, first, the demographic data of human population expansion which tends to proceed uncontrolled and at a geometric rate of progression; second, an ever-growing ecological disparity between the numbers of people and the resources available to support these numbers in the manner to which they are or would like to become accustomed; and third, and perhaps most important, a quite new social emphasis on something which is beginning to be called the quality of life, a something which becomes possible for the first time in human history because of scientific and technological development. These are now being seen by a growing segment of the public as realities which are within the power of humans to control and there is quite evidently an increasing determination to do this.

What is not yet so clearly perceived is that in order to bring this about hard choices will have to be made with respect to what is to be preserved and strengthened and what is not, and that this will of necessity violate and ultimately destroy the traditional Western ethic with all that this portends. It will become necessary and acceptable to place relative rather than absolute values on such things as human lives, the use of scarce resources and the various elements which are to make up the quality of life or of living which is to be sought. This is quite distinctly at variance with the Judeo-Christian ethic and carries serious philosophical, social, economic, and political implications for Western society and perhaps for world society.

The process of eroding the old ethic and substituting the new has already begun. It may be seen most clearly in changing attitudes toward human abortion. In defiance of the long held Western ethic of intrinsic and equal value for every human life regardless of its stage, condition, or status, abortion is becoming accepted by society as moral, right, and even necessary. It is worth noting that this shift in public attitude has affected the churches, the laws, and public policy rather than the reverse. Since the old ethic has not yet been fully displaced it has been necessary to separate the idea of abortion from the idea of killing, which continues to be socially abhorrent. The result has been a curious avoidance of the scientific fact, which everyone really knows, that human life begins at conception and is continuous whether intra- or extra-uterine until death. The very considerable semantic gymnastics which are required to rationalize abortion as anything but taking a human life would be ludicrous if they were not often put forth under socially impeccable auspices. It is suggested that this schizophrenic sort of subterfuge is necessary because while a new ethic is being accepted the old one has not yet been rejected.

It seems safe to predict that the new demographic, ecological, and social realities and aspirations are so powerful that the new ethic of relative rather than of absolute and equal values will ultimately prevail as man exercises ever more certain and effective control over his numbers, and uses his always comparatively scarce resources to provide the nutrition, housing, economic support, education, and health care in such ways as to achieve his desired quality of life and living. The criteria upon which these relative values are to be based will depend considerably upon whatever concept of the quality of life or living is developed. This may be expected to reflect the extent that quality of life is considered to be a function of personal fulfillment; of individual responsibility for the common welfare, the preservation of the environment, the betterment of the species; and of whether or not, or to what extent, these responsibilities are to be exercised on a compulsory or voluntary basis.

The part which medicine will play as all this develops is not yet entirely clear. That it will be deeply involved is certain. Medicine's role with respect to changing attitudes toward abortion may well be a prototype of what is to occur. Another precedent may be found in the part physicians have played in evaluating who is and who is not to be given costly long-term renal dialysis. Certainly this has required placing relative values on human lives and the impact of the physician on this decision process has been considerable. One may anticipate further development of these roles as the problems of birth control and birth selection are extended inevitably to death selection and death control whether by the individual or by society, and further public and professional determinations of when and when not to use scarce resources.

Since the problems which the new demographic, ecologic and social realities pose are fundamentally biological and ecological in nature and pertain to the survival and well-being of human beings, the participation of physicians and of the medical profession will be essential in planning and decision-making at many levels. No other discipline has the knowledge of human nature, human behavior, health and disease, and of what is involved in physical and mental well-being which will be needed. It is not too early for our profession to examine this new ethic, recognize it for what it is, and will mean for human society, and prepare to apply it in a rational development for the fulfillment and betterment of mankind in what is almost certain to be a biologically-oriented world society.

APPENDIX E

The following chronology was prepared by Bonnie Manion, a member of the Human Life Center Board. It was published (without my knowledge) in Orthodoxy of the Catholic Doctrine *vol. 10, no. 1, (Jan.-Feb.-March, 1981). My corrections are shown in brackets.*

The Victim of the Collegeville Coup

*M*INNEAPOLIS, AUGUST 1980 — Abbot Jerome Theisen, OSB, Fr. Alberic Culhane, OSB, Acting President of St. John's University, Fr. Gunther Rolfson, OSB, Academic Dean of St. John's University, Fr. Paul Siebenand, OSB, Acting Executive Director of the Human Life Center, Mr. Norbert Berg, Mr. John Kidwell, Chairman of the Board of Directors of the Human Life Center, Dr. Konald Prem and Mr. Jack Quesnell meet to discuss a sabbatical leave for Fr. Paul Marx, OSB, President of the Human Life Center. [Dr. Prem opposed my ouster.]

MINNEAPOLIS, SEPTEMBER 1980

Another meeting with the above same members to confirm the sabbatical leave. (The decision had actually been made by the "monk members" of the meeting who felt that Fr. Marx took too strong a position on pro-life matters. They wanted the lay members to prevail upon Fr. Marx to graciously accept this decision. Mr. John Kidwell actually stated that if he didn't accept this decision, it would be forced on him. Used at this meeting was Fr. Marx's personal and confidential correspondence that had been removed from his files.)

OCTOBER 1980

Father Marx returns from the Synod meeting in Rome to hear the announcement of the sabbatical leave.

NOVEMBER 8, 1980

A meeting of the Board of Directors of the Human Life Center "rubber stamps" the sabbatical leave. Not present and not voting for this sabbatical leave was one member of the board, Mrs. Bonnie Manion. One other member, Mrs. Jeri Lunzer, voted hesitatingly, not knowing of the Minneapolis meetings or whether Fr. Marx wanted this sabbatical.

NOVEMBER 10, 1980

A memo to the staff of the Human Life Center from the Acting Executive Director, Fr. Paul Siebenand, OSB, is released in which we learn that Fr. Marx "is not to use the HLC stationery, the HLC car, is not to set foot in the HLC offices, is not to speak for the HLC and must vacate his office on or before December 1, 1980." (He was physically removed on this date.)

NOVEMBER 12, 1980

Mr. Dan Lyons and Mr. Andy Scholberg are given a notice in their mail boxes that as of November 14, 1980, their services are no longer required by the HLC. Mr. Lyons was the principal fund raiser [this was not correct] and the editor of Family Life News at the center. Mr. Scholberg was the editor of *Human Life Issues*, the assistant editor of the *International Review of Natural Family Planning*, an author and lecturer for the HLC. (Mr. and Mrs. Scholberg were expecting a baby within a month of his firing.)

Somewhere within this time, Mr. John Kidwell resigns as Chairman of the Board of Directors of the HLC stating that he has been "gutted out." (It is felt by many of the board members that, since Mr. Kidwell was part of the group that started the sabbatical decision, that he should have at least stayed to see his decision through.)

The foregoing scenario gives only a brief description of events and meetings prior to the forced sabbatical leave that Fr. Paul Marx, OSB, received. A contradiction to a nice, clean, restful sabbatical arose immediately with the inept memorandum (11/10/80) that Fr. Paul Siebenand, OSB, released to his staff of the Human Life Center. The almost immediate firing of two key employees at the HLC increased the bungling. Now a different picture is beginning [to emerge] and is contrary to any show of "concern" for Fr. Marx's health and need for rest.

As the articles began to appear in the press regarding this forced leave, funders to the HLC began to question St. John's University about Fr. Marx's sabbatical leave. The Public Relations Department of the University issued statements, in response to the calls, that reinforced "concern" for Fr. Marx's need for a rest. They stated that nothing is to be changed at the HLC and "we promise that your funding will be put to the best possible use." (Remember that two key employees have already been fired and two key publications have been dropped.) Another memo to the staff from Fr. Paul Siebenand has stated that no negative statements regarding Planned Parenthood will be forthcoming from the HLC — "we will keep a positive image."

Finally, the international seminars held each summer are in a state of limbo and the time is too late to conduct them this year. Apparently the funders of the HLC are reasonable people and the "non-function " of the HLC is seen by them, for the funding has virtually stopped. The old pro-life funders that have been inspired by Fr. Marx have ceased, both large and small. The next move by the HLC has been to buy the mailing lists from *Better Homes and Gardens* and *The Catholic Digest* without any Board of Directors approval. [I learned later that a large number of subscribers to *Better Homes and Gardens* wrote back angry letters saying they were for legal abortion.]

At first, when the sabbatical was announced, Fr. Marx responded to the press with "no comment" because Abbot Theisen was out of the country and Fr. Marx was awaiting his return. Upon his return, there were more "guidelines" for his behavior that he is to follow. He is not to associate or support or contribute in any way with former employees Lyons or Scholberg (both now actively involved in resurrecting the newspaper under a different name and working at a nearby location in the community of Avon, Minnesota); he is not to say volatile things to the press but to show mercy and kindness to all his fellow monks who differ from his pro-life stance and he is not to disturb the workings of the HLC. The Abbot thinks that Fr. Marx is suffering from a psychological illness and absolutely demands that he sees a psychiatrist of the Abbot's choosing—Dr. Conrad Baars of San Antonio, Texas. [Wrong: Abbot Jerome had chosen another psychiatrist.]

It should be pointed out here that Dr. Baars made some very unfavorable remarks to an Order priest about Fr. Marx, and in his letter of February 20, 1981 practically telling Fr. Marx that he needed help. [Strange, because Dr. Baars had been my friend and advisor, and said no such thing to me. Nor had I seen the letter referred to, nor is it in the archives.] For a psychiatrist to diagnose a disease without having seen the patient, is a very strange procedure!

JANUARY 10, 1981

A meeting of the Board of Directors of the HLC concluded nothing other than a marked reduction in the funding. The major thrust of the meeting was to consider a proposal from Mr. Robert Joyce, a faculty member of St. John's University. It is a proposal for a search committee to fill the new job opening for a "pro-life liaison." It was noted in this proposal that a person not necessarily of our philosophical goals be included in this search committee so we could be "sensitive and compassionate" to the needs of those who are anti-life! Fr. Marx was given ten minutes of time to state his case (out of a four hour meeting time) and was interrupted several times in the ten minutes. The board then voted to hold the next meeting on February 21, 1981.

FEBRUARY 17, 1981

Through a telephone call from Nancy Phelan (Fr. Siebenand's secretary), the February 21, 1981 meeting was canceled. The reasons for this cancellation were two: the Abbot was away from the university (he is not a member of the Board) and Fr. Siebenand (also not a member of the Board) would have a better financial picture on March 14, 1981. Members of the Board who live other than in the area of

St. John's University were polled to discover that this was a poor date and asked Acting Chairman Alice Brown to set an agreeable date for the meeting. She declined to do so, saying that it was her prerogative to set the date and she chose the "preference of Fr. Siebenand and John Boyle (Director of Finance at the HLC)" for selection of the March 14 date. When she was asked to state the urgency for the meeting at this time rather than a later time amenable to all board members, she refused to do so. When she was then pressed to release the agenda to other board members, she stated that they would receive the agenda just prior to the meeting on March 14. She stated that she had, in fact, polled the members in Minneapolis herself and they agreed that the date of March 14 was agreeable to them. Board Member Manion polled the members in Minneapolis to learn that they had not been polled by Chairman Brown, but had rather simply been informed by mail that the meeting was to be held on March 14. In fact, Manion polled all the members of the Board and learned that none of them had been polled by Acting Chairman Brown. She also discovered in the polling that March 28 would be a date at which all members except Brown and Joyce could be present at a Board meeting.

FEBRUARY 24, 1981

Fr. Paul Siebenand announces to his staff that when the Abbot returns from his recent trip, probably on February 29, that he will announce Fr. Marx's priestly suspension. [This, of course, never happened.] Fr. Siebenand also briefed the Administrative Board of the Catholic Conference of Bishops of the forthcoming removal of Fr. Marx.

FEBRUARY 28, 1981

In a telephone conversation with Board Member Manion, Acting Chairman Brown states that the meeting date will be on March 14 and the "Abbot will announce Fr. Marx's priestly suspension." When Manion objected that this could not be done because Fr. Marx has appealed to the Apostolic Delegate, Archbishop Pio Laghi, Brown insisted that Fr. Marx takes his orders from the Abbot and the suspension is forthcoming.

Consider these documented statements:

1. Some theologians at St. John's School of Theology were signers against *Humanae Vitae*. They have never recanted. Their names are:

> Fr. Godfrey Diekmann, OSB, (at the Seminary),

> Fr. Michael Marx, OSB, (at the Seminary).

[There were two other dissenter theologians teaching in the seminary: Fr. Aelred Tegels, OSB, and Fr. Kieran Nolan, OSB.]

They are in the Diocese of Bishop George H. Speltz, St. Cloud, Minn., and some of these teach in his Seminary at the Collegeville campus. [All did then.]

2. The contraceptionist Human Life Center Board Members were appointed by Fr. Michael Blecker, OSB, President of St. John's University. Fr. Blecker once stated that "contraception is like taking another glass of wine." Three years later he invited the HLC off campus.

3. Fr. Philip Kaufman, OSB, has played a tape of Fr. Bernard Haring's dissent to *Humanae Vitae* in criss-cross travels across this country trying to whittle away acceptance of *Humanae Vitae*.

4. No single theologian of St. John's University, the diocesan seminary, or the Graduate School of Theology has ever published anything against abortion.

It is important to remember that Pope Paul VI, in 1973, told Fr. Paul Marx that in defending *Humanae Vitae*, "You are a courageous fighter." [Correction: The Pope was referring to my international pro-life work.] In October of 1980 [correction: 17 November 1979], Pope John Paul II told Fr. Marx, "You are doing the most important work on earth."

Will the aforementioned "hierarchy" of St. John's University be allowed to silence this priest-defender of *Humanae Vitae*, this defender of orthodoxy of Catholic doctrine?

Bonnie Manion
Member, Board of Directors
of Human Life Center

(*Editor's Note*: *The National Catholic Reporter*, of August 14, 1968, published, according to states, the list of signers of the Statement disagreeing with the encyclical *Humanae Vitae*. The complete list was reproduced "for informational purposes only" in *Orthodoxy of the Catholic Doctrine*, vol. 2, no. 1,(Jan.-Feb.-March, 1973). Under the State of Minnesota, it read:

St. John's Abbey Collegeville:

> Rev. John F. Riley, College of St. Thomas, St. Paul
> Rev. Godfrey Diekmann
> Rev. Michael Marx
> Norman A. Berube, College St. Teresa, Winona
> Rev. Kieran Nolan
> Rev. Aelred Tegels
> Brother J. Frederick Beaudry, St. Mary's College, Winona

An Open Letter

MY RESPONSE TO MARY JOYCE'S LETTER ON FATHER PAUL MARX'S FORCED SABBATICAL

(Sent to all Cardinals and Bishops)
by Mrs. Bonnie Manion, Member,
Board of Directors, Human Life Center

*I*t was stated in a letter recently written by Mary R. Joyce, a member of the Board of Directors of the Human Life Center and which letter was then mailed to all Cardinals, Bishops and donors to the Human Life Center by Acting Director Father Paul Siebenand that a concern for Father Paul Marx's "excessive intenseness" existed.

The solution to remedy this "excessive intenseness" was a forced sabbatical. If this is the most appropriate treatment for a "family member," I hope that I, as a mother of nine who is guilty of the same intenseness in my work as a mother, may be spared the same treatment by those concerned for my welfare. I can assure you that there would be no "return to health" upon isolating one from the comfort of the environment. I think Mary R. Joyce should stay in the field in which she is qualified and credentialed rather than switch to a field of psychology, diagnosis and treatment in which she holds no training.

The "guilty" charge as stated in the Joyce letter arose from past employees who had been fired from the Human Life Center. One does not need any advanced training to realize that one is fired from employment due to incompetence. As one who has worked directly with Father Paul Marx for the past ten years, I have, on at least ten occasions, been given the responsibility to produce and participate in ten major seminars he has conducted. After successfully producing and participating in these seminars he has conducted, we have joked about how overworked Father Marx is! Can any board member or other employee of the Human Life Center, past or present, cite a similar work record? The answer is, "no"! The person, character and ethical commitment of former employees as Joyce mentions invalidly, in her letter, is not in question. This is why people are released from employment—incompetence. Management is not satisfied with the product.

It is untrue that five administrative directors came and left the Human Life Center. Since the job description was written, there has been only one employee who has partially filled the description and that one left due to his health problems. Had a complete *curriculum vitae* been given upon his application, at least several of us board members would not have agreed to that hiring.

As to Dan Lyons' "incompetence," one of his "guilty" charges was to publish an article about the devotion to the Sacred Heart in one of the last issues of the *Family Life News*. It was argued that this was not contemporary religious reading!

As to the facts, both Lyons and Scholberg were very "guilty" of competence. That competence and the competence of Father Marx was a focus that does not find itself in the new direction of the HLC. As a board member, I am more than uneasy about this new focus. It is one belief to uphold *Humanae Vitae*. It is quite another to be anti-Planned Parenthood. It is one belief to be pro-life. It is quite another to be anti-abortion. It is one belief to promote natural family planning. It is quite another to openly oppose contraception and to point out its evils. Why do you suppose that Dr. C. Everett Koop resigned his membership in anti-abortion groups when he was appointed as Surgeon General? Precisely as he named it: a conflict of interests.

Our Lord gave us two mandates. One mandate arises in the first two Commandments and was a positive mandate. The second was in the remaining eight Commandments and was a negative mandate. These are the two mandates that I have watched Father Paul Marx carry out for the Church and in obedience to the Holy Father. Neither shall abandon him in his personal hour but shall open a new window as all the doors close. I continue to be personally inspired and aligned to that work. It may be that, in the future, I might have to resign from the Board of Directors of the Human Life Center if they choose to only carry out the first mandate of Our Lord. Our Lord also said, "You cannot love two masters."

In Defense of Fr. Paul Marx, OSB

AN OPEN LETTER TO FR. PAUL SIEBENAND AND MARY JOYCE AT HUMAN LIFE CENTER, COLLEGEVILLE, MINN.

by Judie Brown, President, American Life Lobby, Inc.

*D*ear Friends:

Recently I received a copy of the letter which you are circulating to those whom you say are concerned about the situation at your Center. Never before have I felt more strongly about the fact that something must be said to put your letter (which is a true insult to Father Marx) to rest along with the other scurrilous things that have been done and said in regard to the matter of "trust."

You state in your letter that people of the movement are supposed to place their "trust" in you — an organization whose Board of Directors turned on the only man who has ever really stood up against the TOTAL ABORTION PROBLEM in this nation and taken a stand which is completely in agreement with *Humanae Vitae*.

Your Board of Directors reminds me a great deal of the Board I once had to deal with during a time of previous experience in the prolife movement. Perhaps that is why I feel so qualified to defend Father Paul Marx. I have witnessed myself how vicious, deceitful, maligning, and even blind a Board of Directors can be when these men see someone come along for whom their only feelings are jealousy and contempt. It would perhaps have been better if your Board of Directors had taken a sabbatical —permanently, perhaps.

First of all, Father Paul Marx is an inspired leader. Because he is so deeply committed and so terribly concerned about the fact that babies are murdered each moment that we delay, he certainly becomes frustrated, anxious and nervous about the task at hand. If that means, as you suggest in your letter, that he is hard to work for, then perhaps it is those who work under him who should have their commitment to the cause of protecting human life brought under examination, rather than be permitted to accuse Father Marx of faults that are not a part of his character. People who are in positions of authority and who have a total grasp of the significance of their involvement are always temperamental and demanding — how else could any of us ever accomplish the small bit that we do? How can this have escaped your prestigious Board of Directors' awareness?

It is my firm conviction that your attempt at the complete character assassination of Father Marx will not work because it is not based upon facts. The Human Life Center was a dream placed into the realm of reality by one man who stood up for what he knew was right and defended the principles of this movement against the greatest of adversity. You are seeking to chastise him for executing the task that he knows he has been charged to perform by the Lord. God will not support you. No single human being or group of so-called Board Members can ever erase the truth and the truth is that this movement will be a far weaker force without the continued persistence and devotion of Father Paul Marx.

Is Father Marx tired? Yes, we are all tired! Is he restless? Yes, who would not be under the circumstances. Is he fatigued to the point of being ineffective? No more so than any of the other great men whom the world has witnessed in its brief history! Will he be defeated by your continued efforts to discredit him? No, he will not, because people like myself and countless others will not allow you or your Board to destroy what has been and must continue to be a driving force in the pro-life movement.

Father Paul Marx has already made his greatest contribution to his Church, the movement, and his religious order, for he has stood the test of courage in a time when his "friends" were willing to do anything at all to destroy him.

I pray that the Lord will bring peace and real Christian Justice to dwell in the minds and hearts of those who have begun this terrible assault on Father Paul Marx. And if the Lord cannot manifest himself in that way, then I pray that He finally delivers Father Marx to another place where Father Marx may continue his apostolate without

this continued attack. The preborn children of the world need him —
can't you hear them cry out for "truth"? God help you all!

With God for Life,

Mrs. Judie Brown
President, American Life Lobby, Inc.

◆〰◆

THE EPILOGUE OF THE CASE OF FR. PAUL MARX, OSB, *vs.* HUMAN LIFE CENTER & CO., COLLEGEVILLE, MINN.

*T*he three preceding articles presented the factual description of
the unfortunate case of the "sabbatical" which some attempted
to impose upon Fr. Paul Marx, OSB, the Founder and Director of
Human Life Center, Collegeville, Minn.

The readers of the *Orthodoxy of the Catholic Doctrine* deserve also
to know the final conclusion of this case.

After Fr. Paul Marx, OSB, made an appeal, through the proper
channels, to the Holy Father himself, all is well now for him!

His Abbot Jerome Theisen, OSB of Collegeville Abbey, offered the
full freedom, for the period of five years, to Fr. Paul Marx, OSB of
accepting and developing, in any place, his apostolate in defense of
human life as he was doing before in his Human Life Center at the
campus of St. Johns University, Collegeville, Minn.

At the present, Fr. Marx, OSB, has eight to ten offers where he is
most welcome to continue his fight for the life of the unborn and
those who are born, but unwanted by some!

He will decide by August 1 of this year where to go and what to
accept. It is to be noted that Fr. Paul Marx, OSB, loves his Benedictine
Order and he remains a Benedictine monk.

Thus, one may say that "the Victim of the Collegeville Coup," instead of remaining as a permanent victim, turns to be a Victor!

Our heartfelt congratulations to Fr. Marx, OSB—the fearless defender of human life and the faithful promoter of the teachings of the Magisterium of the Church!

Fr. Milan Mikulich, OFM, STD
Editor: *Orthodoxy*

Index

Page numbers in italics indicate illustrations.